UNHOLY ALLIANCES

UNHOLY ALLIANCES

WARREN KINSELLA

Terrorists,

Extremists,

Front Companies,

and the Libyan

Connection

in Canada

Lester

Publishing

Canadian Cataloguing in Publication Data
Kinsella, Warren, 1960–
Unholy alliances

Includes index.
ISBN 1-895555-24-8

1. Terrorism—North America. 2. Terrorism—Libya. 3. Qadhafi,
Mu'ammar. 4. Corporations—Corrupt practices. 5. Libya—
Foreign relations—North America. 6. North America—Foreign
relations—Libya. I. Title.

HV6433.N6K55 1992 303.6'25 C92-093042-5

Lester Publishing Limited
56 The Esplanade
Toronto, Ontario
M5E 1A7

Printed and bound in Canada.
92 93 94 95 5 4 3 2 1

This book is dedicated to my family—Lorna, Douglas, Kevin, Lorne, Troy, and Suzanne—who stood by me during some tough times; to my best friend, Pierre; and to Christoph Halens, who died trying to tell his story.

CONTENTS

ACKNOWLEDGEMENTS

Literally dozens of people—friends, family, and acquaintances—have helped me to write *Unholy Alliances*. For three long years, these people endured countless questions about style, content, and the world of laptop computers. Some I can name here; others I can't, for reasons that will soon become obvious. To all of them I owe a debt of gratitude.

So—a heartfelt thank you to the following: all concerned at the Office of the Leader of the Opposition and the *Ottawa Citizen*, for their unflagging moral support and interest; Dan Hayward, for his research skills; Jean Gagné, Ken Campbell, and Randy Coulter, for computer help; Aaron Milrad and the host of libel lawyers who advised me, for their legal skill; Charlotte Gray, Richard Cléroux, Charlie Greenwell, and Brian Milner, for their helpful media suggestions; John Kessel, for his connections; Desmond Gray, Rosemary Knes, and the Halens family, for their candour; Bernie and Stan Farber, for their friendship and kind assistance; Eddie Goldenberg and Jean Chrétien, for giving me the time to flog the thing; Tony Fouhse, for photos and insights; Louis Valenzuela and everyone else at *Ottawa Magazine*, for their enthusiasm; the Replacements, the Pixies, Public Enemy, and Wire, for filling the silence.

I would be remiss if I did not also tip my hat to that small group of people to whom this book owes its existence: Malcolm Lester at Lester Publishing, for his experienced editorial eye and for having the courage to take on a project that has been fraught with difficulty; Helen Heller, who, as Richard Cléroux says, is the best literary agent in Canada; Randy Denley and Scott Honeyman at the *Ottawa Citizen,* for taking a chance on a nosy summer student; and, most of all, Ian MacLeod, my former partner at the *Citizen,* and my friend.

Thank you all.
W.K.
Ottawa, February 1992

PREFACE

One sweltering afternoon in June 1988, not long after I joined the reporting staff of the *Ottawa Citizen*, I received a phone call at the paper's west-end newsroom.

At the time I was investigating a story about the doings of white supremacists and anti-Semites living in the Ottawa area. It was not the first time I had probed organized racism in Canada; two years earlier I had spent a few months documenting the activities of the Aryan Nations for the *Calgary Herald*. The Church of Jesus Christ Christian Aryan Nations, as it calls itself, is a virulently anti-Semitic group headquartered in Idaho and Alberta. Some of its members had been convicted in the United States for racketeering, armed robbery, and murder. From what I had observed, Ottawa's racist right, which could claim about 100 members, was comparatively well-organized and well-funded. But it was not as much of a threat as the Aryan Nations.

On that humid summer day I had just returned from a two-hour interview with a man who at one time was a senior Canadian trade diplomat as well as an advisor to the Grand Wizard of the Canadian Knights of the Ku Klux Klan. His name was Ian Verner Macdonald.

At first the caller would not identify himself. He spoke in a thick

Arab accent. After some prodding he said, "You can call me Abdul."

Abdul told me that he was a member of a Libyan dissident group—a group that was opposed to the dictatorial rule of Libya's leader, Mu'ammar Qadhafi. He added that most of the group's members were students enrolled at universities and colleges in the Ottawa area. He then said that he and his colleagues had Macdonald under surveillance. "We know you have been interviewing him, Mr. Kinsella," Abdul said.

"All right, then, Abdul, or whatever your name is. If I *am* interviewing this Macdonald fellow—and I'm not saying I am—when was the last time I spoke with him?"

"About thirty-five minutes ago, Mr. Kinsella. At his home on Wilbrod Street."

I looked at my watch. Abdul was correct to the minute. I was intrigued—after all, the *Citizen* had yet to publish anything about Macdonald and his far-right friends. Few people even at the newspaper knew about my investigation. So why were a bunch of anti-Qadhafi students interested in the activities of someone like Macdonald? Abdul explained that Macdonald was "a very close friend" of Qadhafi's Tripoli regime and had travelled to Libya often. Moreover, Macdonald was also "a very close friend" of Mousa Hawamda.

"Who is Mousa Hawamda?" I asked.

"Mousa Hawamda is a Palestinian who owns a travel agency in downtown Ottawa, Mr. Kinsella. He is a very evil man."

"You will have to forgive me, Abdul, but what is evil about owning a travel agency?"

Abdul gave a hearty laugh. "Mousa Hawamda is not really a travel agent, Mr. Kinsella. He is a spy. He is a spy for Mu'ammar Qadhafi."

Over the coming weeks and months it would become clear that Abdul was telling me the truth. I would learn that Mousa Hawamda *was* an agent in Qadhafi's intelligence service and that for the past three years he had been Libya's senior spy in North America. In that capacity he had cultivated relationships with Ian Verner Macdonald and with dozens of other extremists from the far left and the far right.

This book is a record of my investigation into Libyan espionage activity in Canada. *Unholy Alliances* will not provide clear answers to every question it raises, but it will sketch the outlines of a story that, to me and my newspaper colleagues in 1988 and 1989, was startling.

This book is also an attempt to examine the unholy alliances that Mu'ammar Qadhafi—through intermediaries like Mousa Hawamda—has forged with white supremacists, hard-core Marxists, black Muslims, radical natives, anti-Semites, and other political extremists around the globe. It tries to show how Canada has come to play a central role in Qadhafi's decades-long war against Israel, the United States, and other Western nations. Most of all, *Unholy Alliances* argues that Qadhafi's regime remains a real threat. By every means at his disposal—chemical weapons, assassination squads, front companies, money laundering schemes, and the co-opting of neo-Nazis and leftist terrorists—the Libyan leader will continue to battle that which he has sworn to destroy: the imperialist West.

As Abdul put it to me shortly before he disappeared in 1989, "Mu'ammar Qadhafi is a madman. He is evil. And you who live in North America will pay a very big price if you do not take him as seriously as he takes you."

UNHOLY
ALLIANCES

At a few minutes past midnight on April 15, 1987, hundreds of people crowded into the shattered remains of the Bab al-Aziya barracks in Tripoli, Libya. Floodlights threw long shadows on the barracks' grimy white walls. Some areas had been roped off, and guards stood here and there, waiting. Broken glass crunched underfoot. Above it all a banner read, THE PEACE GATHERING TO COMMO-MORATE [sic] THE TRAGIC BOMBING OF LIBYA.

One year earlier, at 2:00 a.m., a group of U.S. Air Force F-111 jets had screamed through Libya's dark skies, scattering bombs on Tripoli and Benghazi, that country's two biggest cities. They had been sent by Ronald Reagan, the American president, in retaliation for a terrorist attack on a Berlin disco frequented by American service personnel. One American had died in that attack and many had been injured. One of the jet fighters' targets had been the Bab al-Aziya barracks, occasional home to Colonel Mu'ammar Qadhafi, Libya's leader. Among the 37 Libyans killed in the American reprisal had been Qadhafi's 15-month-old daughter, Hana.

In the centre of the barracks a large stage had been erected. To one side of it, chatting with a group of his black Muslim colleagues, was Akbar Mahamed, a leader of the American anti-Semitic group known as the Nation of Islam. Nearby, Ojibwa leader Vernon Belle-court waited quietly with a few dozen men and women belonging to another radical group, the American Indian Movement. Later, he would lead the AIM members in a song "to honour the people of Libya."

Some of the Indians present—the older ones—had been involved in the bloody two-month standoff at Wounded Knee, South Dakota, in 1973. Scattered through the crowd that night were members of obscure American groups such as the Native American Treaty Council, the All-African People's Revolutionary Party, the New Alliance Party, and the National Mobilization for Survival. Also present were a British Labour MP and senior representatives of the Palestine Liberation Organization and the Irish Republican Army.

Attending from Canada were an official from the Canadian Union of Postal Workers, a few Marxist university professors, and several dozen anti-American activists from the Ottawa area. Also part of this Canadian delegation, but keeping a low profile that night, were a dozen or so members of the Nationalist Party of Canada, a neo-Nazi group based in Toronto.

And above them all, surveying the neo-Nazis and leftists and Irish nationalists and Black Muslims, his dark eyes unblinking, his expression bemused, was Qadhafi himself, the man the evening's program described as "the International Revolutionary Leader." Qadhafi remained hidden from the delegates, watching. Because he is not stupid, Qadhafi knew that this night had no precedent. It should have been impossible to persuade so many fascist, leftist, and nationalist groups to convene to celebrate anything, let alone peace. But he had done it. Armed with generous amounts of cash, anti-Israeli credentials, and a byzantine political philosophy called the Third Position, the Libyan leader had forged his own anti-imperialist rainbow coalition. In other circumstances and in other places, those present in the Bab al-Aziya barracks would have been at each others' throats. On this night they were at Qadhafi's feet.

Some delegates walked the perimeter of the barracks to examine a grisly display: photographs of Libyans said to have been killed during the April 1986 air raid. Others listened attentively as one of Qadhafi's young sons, Saif el-Eslam, lectured them about the imperialist leaders in the United States and Israel. "The aggression has failed," said the boy. "It hasn't realized any of its objectives. Reagan has failed even with his sophisticated war planes. If defence of a country is terrorism, we are terrorists. Bombs can destroy iron but not our determination. Long live Qadhafi!" The delegates applauded when the boy, who appeared to be no more than ten years old, criticized Israel in squeaky Arabic and shook his tiny fist.

This was the evening's predominant theme: the "threat" posed by the Jewish state. Almost without exception the 2,000 Libyan, Palestinian, European, American, and Canadian delegates were resolute opponents of Israel. Although most would have denied it, when their shared philosophy was reduced to its base elements, the bulk of them subscribed to the tenets of classic anti-Semitism. For example, they believed in an international Jewish conspiracy, opposed Israel's right to exist within secure boundaries, and thought that the Holocaust was exaggerated—or that it didn't happen at all.

Some who were present were not bashful about their anti-Semitism; some, like America's Nation of Islam and Britain's far-right National Front, would dutifully spew anti-Jewish bile for anyone who had a few minutes to spare. This anti-Semitic coalition, whose member organizations promoted wildly conflicting views on race, was part of a growing movement called the Third Position. Like Germany's National Socialists before them, the Third Positionists were as anticapitalist as they were anticommunist. They were also largely bankrolled by Qadhafi's regime. Their slogan was emblazoned across the front of one of the pamphlets a National Front leader was distributing that night: HITLER AND MAO UNITED IN STRUGGLE!

But more than Hitler and Mao had brought these people together. What truly united the Third Positionists was a loathing of Israel and its international allies. Through terrorism and subversion, the Third Position partnership was seeking to wipe the slate clean— to expunge all traces of capitalist Western nations, and all traces of Soviet-style communism. The Third Positionists dreamed of emerging from the wreckage of the political forces that had shaped the twentieth century to establish a racist and anarchist society free of Jews, non-believers, and governments.

Those who march under the Third Position banner do not number many, but their movement is growing. Unlike others who reside at the political fringes, they have not been left in disarray by the collapse of the Berlin Wall. To them, the lifting of the Iron Curtain that once separated capitalism from communism merely confirms that, as the end of history approaches, those two competing ideologies deserve each other. Communism and capitalism are "falling apart at the seams," as one British Third Positionist newspaper recently put it. With the collapse of communism, they say, the collapse of capitalism cannot be far behind.

After the protests in Tripoli were over, some of the Third Positionists would leave Qadhafi's Libya, and with the amount of reflection most people reserve for flicking on a light, proceed to commit acts of terror around the globe. For example, the IRA would use Libyan money to purchase armaments, and the Nation of Islam would print pamphlets asserting that Jewish doctors were "injecting AIDS" into black babies. These men and women, and many others like them, are the shock troops in Qadhafi's decades-long war against the West, the well-paid mercenaries he sends out to do battle with the forces he imagines are arrayed against his small North African republic.

———————

Few are certain exactly when, but it is known that Mu'ammar Qadhafi was born in a goatskin tent near Sirte, midway between Tripoli and Benghazi. Most of his biographers agree that the year was in or around 1942, but even Qadhafi himself is not sure. In 1989 he told an interviewer, "When I was born, our country was under occupation. There were no records." In the Bedouin culture that formed him, such things matter little.

His parents, Abu Minyar and Aisha, named their only son Mu'ammar Muhammad Abu Minyar al-Qadhafi. Mu'ammar spent much of his childhood in the company of his mother and two sisters. Whenever Abu Minyar returned home to spend time with his family, he would tell his son about the role he had played in the guerrilla war against the Italian invaders in the late 1920s and early 1930s. The Italians, under their fascist leader Benito Mussolini, committed many atrocities against the Libyan people, Mu'ammar was told. Their troops machine-gunned tribesmen on horseback from airplanes. They forced Libyans off their land and into concentration camps. In the end, Abu Minyar and his brethren in the resistance had failed in their struggle—Libya was officially integrated into Italy in 1930. Even so, to the young Qadhafi, his father's tales of battles with the corrupt forces of imperialism were very heady stuff. He would not soon forget them.

The Qadhafis were not a wealthy family, but they scraped together enough money to send their son to a Muslim elementary school. There, many of his teachers were enthusiastic supporters of Gamal Abdel Nasser, who led Egypt's revolution in 1952 and was a fiery exponent of Arab nationalism. Qadhafi regularly tuned in to "Voice of the Arabs," Nasser's anti-Zionist radio program broadcast from Tripoli. The Egyptian revolutionary was almost a god to Qadhafi, who became a lifelong Nasserite. Even today, enormous photographs of Nasser can be seen along Tripoli's dusty streets, beside those of Qadhafi himself.

Qadhafi says that it was around 1954, when he was no more than 13 years old, that he started laying plans to overthrow Libya's reigning monarch, King Idris. It is reported that he once asked his Egyptian teacher, "Does the possibility of organizing a revolution in Libya exist? If a revolution were to be carried out in Libya, would Egypt come to the assistance of the Libyan people?" Many of the men who have been helping Qadhafi to rule Libya since the 1970s were his boyhood friends. Among them are Abdel Salem Jalloud, Qadhafi's second-in-command and Libya's former prime minister; Ali al-Houdery, who was head of the People's Committee for Libyan Students in Washington until his expulsion in 1981; and Abu Bakr Yunis Jabir, who was once chief of staff of the Libyan armed forces.

By the time he enrolled in Sabha High School in Fezzen, in Libya's southwest, Qadhafi was holding secret meetings with his peers to promote Nasserism and militant Arab unity. His enthusiasm got him in trouble: he was expelled in his third year for leading a student demonstration. After completing his high school education in Musurata in 1961, Qadhafi spent two years at the University of Tripoli, studying history. He dropped out in 1963, a decision he does not regret: almost 20 years later, he would say that compulsory education "suppresses freedom because it deprives man of free choice, creativity and brilliance."

In that same fateful year, Qadhafi was encouraged by his Nasserite friends to enter the Benghazi Military Academy. Later, he would claim that he only joined the academy to infiltrate King Idris's armed forces, with the goal of leading an eventual coup. Whatever is the case, Qadhafi graduated in 1965 and was sent to a British training academy at Beaconsfield in Buckinghamshire, England. He lived there for five months, studying British signal corps techniques. It was in Beaconsfield that young Lieutenant Qadhafi learned some English, which he now speaks—when he speaks it at all—in a husky and heavily accented bass.

Back home in Libya, Qadhafi's countrymen were growing resentful of King Idris's rule. Corruption in the bureaucracy was rampant, and Arab nationalism was gaining wider support. Perhaps most significantly, the Libyan people were not sharing in any of the wealth that had been flowing into their country since the discovery of huge oil fields there in the late 1950s. Instead, that wealth was being diverted into the pockets of the king and his entourage. When he returned to Tripoli in 1966, Qadhafi found a country on the edge of revolution. He and his high school friend, Abdel Salem Jalloud, then an army lieutenant, along with ten other like-minded Libyans, started planning a coup d'état.

The group of young Libyan military men called themselves the Free Unionist Officers. Lieutenant Mu'ammar Qadhafi was their obvious choice for leader. He was charismatic, intelligent, and a mesmerizing speaker. Women liked his looks: with his strong jaw and penetrating gaze, he might have stepped out of the screen of a Hollywood movie. He could sometimes be cruel and idiosyncratic— years later, Egypt's president Anwar Sadat would describe him as "one hundred per cent mad and possessed of the devil"—but he also possessed the qualities the plotters were seeking.

Time after time through the spring and summer of 1969 the plotters set the coup in motion. On each occasion they drew back at the last opportunity to wait for an even better moment to present itself. Finally, in late August of 1969, that moment arrived. King Idris and Queen Fatima were at a spa in Turkey, where the monarch was receiving medical treatment for a leg ailment. In the space of a few hours on the evening of August 31, 1969, several hundred Free Unionist Officers occupied airports, radio stations, and police stations in Tripoli, al-Bayda, and Benghazi. They encountered little resistance.

At dawn on September 1, 1969, in a revolutionary bulletin broadcast from a Benghazi radio station, Qadhafi announced the end of "the reactionary and corrupt regime, the stench of which has sickened and horrified us all." He was 27 years old.

Qadhafi, who did not identify himself during the radio broadcast, called for "freedom, socialism and unity." Shrewdly, he also extended an olive branch to the West, which was then regarding the coup with equal measures of amusement and apprehension. He proclaimed that all international treaties and agreements would remain in effect and that neither diplomatic personnel nor their property would be harmed in any way. A week later he was promoted to the rank of colonel and named commander-in-chief of the armed forces. Until that day the Libyan people had not known the name of the leader of the Free Unionist Officers.

King Idris never returned to Libya. He was sentenced to death *in absentia* in 1971; he died of natural causes in Egypt in 1983 at the age of 93. His son, the crown prince Hasan al-Rida, had by then renounced all rights to the throne.

Loath as some Western governments are to admit it, the early days of Qadhafi's rule were good ones for many Libyans. He reduced rents, doubled the minimum wage, and made education, child care, health care, and other benefits available to even the poorest in Libyan society. The Leader, as he came to be known, transformed Libya from a backward Third World country into a comparatively progressive Islamic republic.

In the midst of this new-found prosperity and benevolence there were portents of the tyranny and terror to follow. Jews living in Libya were encouraged to leave, and their property was confiscated by the government. Political parties were banned—an empty gesture, since King Idris had banned them years before. Trade unionism was declared a criminal activity, and women's and lawyers' associations were dissolved. Political dissenters were subject to intimidation and threats.

The Libyan parliament was abolished and a 12-man committee was established to run the new republic. It called itself the Revolutionary Command Council, and its powers were immense. For a time the council's membership was in a state of flux. Qadhafi himself did not join it formally until early 1970.

True to its Nasserite principles, the council drew its authority from the institution that had produced it—the Libyan armed forces. It promoted those young officers who were unequivocal in their support for the September 1 revolution, and it disposed of those who were not. The council also made clear its belief that the monarchy had permitted Libya's three million citizens to stray too far from traditional Islam: it quickly forbade the consumption of alcohol and ordered non-Muslim religious institutions to shut their doors. By 1970 the council had enacted a number of laws permitting punishments based on the teachings of the Koran. These ranged from amputation of limbs to death by stoning.

The council had turned Libya back to the precepts of traditional Islam and increased the influence of the military; in other respects it differed little from the court of King Idris in its approach to governing. For example, the new republic, though it called itself socialist, permitted Western petroleum companies to continue removing high-quality Libyan crude from its soil, just as Idris had done. The new Libya was touted as a true democracy, but in many respects civil liberties were more heavily curtailed under Qadhafi's rule than they had been under the monarchy.

There was, however, one key difference between the new republic and the old monarchy: leadership. King Idris had been seen as corrupt by most ordinary Libyans; the young Qadhafi was regarded as honest, and as a devout Muslim, and so maintained his popularity. Some of his ideas may have been hare-brained, but at least he was not a crook.

On April 15, 1973, during a speech in the Libyan town of Zuaza, Qadhafi unveiled his political and social philosophy, later known as the Third Universal Theory. (Its adherents in the West would call it the Third Position.) Collected in three volumes, the precepts he outlined that day would be known as *The Green Book*. This book was to be the blueprint for Libya's Green Revolution. Qadhafi would threaten to resign if it was not followed to the letter.

Qadhafi has characterized his theory as "an alternative to capitalist materialism and communist atheism." It is a mind-numbing mishmash of anti-Semitism, Maoism, racist theory, Arab nationalism, and the Koran—and, according to Qadhafi, just what the world needs. *The Green Book*'s first volume is called *The Solution of the Problem of Democracy.* Qadhafi describes it as no less than "the final solution to the problem of the instrument of governing."

The problem, Qadhafi writes, is that current political systems are inevitably the result of a struggle between competing groups, most often partisan groups. This dialectical process, he says, leads to "the defeat of genuine democracy." For example, if a person is a citizen of a nation with a parliamentary system—what the Libyan leader calls a "false democracy"—then that citizen is always obliged to abide by the wishes of the majority: "Forty-nine per cent of the electorate is ruled by an instrument they did not vote for." This is wrong, Qadhafi writes: "The most tyrannical dictatorships the world has known have existed under the shadow of parliament."

The solution to the antidemocratic dilemma, Qadhafi concludes, is "direct democracy." To achieve direct democracy in the Libyan style, one must establish popular congresses made up of average citizens, not politicians or bureaucrats. "Democracy," he writes, "is supervision of the people by the people."

In Libya a General People's Congress has been meeting since the mid-1970s to promote Qadhafi's direct democracy. This congress is made up of more than 2,000 "basic" congresses, which are classified according to geographic region. These small-scale congresses send delegates to the GPC, which meets once or twice a year and, theoretically, is Libya's supreme legislative and executive body. In reality,

Qadhafi holds a veto over all that the GPC does, despite the fact that he abandoned all his formal titles in 1977. In January 1984, for example, the GPC refused to bow to Qadhafi's suggestion that Libya introduce compulsory military training for all men and women. Within a matter of weeks Qadhafi had organized a series of well-attended demonstrations that angrily denounced the GPC's stance. By March the GPC was meeting in a special session to hastily approve compulsory military training for all. In their drive to forge direct democracy the GPC delegates had forgotten one of the lesser-known precepts in the first volume of *The Green Book:* "The stronger part in the society is the one that rules." And Qadhafi rules.

The Libyan regime's version of popular democracy was abandoned in March 1990. After an eight-day meeting in Tripoli, the GPC passed a law stating that Qadhafi's role in the 1969 revolution gave him a legitimacy from which all of Libya's institutions derived their authority: "So instructions issued by the leader of the great revolution, brother Colonel Mu'ammar Qadhafi, are binding and it is a duty to carry them out." With the passing of that law, Qadhafi stopped playing his political shell game: he was now Libya's supreme leader, with the power to overrule virtually any GPC decision.

The second volume of *The Green Book* was written by Qadhafi in 1976 and 1977. Libya's leader, who has never been noted for understatement, called it *The Solution of the Economic Problem.* The problem, Qadhafi writes, is that "the wage-worker is like a slave to the master who hires him." As a Third Positionist, Qadhafi does not distinguish between the capitalist exploiter and the communist exploiter; to him, there is no material difference between the two. He who produces goods should be the one who consumes those same goods, Qadhafi concludes. This idea forms the basis of the most celebrated of Qadhafi's slogans: "Partners, not wage earners."

All citizens are entitled to a home, a vehicle, and a salary. But at the same time, Qadhafi insists, they should not be permitted to act as landlords, nor should they dispense wages to others. It is not "natural," he writes, for one man to profit from the unequal distribution of wealth or goods. This is the "beginning of distortion and corruption," which leads to exploitation. (It is worth noting that Qadhafi's regime permitted major American petroleum companies to employ Libyans throughout most of the 1970s and 1980s and to realize huge profits extracting high-grade "sweet" crude from Libya's oil fields. It seems that the economic principles Qadhafi proclaims in the second volume of *The Green Book* are not as universal as he asserts—not even in Libya.)

The third volume of Qadhafi's *magnum opus* is *The Social Basis of the Third Universal Theory*. It is more of a running commentary on the headlines of the day than a philosophical statement. In it, the Libyan leader attempts to justify his well-known willingness to fund international terrorist movements. "Contemporary liberation movements are themselves social movements," he writes. "They will not come to an end before every other group is liberated from the domination of another group. The world is [now] passing through one of the regular cycles of the movement of history, namely, the national struggle in support of nationalism."

In this third and final text Qadhafi offers his wisdom on a wide range of subjects. In many cases he indulges himself in the most banal of generalities. On religion: "The religious factor ... may divide the national group or unite groups with different nationalisms." On families: "The social bond, cohesiveness, unity, intimacy and love are stronger at the family level than at the tribal level." He sometimes shows a perceptive grasp of human history: "National fanaticism is essential to the nation, but at the same time it is a threat to humanity." Women, meanwhile, deserve better than they are getting: "The East regards her as a commodity for buying and selling, while the West does not recognize her femininity."

To an outsider and even to many Libyans, *The Green Book* is bizarre, contradictory, and naïve. To Qadhafi it is the wisdom writ large. As the Libyan leader said in 1979, "*The Green Book* is the guide to the emancipation of man. *The Green Book* is the Gospel. The new Gospel. The Gospel of the new era, the era of the masses. In your gospels it is written, 'In the beginning there was the Word.' *The Green Book* is the Word. One of its words can destroy the world, or save it. The Third World only needs my *Green Book*. My Word."

In the years that followed the Green Revolution, Qadhafi became distant and eccentric. A 1982 CIA profile describes the Libyan leader as suffering from a "borderline personality disorder.... Under severe stress, he is subject to episodes of bizarre behavior when his judgment may be faulty." But Richard Helms, who once ran the CIA, refuses to dismiss the Libyan leader. "Qadhafi is in some respects crazy like a fox," he said in 1986. "His various moves, although seemingly outlandish, appear to have some strategic or tactical motive behind them. I think he's peculiar, quixotic, eccentric. But I don't think he's crazy by any means."

Whether he is crazy or not, Qadhafi can hardly be regarded as a run-of-the-mill dictator. He does not surround himself with the trappings of luxury; in fact, he favours an austere lifestyle and spends many nights alone in the desert, just as his Bedouin ancestors did. He wears brightly coloured capes and uniforms. He does not enjoy socializing and is not known to have any close friends. For companionship, he prefers women to men. He surrounds himself with female bodyguards.

Fearing assassination attempts—he has survived at least nine— he now travels in armoured busses and sleeps in tents at different locations in and around Tripoli. He never stays in one place more than two nights in a row. When he flies, which is not often, all other planes in Libya are grounded.

He thrills in making outrageous statements, most often about his despised foes, Israel and the United States. Moderate Arab leaders will one day be obliged to "drink the blood of the Zionist and American enemies," he once said. More recently, in July 1990, he accused the United States of deliberately introducing flesh-eating flies into

Libya as part of a campaign against his republic. "The Americans continue to wage war against us by sending these flies that they conceal in the products that we import," he told JANA, the state-run Libyan news agency.

––––––––––

Considering Qadhafi's character and beliefs, it is no surprise that nestled in his political bed is the strangest collection of kooks and extremists on the planet. In his two decades in power Qadhafi has patched together a coalition of startling variety. It includes terrorists and peace activists, dictators and the downtrodden. The oddest additions by far to his retinue are among the most recent—the white supremacists, the neo-Nazis, and the anti-Semites.

Qadhafi provides these groups with equal measures of material and rhetorical support. He relies upon agents and front companies around the world to promote the growth of violent ultra-rightist and ultra-leftist movements in Australia, Europe, the United States, and Canada. His basic objectives are clear: he wants to terrorize Jews around the globe, and he wants to cement his reputation as a global bad boy. Israel and its strongest ally, the United States, remain for Qadhafi the biggest obstacles to the establishment of a pan-Arab nationalist state. He believes that he hurts Israel by promoting anti-Semitism, and that he hurts the United States by funding terrorism.

But it is also clear that Qadhafi is much more than a gun-toting terrorist. The Libyan leader clings to the fierce hatred of the colonial mentality that he learned at his father's knee. Like many other modern African and Asian leaders, Qadhafi is driven by the need to assert his nation's independence, to establish and lead a society that is free from Western influence. But unlike many other Third World leaders, he has an almost obsessive desire to exact revenge for the real and imagined misdeeds of the past.

Some Western observers concede—reluctantly—that Qadhafi's

anti-imperialist strategy is a shrewd one and that he is good at what he does. They admit that forging a political alliance between fascists and Marxists around the globe is no easy task. The Libyan leader has accomplished exactly that by making huge payouts of Libyan petro-dollars with one hand, while insinuating the other into extremist politics.

Fearing direct confrontations with American military might, Qadhafi has embraced those tactics with which his regime is now synonymous. Western intelligence agencies report that, since coming to power in 1969, Qadhafi has channelled an estimated $100 million every year to extremist and terrorist groups all over the world, using Libyans and non-Libyans as couriers. In Europe, Libyan government funds have been passed to the Provisional Irish Republican Army, the Armenian Secret Army, the Basque Separatist Movement, Germany's Red Army Faction, and the Popular Forces of April 25 in Portugal. In the volatile Middle East, huge portions of Libya's oil wealth have been distributed to terrorist groups such as Black September, the Abu Musa faction, the Abu Nidal organization, and the Popular Front for the Liberation of Palestine. Other beneficiaries have included the Japanese Red Army, the Moro National Liberation Front in the Philippines, the American-based Nation of Islam, the militant American Indian Movement, and white supremacist groups like the Nationalist Party of Canada.*

Sometimes, as with the Nationalist Party of Canada, the Libyan money is used to finance relatively harmless activities such as the publishing of pamphlets and the sending of delegates to conferences in Tripoli. But at other times, the Libyan leader has been a major financial backer of Palestinian terrorist groups opposed to the relatively

---

*More recently, in July 1990, the *New York Times* reported that the Muslim mastermind of a bloody failed coup in Trinidad had received military training in Libya only months before: rebel leader Abu Bakr claimed to be a "personal friend" of Qadhafi and told British journalists he had visited Libya many times.

moderate policies of PLO chairman Yasser Arafat. Libyan money has paid for the killing or maiming of hundreds of innocent people around the globe.

Even when a mid-1980s oil glut pushed Libya's annual petroleum revenues down to $7 billion from $20 billion, Qadhafi continued to fund extremism. As the Libyan leader said in November 1986, "We have increased our support for the liberation movements of the Palestinians and for all liberation movements throughout the world. To react to aggression, we have doubled our efforts with the liberation movements."

In October 1991, a French judge issued arrest warrants for four Libyan officials—including Qadhafi's brother-in-law—relating to their suspected involvement in a bloody terrorist attack on a Union de Transports Aériens flight over the Sahara in September 1989; 170 people were killed in that attack. The French warrants were issued shortly before two Libyan agents were charged with complicity in the bombing of a Pan Am flight in December 1988 over Lockerbie, Scotland; 270 people were killed in that bombing, which at first had been thought to be the work of Iranian- or Syrian-backed terrorists.

The United States and Britain demanded that the Tripoli regime hand over the two suspects named in the Lockerbie case. Qadhafi refused, telling a press conference, "The evidence against Libya is less than a laughable piece of fingernail." He even claimed that the plane had crashed due to bad weather. By April 1992, Libya's government was still refusing to extradite the two men: the U.N. Security Council voted to impose air, arms, and diplomatic sanctions against Libya.

In October 1989, Qadhafi had reluctantly admitted that he *had,* in fact, been supporting terrorism. "We erroneously thought that these groups could be part of the Arab national liberation movement," he admitted in a magazine interview. "But we found out that they were practising terrorism for the sake of terrorism and for other objectives that had nothing to do with our national cause."

In many cases, the extremist groups that Qadhafi funds are

laughing up their sleeves at his eccentric policies. But for the most part they have resisted the impulse to criticize him publicly: Libyan money buys their collective silence. For many terrorist cells Qadhafi's benevolence has meant the difference between political life and political death. In return for the Libyan leader's crucial support, leftist and rightist organizations have agreed to mount clandestine joint operations, to exchange intelligence information, and to adhere in general terms to Libya's unique view of the world. One result is that Qadhafi has been able to cling to the fantasy that he is a key player on the international political stage.

Qadhafi is not the Arab world's kingpin of international terrorism: the governments of Iran, Iraq, and Syria fund far more organized butchery than Libya. But unlike those nations, Libya has managed to bring together groups that in any other circumstances would be devoting their considerable energies to murdering each other—groups as disparate as the violently anti-British Irish Republican Army and the fiercely anti-Irish National Front in Britain; or the ultra-leftist Red Army Faction in West Germany and the ultra-rightist National Democratic Front in the United States.

Qadhafi has bought the extremists' complicity with millions in Libyan dinars. But his success cannot be attributed to money alone. In no small way it also testifies to the Libyan leader's skills as a political manipulator. Key to his success has been his doctrine of the Third Position, which, some have noted, is similar to China's "Theory of the Three Worlds." The basis of this latter theory is that the Third World must co-operate to counteract the pernicious influence of the superpowers. When Qadhafi writes that "man's freedom is lacking if someone else controls what he needs," he is criticizing both capitalism and communism.

The Third Position, though an ideology, is anti-ideology. It is also vague enough to admit groups holding starkly contrasting views. Any group that is anticapitalist, anticommunist, and anti-Israel can call itself Third Positionist.

Little has been written in the mainstream media about the Third Position, which does not usually court publicity. It is made up of men and women who lack the public relations skills of the Black Panthers or the Ku Klux Klan. But with its anticapitalist and anti-communist credo, the Third Position is a racist alliance designed for the 1990s. To those within the movement, the political collapse of the Soviet Union (the heart of communism) and the social collapse of the urban United States (the heart of modern capitalism) are not unforeseen events. They are prophecies come true.

Understandably, for many reporters, a fusion of far-right and far-left lunatics sounds too bizarre to be credible. But it is a fact: the Third Position exists. And it is growing.

In Europe one of the most active Third Position organizations is the virulently anti-Semitic International Third Position, led by Nick Griffin. The ITP has actively sought Libyan and Iraqi funding. Griffin, a Cambridge graduate who was at one time a leading figure in Britain's racist and anti-Semitic National Front, has purchased property in the Normandy countryside to be used as a Third Position "commune." His group has also published glossy anti-Jewish hate sheets and printed stickers that call the United States "a Zionist state." The ITP is dedicated to the destruction of Israel. It favours changing society through violence and supports the forced repatriation of non-whites to their countries of origin.

Another Third Position movement gaining strength in Britain calls itself Liberation. Like the ITP, Liberation began as a splinter group from the National Front and is more radical than its parent. Led by a convicted criminal named Colin Todd and a former National Front activist named Phillip Andrews, Liberation's members made an eight-day visit to Baghdad in the fall of 1990. There, they and some members of the ITP met with the Speaker of the Iraqi Parliament, the Deputy Minister of Information, and the Minister for Religious Affairs. It is alleged that both groups were seeking funding to train a Third Position army filled with what Todd calls "political soldiers."

Libya has also managed to secure the support of the National Front, Britain's most powerful fascist organization in the postwar years. This group was formed in the winter of 1966 out of a number of racist and anti-Semitic groups, the largest being the League of Empire Loyalists, the Racial Preservation Society, the National Party, and the Greater Britain Movement. Its original membership was around 4,000. Within seven years this figure had grown to 17,500 and the Front was enjoying a degree of success at the ballot box in local elections. Its anti-immigrant themes were attracting voters.

This all changed when Margaret Thatcher's Conservatives were elected in 1979. Thatcher's right-wing policies robbed the National Front of much of its natural base of support. The group's leaders reasoned that democratic reform was a waste of time and that a more forceful approach was needed if they were ever going to establish a Fourth Reich. They called this new approach the Third Position. (Ronald Reagan's 1980 electoral victory would have much the same effect on the far right in the United States.)

The Front took its catch phrase from Terza Posizione, an underground terrorist cell associated with Italy's right-wing Armed Revolutionary Nuclei (NAR). The NAR claimed responsibility for an August 1980 bombing in a Bologna railway station that left 85 people dead and over 200 injured. A few weeks after the Bologna murders, Terza Posizione's organizer, Roberto Fiore, fled to London. There he would go on to transform the National Front into a sleek paramilitary organization.

In May 1987, American journalists Martin A. Lee and Kevin Coogan reported in *Mother Jones* that the Third Position was a "bizarre Nazi-Maoist doctrine." They predicted that it would soon become the dominant ideology among neo-Nazis throughout Western Europe. According to Lee and Coogan, the Third Position activists had "adopted an incongruous set of heroes—Hitler, Mao, Qadhafi, and Peron—and shouted slogans like, 'Long live the fascist dictatorship of the proletariat!'" One Third Positionist had even written a letter to Qadhafi asking him to join the battle against "atheistic Soviet Marxism and American capitalist materialism," both of which, he said, were "controlled by international Zionism."

Such sloganeering enthralled Qadhafi. The revitalized National Front was soon receiving direct funding from the Libyan government. It could now publish vicious anti-Semitic propaganda and hold white supremacist rallies. In return for the money, the National Front printed glowing reports on Qadhafi. Some Front members even sold copies of Qadhafi's *Green Book*—and turned a profit at it.

In the March 1988 edition of the *National Front News* a "new alliance" was heralded: its members included Qadhafi, Iranian leader Ayatollah Khomeini, Nation of Islam leader Louis Farrakhan, and the National Front. The front-page article read,

> Revolutionary nationalist groups, racial separatists and the anti-Zionist nations of the Middle East, are beginning to recognize a common set of interests and enemies which make closer co-operation both beneficial and inevitable. Against our common enemies—capitalism and communism—we are at last beginning to develop a credible alternative: the Third Way.

The big rally finally finished. Shortly after 2:00 a.m. on April 15, 1987, hundreds of peace conference delegates started to leave what remained of Qadhafi's Bab al-Aziya barracks. While they lined up to board the busses that would take them back to Tripoli, they did not talk much. They were tired. It had been a long day filled with chanting and speeches and revolutionary fervour.

Some delegates, however, were more than tired—they were also terrified. They kept silent, worried that they would be overheard by one of the "companions" Qadhafi's government had assigned to shadow them. Many would remember how a cloud of gloom was descending on the peace conference, thickening with each hour.

One delegate, a young woman from Montreal named Michelle Tardif, searched the crowd for the face of a friend, a journalist from Ottawa. She could not see him. A few days earlier the journalist had predicted that the bizarre peace conference, with its volatile mix of neo-Nazis, leftist terrorists, and other extremists, was going to end in tragedy. The young woman had not believed him. They had bet a bottle of scotch on it.

The young woman squinted into the dense Tripoli night. "Where is he?" she asked another delegate. "Where *is* he?"

2

THE DEATH
OF CHRISTOPH

Michelle Tardif had just turned 25 when she met an Ottawa journalist named Christoph Halens in a waiting room at Montreal's Mirabel International Airport. It was Thursday, April 9, 1987. Tardif, whose friends called her Mimi, was an occasional columnist for a small-circulation arts paper called the *Montreal Mirror*. She was outgoing and talkative and hard to miss in a crowd. That day she was sporting long, dark hair pulled back in a ponytail, purplish make-up, and a miniskirt. She was pleased, she later recalled, that a bona fide Canadian journalist was travelling to Tripoli for Mu'ammar Qadhafi's April 1987 "peace conference." The two struck up a conversation while trip organizers checked the list of delegates and distributed plane tickets.

"I had befriended Christoph at the airport because he was a reporter," she remembers. "As far as I could see, he was the only guy who was. Being a reporter myself, I just got friendly with him."

Tardif was bright but not very political. She admits that she regarded the free trip to Tripoli as a lark. Halens impressed her as a reflective but friendly man with a "scholarly" bent. She remembers his neatly trimmed beard, and that his eyes were bright with good-natured curiosity. The two chatted amiably.

Halens had a sharp intellect and was a well-read observer of international affairs. As he and Tardif talked, Halens suggested that the conference he was being sent to cover likely had more to do with propaganda than with peace. But in and of itself, such an assignment was not unusual: people like to read about peace, and newspapers are generally happy to oblige them. That the Libyan regime was funding and organizing the peace conference—*that* was unusual.

Libya had rarely if ever been associated with peace. Western spy agencies estimated that between 1975 and 1985 Libya had initiated 200 terrorist operations that had killed 100 people and wounded 500 more. As Ronald Reagan had said in his April 14 televised address that announced the American bombing raid, "Colonel Qadhafi is not only an enemy of the United States. His record of subversion and aggression against the neighbouring states in Africa is well documented and well known. He has ordered the murder of fellow Libyans in countless countries. He has sanctioned acts of terror in Africa, Europe, and the Middle East, as well as the Western Hemisphere."

But Halens also suspected that Qadhafi's peace conference was much more than an opportunity to bash Reagan. According to his friends and colleagues, Halens had heard from sources that the conference was a smokescreen designed to divert attention from Libya's real goal, which was to secretly pass on funds to extremists based in the United States. The American radicals feared detection, Halens knew, because receiving Libyan money was now against the law in the United States. In January 1986, Reagan had made any kind of financial transaction with Libya—or even travel to that country—a serious criminal offence punishable by lengthy jail terms and stiff fines.

As Halens and Tardif killed time in Mirabel's lounge, four dozen other Canadians milled about, waiting to board the Alitalia red-eye flight to Rome. It was, to put it mildly, an eclectic group. Among those travelling to Libya were Ian Verner Macdonald, who frequently discussed policy with the Grand Wizard of the Canadian Ku Klux Klan; Ingrid Beisner, a housewife from Kemptville, Ontario, who raised funds for Ernst Zundel, a Toronto publisher of anti-Semitic materials; and, later, Anne Ladas, director of the Nationalist Party of Canada, the biggest white supremacist organization in eastern Canada.

Also bound for Libya, but representing the opposite end of the political spectrum, were Eibie Weizfeld, the founder of the Parliament Hill Peace Camp, which was established to protest cruise missile testing in Canada; and a smattering of Marxists and peace group organizers from Ottawa and Montreal. The leftists waited, reading magazines, chatting amongst themselves, impatient for the great adventure to begin. None, it seems, had been told that more than a dozen white supremacists and professional anti-Semites had also been invited to the conference.

The Canadians' air fare and accommodation were being paid entirely by the Socialist People's Libyan Arab Jamahiriya (a Libyan neologism meaning, literally, "State of the Masses"). Partly because Libya maintained no embassy in Ottawa, Ian Verner Macdonald had been asked to find 90 or so delegates to attend the four-day peace conference. Credentials were easy to obtain: for the price of a single phone call, those who contacted Macdonald at his home in Ottawa's embassy district were guaranteed a return flight to Libya.

Rumours about the conference had been circulating in peace organizations in Montreal and Ottawa for much of March and April. Halens, a founding member of Ottawa's Disarmament Coalition, had discussed the planned conference with two of his bosses at Southam News and suggested that it might make for a good news story. To Halens' surprise, managing editor Doug Fischer and general manager Nick Hills asked him if he wanted to cover the conference himself. Southam, they told him, would gladly pay his expenses and air fare. They gave him a laptop computer and told him to write about the peace conference when he returned to Canada.

The peace conference was Halens' first chance to do any reporting for Southam. He had been looking for the opportunity ever since joining the national news service in 1983. The Carleton University graduate had been that agency's chief librarian and researcher but had done no actual news gathering, so the peace conference was his big break. After Ian Verner Macdonald agreed to let him attend—he would be the only accredited Canadian journalist to do so, Macdonald told him—Halens wrote a letter to his family at their home in Barntrup, West Germany. In it, he promised to visit them for his father's seventieth birthday party on April 24.

The Libyan peace conference generated a good deal of media coverage in eastern Canada—after all, it was not every day that a foreign nation paid out more than $1 million to fly 95 Canadians across an ocean to march in a parade.

The conference also stirred up plenty of controversy. Many of those who had agreed to take part were being strongly criticized by other peace activists. Some argued that anti-Israel sentiment was fine, but that Qadhafi's well-documented support of international terrorist movements proved that he was hardly interested in peace. But the 95 delegates—some of them sincere, some naïve, and some (like Tardif) merely interested in a free trip—were not swayed. The risks were worth it. Some now say that a small news story in the early editions of the April 9 *Globe and Mail* should have changed their minds. On page 9 of that morning's paper a headline read, "Zundel Supporter in Libyan Peace Trip Group."

The news item stated that a Toronto man called Jurgen "Jerry" Neumann was expected to be one of the conference delegates. Neumann had served as Ernst Zundel's aide and bodyguard in 1985, while the Toronto publisher was being prosecuted for spreading false news about the Holocaust—namely, that it did not happen.

"The reason I'm going [to Libya] is because it's free and I've never been to North Africa," Neumann was quoted as saying. "Personally, I think the U.S. bombing was the act of a bully. They now admit Syria is involved in all the terrorism. And so the Americans murdered Qadhafi's daughter for nothing."

Sensing a public relations disaster in the offing, some of the peace conference's Canadian organizers told the *Globe and Mail* that Neumann would not be permitted to attend the event. This, like the peace conference itself, turned out to be a lie. Michelle Tardif recalls seeing Neumann on the plane to Rome, though at the time she did not know who he was. "I remember seeing these weird-looking guys climbing aboard, but I didn't think much of it."

———————

Twelve hours later, on Friday, April 10, the Canadian peace conference delegates stood in the lobby of the Hotel Portamaggiore in Rome, their bags at their feet, waiting for Ahmad Eed Murad to return. It had been a long flight. They were bone-tired and irritable.

Murad was a member of Ottawa's Association of Palestinian-Arab Canadians. He was a big man with blunt features and had a distracted air about him. His association had aggressively lobbied against an Ottawa Board of Education proposal to develop a Holocaust Studies program. He spent much of his time advancing the interests of Qadhafi's quixotic regime in Canada. Working out of a tidy bungalow in Ottawa's suburban south, Murad was Libya's "agent"—his term—in Canada's capital.

It was while making the rounds on Ottawa's endless circuit of embassy parties that Murad met Ian Verner Macdonald. The two got along well. In 1987 they joined forces to fight the Ottawa board's Holocaust Studies proposal. Later that year Murad suggested to the

Libyans that they retain Macdonald to find Canadian delegates to the peace conference. The Libyans agreed.

Murad ambled over from the hotel's reception desk, clapping his hands as he approached the group. "Our rooms will not be ready for another couple of hours," Murad said to a chorus of groans. "Now might be a good time to meet each other."

Tardif introduced herself, as did Halens. Then Anne Ladas addressed the group. "I'm here because I'm pro-Qadhafi, anti-Zionist, pro-Palestinian, and I'm from the Nationalist Party of Canada," Ladas said. Most of those present had never heard of the Nationalist Party. But Halens was well-read on the subject of Canada's far right. He inched forward as if to make sure he had heard Ladas correctly. In rapid succession eight other delegates proclaimed that they, too, were members of the Nationalist Party. Then a tenth member of the group stepped forward to speak, complaining that he could not make out what anybody was saying.

This strapping older man—at 6 feet, 6 inches and 220 pounds, he towered above every other delegate—said his name was Jacob Prins. "Jack" Prins was the "international ambassador" of the white supremacist Western Guard in the 1970s and had twice been a Toronto aldermanic candidate. As they listened in stunned silence, Prins told his fellow delegates that he had "fought in the streets" for freedom during World War II. "And it is well-known," he added, "that Jews control the Soviet Union's secret police, the KGB."

If there had ever been any doubts about the ideological outlook of the Nationalist Party members, there were none now. Within minutes a group of outraged delegates—one Canadian jokingly labelled them "the Yappies"—had cornered Ahmad Eed Murad, demanding to know why Prins, Ladas, and their ilk were considered worthy of Tripoli's hospitality. Murad told them the Nationalist Party delegates had picked up their airline tickets before he could intercept them. Few were satisfied with his explanation. "Right off the bat, it was a freaky story," Tardif recalled. "I mean, those guys were sympathizers of Ernst Zundel, for Christ's sake! How could they be there?"

How, indeed. Moments after Prins concluded his anti-Semitic rant, a number of delegates were huddling to discuss ways to deal with the ultra-rightists. Halens listened, but like any good journalist, he did not participate. The deliberations would continue through the day, with the Yappies periodically demanding that Murad expel the Nationalist Party members from the Canadian delegation. Murad repeatedly refused to do so.

Tardif was less upset than most by the controversy. She dropped off her bags in her room and then headed downstairs to meet up with a Roman friend. On her way through the hotel lobby she stopped to talk with Halens and an Ottawa lawyer named Terry Jabour. The two were sitting on a bench, eating cashew nuts and listening to the other delegates debate the threat posed by the white supremacists.

She remembers, "I said to Christoph, 'Boy, you've got a hot story here, don't you?' Since Ernst Zundel was kind of hot in the news right then, Christoph thought this was a big deal, you know?"

After a moment's thought, she adds, "But that story was going to backfire on him later on."

————————

One of the Yappies was Peter Bleyer, a 23-year-old Montrealer studying at the London School of Economics. Bleyer, who calls himself a progressive activist, had been visiting friends in Ottawa in late March when he heard about the Libyan peace conference. After a bit of soul-searching, he decided to attend. The decision was a tough one, he says now: his family is Jewish, and Qadhafi is not fussy about Jews. He decided to go because he believed Arabs were being denied a proper role in the debate over a Palestinian homeland.

By 2:00 a.m., after listening to 12 or so hours of brain-numbing argument between the white supremacists and the peace activists, Bleyer had made up his mind: he would not go to Libya. When he told Murad about his decision, Halens was sitting beside him, sipping an Italian beer.

"Murad was giving me this spiel," Bleyer remembers, "saying I shouldn't worry, that a whole delegation of Jews was coming to the conference. He said: 'Maybe you know one of them, he's a friend of mine. His name is Eibie Weizfeld'."

Bleyer knew him. Weizfeld was a 37-year-old Montrealer who, when not promoting peace, owned and ran an avant-garde art gallery. He and another man achieved national notoriety in 1985 when they used sledgehammers to batter a statue near the entrance to Parliament's Centre Block. The two claimed they were promoting the peace movement. They caused $15,000 in damage and were each sentenced to 30 days' imprisonment. Bleyer recalls, "When Murad said Weizfeld was coming, that's when I knew for sure that I wasn't going."

Bleyer was unable to exchange his airline ticket and didn't know how he was going to make it back to London. Halens was sympathetic, Bleyer remembers. "Christoph said to me—and I'll never forget this—that he supported my decision. 'If I wasn't going as a journalist, I'd do what you are doing,' he said."

Later on, after taking in a few ideological screaming matches, Halens sat on his bed at the Portamaggiore while Jabour, his assigned roommate, read. Halens was frowning. Before leaving Canada he had anticipated that he would be filing a few news stories about the presence of radical delegates at Tripoli, and that the American Indian Movement and the Nation of Islam would be represented there, and that the presence of Canadian Marxists at the same conference would be an interesting local angle. But a delegation comprised of far-left types *and* fascists? Somehow he knew that this "Third Position" he had heard about was worth a hard look. He suspected that his editors would want him to explain why the Qadhafi government was playing footsie with both the ultra-left and the ultra-right. But he did not have that explanation—not yet.

Halens flipped through his note pad. Before leaving Ottawa he was extensively briefed by Jonathan Manthorpe, a Southam veteran, on how to keep himself out of trouble while reporting from abroad. Keeping oneself out of trouble was particularly important in a country like Libya. In the early days of the Green Revolution the ubiquitous People's Courts often prosecuted journalists for writing stories that criticized the new regime. The Libyans considered such stories treasonable. Halens was also well-briefed on Qadhafi's readiness to fund extremist political organizations. One of Halens' friends recalls, "How the money was coming in to the extremist groups in Canada and the United States—*that* of course was the story to be found. And that would have been a big story."

The next morning, Saturday, April 11, the remaining delegates were driven to Rome's Leonardo da Vinci airport in a chartered bus. The mood of the Canadian group was decidedly sour and growing worse. Terry Jabour, who had spent much of the previous day sightseeing along Rome's Via Veneto with Halens, recalls that some of the delegates were forming cliques and that some were even sneaking photographs of other Canadian delegates. "Everybody was imagining undercurrents," Jabour remembers. "It was a very oppressive atmosphere. You had the so-called neo-Nazis and the so-called radical leftists. And there was this clash of right versus left.

"And underlying the whole trip was a total lack of organization. It was chaotic from the word go in terms of what to do, where to go, who was on the trip, that kind of thing. I don't think they even knew how many people they had on that trip. They kept doing head counts, and they were constantly losing passports, or people, or tickets." He shakes his head as he remembers. "I was thinking to myself, 'What the hell am I getting myself into!'"

Some of the delegates, including Halens, were equally curious about Jabour, who says he was told about the conference by his client and friend, Ahmad Eed Murad. Jabour, who considers himself an "adventurer" with no strong political views, states that he joined the Canadian delegation as a last-minute replacement for a delegate who made other plans.

Halens had a girlfriend named Rosemary Knes, a Southam News editor in Ottawa. He called her twice from Rome. During one of those calls he admitted to being worried about filing a story on the confrontations between the white supremacists and the leftists. She asked him why. "My room-mate is always hanging around," he told her, "always looking over my shoulder. I get the definite feeling he was assigned to me, to keep an eye on me."

———————————

Much later, Terry Jabour stretches out in a chair, his hands clasped behind his head. Jabour, a third-generation Lebanese Canadian, is wearing wire-rimmed glasses, a baggy brown corduroy jacket, and a few days' growth of beard. He shrugs, almost amused. He has just been asked if he spied on Christoph Halens.

"I was a last-minute addition," he answers in his resonant baritone. "A few days before the trip, I was asked if I was interested in going to Libya, and I said sure. But I wasn't part of any group, and I didn't really know anybody."

Jabour is told that Halens called Rosemary Knes two days before flying to Tripoli. According to Knes, Halens believed that Jabour may have been brought along to shadow him. When Halens' allegations are read back to him, Jabour rolls his eyes. "Yeah, I heard later on that he had phoned her from Rome," he says. "Maybe he thought I was too pushy."

In person, Jabour does not seem very pushy. He does not raise his voice; he is polite; he tells self-deprecating jokes. He presides over a one-man legal practice—mostly to do with real estate—that gives him little spare time. He has an office in downtown Ottawa and owns a restaurant in Wakefield, Quebec, and is unmarried. He says he has few political beliefs. He went to the peace conference merely because he was curious, he says.

He derides allegations that he was a pro-Libyan spy and—as a CBC journalist would say—that he was "part of a conspiracy" to cover up criminal activity at the Libyan peace conference. He and Halens became room-mates by coincidence, according to Jabour. There was no conspiracy. He adds that he was pleased to be assigned a room with someone who was "normal."

Christoph Halens was "a nice guy," Jabour says pleasantly.

Christoph Halens—his full surname was Lehmann-Halens—was born in 1955 in Munich, Germany. His father, Horst, was a technician for UNICEF; he and his wife Cybil have three other children, one of whom, Stefan, is Christoph's twin. The Halens family lived in Rye, New York for ten years, until Christoph was 12. In 1969, Horst Halens was transferred to New Delhi, where Christoph developed a love of Indian art. (His apartment in Ottawa was full of it.) In 1972, Christoph and Stefan were enrolled in a boarding school in Bavaria near the famous Schloss Neuschwanstein castle. A year later the entire family returned to the United States, this time to Greenwich, Connecticut.

In 1974, after graduating from high school, Halens moved to Ottawa, where he buried himself in philosophy and political science at Carleton University. In 1975, while still there, he married Donna Jowett, a Carleton Ph.D. student. They separated on amicable terms two years later. After graduating from Carleton, Halens engineered a student referendum to set up a Carleton branch of the Ontario Public Interest Research Group, an environmentalist lobby. The referendum succeeded. He was OPIRG's first co-ordinator.

By all accounts, Halens *was* a nice guy: friendly, unpretentious, bright.

"He was very smart, very sharp, a very fast thinker." So says Desmond Gray, a bureaucrat at Statistics Canada who was Halens' best friend. "He was a very good speaker, and he was very funny. He had a very fine wit. He was a very good debater, and he was excellent at presentation. I wouldn't say he was a saint—he had his good days and his bad days, like all of us. But he was a good person."

In 1983, Rosemary Knes helped Halens to get a librarian's job at Southam's Ottawa bureau. According to Knes, Halens was well-liked at the news service. He contributed a lot of story ideas and was known to be thorough in the research he produced. Nick Hills, who is now editor-in-chief of the *Vancouver Sun,* says he had a high regard for Halens: "He really contributed a lot. He was always one of those people you could rely upon." There was talk of making him the news bureau's Access to Information writer. Knes says that Halens was happy.

The Canadian delegation arrived in Tripoli on Saturday, April 11, and booked into the Zanzour Tourist Village. Throughout the peace conference, Halens and Tardif—and sometimes Jabour—would meet in the room the two men shared, room 134, to pool information or discuss Halens' story. The bid to expel the white supremacists in Rome had failed. The three talked about what was going to happen next. They would drink late into the night. Alcohol is forbidden in Libya, but Jabour had managed to smuggle in some cognac and two bottles of scotch. Most of the time the three delegates had nothing to do, so they conferred with each other. At all hours of the day they held meetings, "like cub reporters in the midst of an international conspiracy," Tardif says.

Halens, Tardif, and Jabour were bored, as were many of the delegates. The conference had no agenda and had scheduled no significant events except the rally at Bab al-Aziya barracks, which would last only two hours. Tripoli and its environs offered little excitement. The conference organizers offered excursions to the capital's old shopping district, the Roman ruins at Subrata, the Geryan mountains, the municipal zoo, and a children's festival. The delegates, most of whom had travelled around the world to attend a political conference, did not consider them worth seeing. Generally they found Libya to be a dull, uninspiring place. Its people plodded through grey, dusty streets. The stalls in the marketplace were empty of goods. The countryside was as sterile and craggy as a lunar landscape.

"The [conference] was disappointing, in that there was very little substance to it," recalls Michael Marsh of the War Resisters' League, an American peace group. "At no time were we offered the opportunity to have an exchange with someone knowledgeable about the achievements of the Libyan revolution. Instead of visiting schools, hospitals and development projects, the majority of our trip focussed on tourist sites, such as the Tripoli Zoo. Though it is a very nice zoo, seeing it did not give me a deeper understanding of Libyan society." The Libyans were not at all concerned that the North Americans were unimpressed with their organizational skills. Complaints were met with blank stares and indifference.

Many delegates were beginning to suspect that the Libyans had duped them. Halens and Tardif had grown certain that the entire event was a hoax and that the Libyans "were up to no good," as Halens himself put it. The layout of the Zanzour Tourist Village, where they were staying, did little to diminish their fears. The state-run villa, on the Mediterranean coast just outside Tripoli, was surrounded by a chain-link fence, a guarded gateway, and an indeterminate number of plain-clothes security men. Albert Nerenberg, a colleague of Tardif's in Montreal who is now a columnist for the *Montreal Gazette,* recalls watching two delegates attempt to visit what appeared to be a missile silo down the road from the hotel. Within minutes, according to Nerenberg, "they were intercepted and brought back to the compound. There was a feeling we couldn't leave."

Tension grew when the Libyans arranged for "companions"— most of them students from Tripoli University—to follow delegates around the conference sites. When one New York representative of the National Mobilization for Survival eluded his guards during an excursion to Tripoli, he was arrested for being "a suspicious foreign photographer."

The character of their fellow delegates worried Halens and many other North Americans at the conference. Hundreds of people were attending from all over Europe, the Middle East, and the United States. Rumoured to be rubbing elbows with the leaders of the PLO and the IRA were terrorists from France's Action Direct and West Germany's Red Army Faction.

When members of the 200-member American delegation learned that Canadian white supremacists were present, one senior Black Muslim, Akbar Mahamed, requested a meeting with the conference organizers. At a raucous summit on the morning of Sunday, April 12, American delegates threatened to leave Libya unless the white supremacists were ejected. That afternoon a dozen ultrarightist Canadians, including the Nationalist Party members and Ian Verner Macdonald, were quietly bussed to the Bab Al-Bahar hotel in downtown Tripoli.

For most of the Canadian delegates, the expulsion of the white supremacist group was long overdue. For Halens and others, it ultimately meant little: the peace conference was growing more hellish with each passing hour; gloom hung over it like a poisonous fog. Grim-faced, Halens told one delegate, "I feel like cannon fodder."

No one will ever know what Christoph Halens was going to write about Libya. The key notes he kept are gone, as is anything he may have written on his laptop computer.

There is evidence, however, that Halens' story would have embarrassed Qadhafi's regime. The Libyans had plenty to lose: they had spent millions of dollars transporting delegates to the peace conference and another $200,000 to pay for a two-way video transmission of the conference's most newsworthy event—the April 15 parade in front of Bab al-Aziya barracks, featuring a few hundred chanting Western delegates. Almost as much money had been disbursed to organize a concurrent demonstration in front of Washington's White House. A great deal had been invested in the planned propaganda coup, and the Libyans were not about to let a nosy Canadian journalist spoil it all.

Halens took pains to avoid offending his Libyan hosts while in Tripoli. Michelle Tardif recalls that when he conducted interviews in Libya, he was tactful to the point of secretiveness. Rosemary Knes remembers that when Halens called her from Rome, he was worried about attracting the attention of what he called "gangster types." When Knes pressed him to write a story before he arrived in Tripoli, Halens balked. "No," he told her, "you don't fool with these people."

Tardif says that Halens was exercising profound caution: "His main worry was, if he overshadowed the conference with this Nazi story, that wasn't going to please our Libyan hosts. He was worried about his story, but he was also worried about his own life." She adds that he was not alone—many other delegates were starting to wish they had never come.

On the evening of Sunday, April 12, Halens, Tardif, and Jabour assembled to drink scotch and talk. Halens seemed pensive. "Tomorrow is the big day," he said. "I think there's going to be a People's Court." He told Tardif and Jabour that the Canadians were being blamed for disrupting the peace conference. He noted that some of the Black Muslims had learned about the presence of the white supremacists and almost scuttled the entire event. "Maybe because [the Canadians] disrupted the conference so much, they're going to punish us. They're going to try us for that." Darkly, he added, "No matter what happens to me, Southam stock is going to skyrocket."

At around 8:00 a.m. the next day, Monday, April 13, Halens and Jabour went shopping in Tripoli's Old City. Halens wanted to buy a bracelet for Rosemary Knes. He found nothing he liked. Later he returned to the tourist village for a stroll on the beach. Tardif, meanwhile, elected to attend an anti-American rally at a stadium in Tripoli's Souk al-Joumaa suburb, by herself. On the bus to the rally site she was confronted by a Libyan man she did not know. He was aggressive and angry.

"I was completely terrified by him," she says. "This was the People's Court Christoph had talked about. The questions he was asking me were not casual at all—who funded the paper I worked for, what I was going to write about. I said to him I wrote mostly about entertainment and movies. I was playing dumb. At the end of it, he relented. He said, 'Well, maybe you can be important in our organization. Maybe you can be invited by the People's Committee. You can be a guest of the government of Libya again'."

Tardif was horrified. At 6:00 p.m. she returned to the tourist village and immediately went to Halens' room. She found the writer sitting on his bed, gazing at the ceiling. He was alone. "I lay down on the next bed and I told him how the Arab guy had interrogated me, and how they wanted me to be their guest."

"I'm glad to hear they feel that way about *you*," Halens told her.

Tardif explains: "He meant I was off the hook. At least *one* of us had fooled the Libyans." She adds that if the Libyans had been worried about what she planned to write, they must have been doubly worried by Halens, the event's single accredited journalist from a major news organization.

After dinner that night, Halens, Jabour, and Tardif joined a small group of Canadian delegates in the hotel's lounge for a question-and-answer session with three Libyan engineers. Halens peppered the Libyans with questions about Qadhafi's war with neighbouring Chad. He was seen busily recording the Libyans' comments in a notebook.

Later, at about 10:00 p.m., Tardif paused to talk with one of the engineers. Halens, meanwhile, loitered by the hotel's stairs, waiting for her. Tardif remembers him slowly going up the stairs, looking back to see if she was going to follow. After a few minutes he disappeared from view. She never saw him again.

At 11:00 p.m. Jabour encountered Halens in their room. He had showered and trimmed his beard and was getting dressed. Jabour asked him, "Why trim your beard? Who cares what we look like over here?"

Halens left the room and was gone for more than two hours. At around 11:45 p.m. another Canadian spotted him outside the hotel's cafeteria. He appeared to be waiting for someone. When he returned to the room at about 1:30 a.m., Jabour was awake. The two talked until near 2 a.m., at which point Jabour fell asleep. Four hours later, Christoph Halens was dead.

———

According to Libyan officials, it was around 6:10 a.m. that Christoph Halens landed on the grey patio tiles two metres to the left of the entrance to Tripoli's Zanzour Tourist Village.

Halens had landed on his back a short distance from the grimy walls of the sprawling three-storey hotel. There was silence. A strong wind was blowing across the Gulf of Sidra and out into the Mediterranean. Above the parking lot, not far from Halens, a soggy banner read, IMPERIALIST TERRORISM YELDS ANTI-TERRORISM.

A member of the hotel's night staff found the journalist's body at 6:25 a.m. Halens was wearing a clean shirt, a sleeveless pullover, and a windbreaker. His eyes were open and a large pool of blood was forming under his head. In his pocket was his hotel room key, number 134.

Gone was the notebook he had been carrying with him for two days—the notebook he had crammed with bits and pieces of a story about neo-Nazis, and militant leftists, and Libyans living in North America, and something called the Third Position.

Gone was the story Christoph Halens had died for.

Later that morning Michelle Tardif knocked on the door of Christoph Halens' room. Inside she found an agitated Ahmad Eed Murad and a group of Libyan men she did not recognize. Tardif asked Murad where Halens was. Murad lied: "He is interviewing Colonel Qadhafi." Feeling uneasy, Tardif left.

Minutes later, Murad phoned Halens' parents in West Germany, using a number he had located in the dead journalist's address book. Horst Halens answered. Murad said, "I am Ahmad. I'm with a group. I call you because my wife is a German. Your son committed suicide. Where shall we send the body—to Canada or Germany?" He then hung up.

At about the same time, across town, Terry Jabour was sitting in a room at the Zanzour police station, answering questions about Halens' death. He would spend ten hours there, almost five of them being questioned by two Libyan magistrates. Jabour told them that Halens had been despondent since arriving in Libya. Hearing this, the magistrates smiled broadly. Later Jabour was driven back to the tourist village in an unmarked car. He refused to answer other delegates' questions about Halens' whereabouts.

Later that day, all of the delegates were forced to attend the rally at Bab al-Aziya barracks. The Libyan leader was there himself, as were his wife and son. After listening to speeches excoriating Israel and the United States, Jabour encountered Michelle Tardif, who was frantic. She told him that rumours were flying that a member of the Canadian delegation was dead.

While they stepped onto a bus together, Jabour said to Tardif, "Did you hear what the rumour is?" He appeared to have been crying.

"Yes," Tardif said. "You don't believe it, do you?"

"Yes," Jabour said, starting to sob, "because it's true."

As the bus lurched down Tripoli's streets, Tardif was speechless. After a long time, she whispered, "Why did they do it?"

Jabour whirled on her. Forcefully, he told Tardif that Halens had killed himself. But Tardif did not believe it. "To me," she says now, "it all confirmed Christoph's paranoia. It was as if he knew too much. The day before, I had been grilled by that Libyan guy [on the bus to the rally] so I just believed it was all coming true, that Christoph was right. I have never been so mortified in my life."

The Libyan government covered up Halens' death for an entire day. Their objective was obvious: Wednesday, April 15, was the first anniversary of the American bombing raid. The Libyans did not want to see their propaganda machine derailed by the death of a meddlesome Canadian newsman. Months later, Ahmad Eed Murad would say that the Libyans were concerned that news of Halens' death would "ruin the celebration."

Despite the Libyans' best efforts, the death rumours persisted. Finally, late on Wednesday, the state-controlled Libyan news agency issued an almost incoherent statement on Halens' death. It declared that after touring the remains of Qadhafi's barracks early on Wednesday, April 15, "Christopher Lahmann Halns [sic] ... committed suicide under the effects of what he saw of the damage caused by the American aggression." The problem with this story, of course, was that by the time that tour took place, Halens had been dead for about 18 hours. The JANA press dispatch was bizarre even by Libyan standards.

The strange events grew stranger. On Wednesday evening Ahmad Eed Murad called a meeting of the Canadian delegation, during which he announced that Halens had thrown himself off the hotel roof. For two hours the Palestinian nationalist gave a rambling, disjointed speech on Halens, Libya, and the peace conference. Albert Nerenberg recalls that "at no point were people given a chance to ask what the fuck was going on."

Eibie Weizfeld also spoke to the delegates. By turns yelling and whispering—"his deep-breathing routine," Nerenberg calls it—Weizfeld warned the Canadians to keep their criticism of the Libyans to themselves, particularly when journalists were present. Recalls Nerenberg, "Weizfeld's first reaction to this poor guy dying was to say, 'I hope nobody uses this to make the Libyan revolution look bad.' He said he feared this would be used by what he called the Western reactionary media to hurt the Libyan revolution."

That night, many of the Canadian delegates barricaded their doors, terrified that they too would be murdered.

Early on Friday, April 17, Michelle Tardif made her way to Tripoli's airport. She could no longer bear the peace conference, or the Libyans, or Libya—she just wanted to go home. Christoph Halens' words were ringing in her head: You don't fool with these people.... We're going to be tried in People's Court.... Cannon fodder.... Southam stock is going to skyrocket....

Something *big* is going to happen.

While she was standing in the ticket line-up at the airport, a Libyan man walked up to her. She recognized him as one of the conference organizers, one of the nicer ones. Today, however, he was not smiling. The man pointed at Tardif's purse—a large black bag she used to carry money, her passport, her make-up, her notebook. Says Tardif, "He said he wanted to weigh it. He said he needed to find out how much weight was going to be on the plane. I said, 'No, this is personal,' but he said they needed everything."

After a heated argument, the Libyan snatched the purse out of Tardif's hands. "You will get it back," he said. But an hour later, the purse had not been returned to her. Tardif felt panicky and started to cry. When the Libyan man saw her, he smirked. "You will get it," he said.

The purse was returned to her only moments before she boarded her plane. Exhausted, she did not bother to examine its contents. "When I got home, I discovered that my notebook was missing. Ironically, I hadn't written a single line about the whole incident with Christoph."

After a long silence, she adds, "You know, I cannot discount the fact that Christoph had a little notebook, and that he had information in it. And it disappeared."

––––––––––––––

For the next week or so, Christoph Halens' mysterious death was the subject of many reports in the Canadian news media. "Reporter found dead in Tripoli," said a *Globe and Mail* headline. "Ottawa researcher's death accident, Libyans say," read a front-page story in the *Ottawa Citizen*.

When Tripoli's deputy district attorney, Saleh Abdul-Jalil Orerbi, finally got around to issuing his report on Halens' death, he did not have much to say. No traces of drugs or alcohol were found in the body. Halens "had been suffering from a psychological illness," his two-page report stated. He did not say how he reached this conclusion, nor did he offer any evidence to justify it. He continued: "The attorney's office [finds] the deceased committed premeditated suicide.... There was no conspiracy behind the suicide." Halens, he said, told his room-mate that "he would disappear, and with this, no change in the stream of life would occur."

Many readers considered Orerbi's bizarre report more interesting for what it did not say. It did not, for example, attempt to explain why there were scuff marks on the hotel parapet, above the walkway where Halens' body was found—as if Halens had struggled before falling. It did not explain why his room was not sealed, or why no forensic evidence of any type was taken. It did not explain why Ahmad Eed Murad and Terry Jabour were the only foreigners interviewed by Libyan authorities. It did not explain why the state-run news agency issued a release that was plainly false.

And it did not explain what happened to Halens' notebook—the notebook that, according to Tardif and to Halens' friends, was full of facts and figures about Qadhafi's Third Position alliance.

Not surprisingly, few believed a word of what the Libyans had to say. Halens' family called suicide impossible. Joe Clark, Canada's Secretary of State for External Affairs, told the House of Commons that the government was prepared to consider arranging a second autopsy for Halens. On April 28, after Halens' body was returned to his family, that second autopsy was performed by Professor Hans-Dietrich Troger of the Institute of Forensic Science at the Medical University of Hanover. Troger concluded that suicide was highly unlikely. The same conclusion was reached by a Toronto forensic expert, Dr. Frederick Jaffe, who later examined all reports and photographs dealing with Halens' death.

Dr. Troger told Southam that "the injuries are not classic for a case of suicide.... The nature of his injuries was very unusual for a case of suicide." He added, "In cases of suicide, most people do not have head injuries. In this case, the injuries were to the head, the left shoulder, and chest. In suicide, because of the way they throw themselves off buildings, we expect injuries to the arms and legs."

And Dr. Jaffe told Southam, "What bothered me was if these [photographs show] his footprints, he was standing on the parapet, his back to the courtyard, someone came along and gave him a gentle push. That is something one cannot establish or exclude. He could have fallen over accidentally or he could have been pushed. Nobody could tell the difference.... Looking at it—and I have seen many suicides—just looking at it, it doesn't look like a suicide."

Despite the evidence, and depite the conclusions of Jaffe and Troger, the Canadian government abruptly closed its file on Halens in February 1988. "It's not a good incident," said Denys Tessier, a spokesman for External Affairs. "We're sorry about it, but as far as we are concerned, the case is closed."

Rosemary Knes and Desmond Gray are critical of how the Canadian government handled the Halens case. "The response of the Canadian government was outrageous," says Knes. "Their only interest seemed to be how to disentangle themselves from it." Gray agrees: "They had a very dismissive attitude. And it doesn't do Canadians any good at all, that they can go abroad and die under mysterious circumstances, and the Canadian government says they can do nothing about it."

Asked if Halens was murdered, Knes and Gray do not hesitate. "I know that he was killed for some reason, but I don't know why," Knes says. "Was it because of something he was finding out? I don't know. I don't know whether his story was about drug smuggling, guns, or whether it was politics. I don't know. I don't know if it was deliberate, either. It may have been a situation where they didn't intend to kill him, and it went too far. All I know is it wasn't an accident—and it wasn't suicide."

At the conference some Canadian delegates, including Halens, heard rumours that Qadhafi was using the event as a smokescreen to pass on $1 million to the American Indian Movement and $2 million to Louis Farrakhan's Nation of Islam. Friends speculate that Halens may have been murdered by members of a Libyan revolutionary committee. Their scenario is that these Libyans learned about Halens' plans to write news stories about the rumours.

It is known that before leaving for Tripoli Halens thoroughly acquainted himself with Qadhafi's penchant for funding AIM, the

Nation of Islam, and other extremist organizations in Canada, Europe, and the United States. It is also known that on the flight from Rome to Tripoli, Halens quizzed a Nationalist Party of Canada member on this issue. What remains a mystery is how much more information Halens was able to dig up once he reached Tripoli. Ian Verner Macdonald, who helped to recruit the Canadian delegates, suggests that Halens was murdered by members of a far-left group who were worried about the impact his news stories would have on their fiscal health.

Knes, Gray, and others agree that it is unlikely anyone will ever know what really happened at Zanzour Tourist Village in the early morning of April 14, 1987. Was Halens, a writer, so depressed that he would kill himself, leaving no note? Or did he go for a stroll on the hotel roof in the middle of the night—while the rain poured down on him and a strong wind swept out across the Gulf of Sidra—and fall by accident? Or—as is likely—was he murdered for learning too much about Libya's dealings with Western extremists?

Albert Nerenberg did not know Halens, but he knows this much: "There was a really strong feeling there that normal laws and normal culture didn't apply. It was like the fifth dimension, you know? It was the perfect scenario for murder—because they knew they could get away with it."

———————

To this day, rumours persist that Christoph Halens killed himself. To this day, no Canadian delegate to the Libyan peace conference can provide a single compelling reason why he would have—but some delegates insist that it was suicide, just the same.

There is no doubt: Halens *was* worried in the days leading up to his death. He knew that if he "overshadowed the conference with the neo-Nazi story," as he put it, he was not going to please his Libyan hosts. He told Michelle Tardif about his concerns.

Some delegates misinterpreted Halens' demeanour. Although they were acquainted with him for only three days, a few, including Jabour, later claimed that the Southam writer was deeply depressed, even suicidal. Halens' family and friends reject such claims as utter nonsense. Why, they ask, would a suicidal man trim his beard hours before his death? Why would he take time on the same day to confirm his plane departure date? Why would he bother to shop for a gift for his girlfriend? No—Christoph Halens was not suicidal. He was simply nervous: it was not wise, Halens told fellow delegates, to antagonize Libya's government while visiting Libya.

"[The Libyan peace conference story] was a very positive development for him," says Rosemary Knes. "Everything in his career was looking up, and I think it was very important for him to be able to go back to his family and to be able to bring this very positive news about his life. The peace conference wasn't a specific assignment. The focus of it was to give him this opportunity, and whatever he wanted to do with it, he could."

Before Halens' death, Rosemary Knes and Desmond Gray had not known each other very well. Afterwards, they found themselves drawn together by the tragedy; as two of the people who were closest to Halens, they spent a lot of time talking about his death. In September 1988 they were married. Mounted on a wall in their tidy Ottawa home, just a few blocks from where Halens maintained his apartment, there is a framed photograph of the dead journalist. He is holding a collection of poems by T.S. Eliot. Her eyes lingering on the photo, Knes says, "I have probably thought about Christoph every day since his death. I don't think his presence will ever leave me."

Gray waits a moment, then adds, "It's almost like he was taken from himself, and there was nothing to prepare anyone for it. It was worse than an accident, because at least with an accident, you know what's happened. So, coupled with the loss of Christoph is the loss of knowing what really happened to him that night.

"In a sense, what has taken over is uncertainty."

3

OPERATION FRIENDLY SKIES

On July 20, 1988, Washington, D.C., was a sauna. It wasn't yet noon but the temperature in the American capital was at least 35°. With the humidity it seemed hotter.

Donald Bartnik did not seem to mind. Bartnik had been a special agent with the Federal Bureau of Investigation for 16 years. He was a cheerful man who liked to laugh and had a folksy, upbeat approach to his job. Down at the FBI's Washington field office, on the banks of the Potomac southwest of Capitol Hill, Bartnik was regarded as an authority on terrorists and spies. He had many years' experience in counter-espionage work. That is why he had been assigned to Operation Friendly Skies.

Operation Friendly Skies was about spies. Libyan spies.

For over a year Bartnik had been quietly observing the comings and goings of eight men he believed to be Libyan agents. All of them lived in or near Washington. Most of them were directors of the People's Committee for Libyan Students (PCLS). The PCLS was incorporated in nearby McLean, Virginia in 1981, after the closing of the Libyan embassy, which the American government had linked to illegal espionage activities. The PCLS provided financial support for the 4,500 Libyans studying in the United States and Canada—in theory. In practice it did a great deal more.

For over a year Bartnik had been watching the group's directors—tapping their telephone conversations, cultivating a network of Libyan informants. He had done his job well. Within hours the PCLS directors would be behind bars and the American media would be filled with news stories about Libyan espionage, assassination plots, and money-laundering conspiracies. Joining them there would be their ally, a Palestinian travel agent named Mousa Hawamda—who, as it turned out, was the man who had given Christoph Halens his plane ticket to Libya.

That day, despite the potential for things to go dramatically wrong, Bartnik was in an especially cheerful mood. All the hard work was paying off: no more bogus peace conferences, no more assassination plots, no more money for Third Position types from the ultra-left and the ultra-right. Operation Friendly Skies was going to be a big success.

It is somewhat astonishing, in retrospect, that the counter-intelligence operation very nearly never happened. The FBI and the CIA had known about Qadhafi's Washington spy ring since at least 1986. By early the following year both those agencies had enough evidence to shut down the Libyans for good. Some members of the American intelligence community wanted to move on the Libyans immediately. The Republican and Democratic national conventions were on the horizon, and the FBI and CIA feared some spectacular Libyan-sponsored act of terrorism. Many FBI agents—Bartnik included—fought against such a move: the bureau had been given an unprecedented window on Libyan espionage activity, they argued, so why not wait a few months and see what Qadhafi's troops were up to?

In the end Bartnik's point of view had won out. In February 1987 he was assigned to lead Operation Friendly Skies. Now, 16 months later, he was about to haul in his catch.

―――――――

Almost from the moment he seized power in 1969, Qadhafi has presided over a dramatic and probably irreversible decline in relations between Libya and the United States. American annoyance with Libya can be traced back to the early-morning hours of December 2, 1979, when more than 2,000 angry Moslems surrounded the American embassy in Tripoli. Eager to show their support for the Iranian militants who were then holding 50 Americans hostage in Teheran, the chanting mob ransacked the mission and burned it to the ground. Five months after the attack, the Americans formally closed down their diplomatic mission in Libya. They have not attempted to reopen it.

Relations between the two nations grew worse. Qadhafi is not entirely responsible for the rift; Ronald Reagan nursed a poisonous dislike for the Libyan leader, calling him at different times a "barbarian" and a "mad dog." Generally, however, Qadhafi has been responsible for the bitter relations. In May 1981 the Americans closed down the Libyan embassy in Washington, charging that Libya had been using it as a base for assisting terrorist organizations. The following year Reagan outlawed the importation of Libyan crude oil. Still later, on January 7, 1986, he took a final, decisive step: calling Qadhafi "flaky," he imposed a comprehensive trade embargo on Libya, citing Qadhafi's long-standing involvement in terrorism as his justification. In a statement that would have particular relevance to Canada, Reagan added, "We call on our friends in Western Europe and elsewhere to join us in isolating [Qadhafi]. Americans will not understand other nations moving into Libya to take advantage of our departure."

In the same breath Reagan announced that any type of travel by American citizens to or from Libya was now prohibited and that all financial dealings between Libyans and Americans were henceforth illegal. The following day Reagan signed yet another executive order; this one froze all Libyan government assets in the United States. With that order Reagan had hit Qadhafi where it hurt most.

The following month the Americans relented slightly. On February 21 the U.S. Treasury Department granted special licence L-66 to the PCLS. This licence permitted $2 million to be deposited each month in the committee's two bank accounts at the First American Bank. This money was to pay for "all legitimate expenses of Libyan students in the United States and Canada." Unless specifically authorized by the Treasury Department's Office of Foreign Assets Control, no single PCLS cheque could exceed $2,000. A few days later another licence, L-66A, allowed the $2,000 limit to be exceeded for "travel tickets ... bought by or on behalf of Libyan students."

The Americans had been persuaded to modify their hard-line stance by Richard C. Shadyac, a Washington lawyer who represented the PCLS and was Libya's official representative in Washington. On behalf of the Libyan students he had written to the Treasury Department explaining that thousands of Libyan students depended on the PCLS for money to pay their travel, tuition, rent, and food costs. "It is my clients' desire to fully comply with the Presidential directives," Shadyac wrote. He referred to the students' plight as of "the utmost urgency." So the Treasury Department softened its stance.

———————

Many people, Libyan and non-Libyan, see Qadhafi as a maniacal despot—a nut, plain and simple. The Sudanese leader Gafaar Nimiery, himself no paragon of orthodoxy, has concluded that the Libyan strongman has "a split personality, both evil." After enduring a number of years of Qadhafi's erratic style of leadership, his detractors both inside and outside Libya redoubled their efforts to rid themselves of him. In October 1981 a deposed Libyan diplomat named Muhammad al-Muqarief formed the National Front for the Salvation of Libya (NFSL). Muqarief was Libya's auditor general until 1979, when he denounced Qadhafi as a corrupt tyrant who was squandering the nation's oil revenues. At that point Muqarief had to seek exile in Egypt.

The NFSL is the largest and best-organized of the dozens of Libyan dissident groups now in existence. It is said to have received funding from Egypt, Sudan, and the CIA. It has claimed responsibility for the attempted coup of May 1984 at the Bab al-Aziya barracks in Tripoli, and for a number of other guerrilla operations that were equally unsuccessful. Some CIA operatives say the NFSL is populated with "Boy Scouts" who could not land a canoe on Libya's shores, let alone overthrow its government.

But for the most part, it is a reliable source of information about the Libyan regime. The NFSL's spokesman in London, Abu Abdullah, contends that Qadhafi has largely become a figurehead in recent years and that the real power now lies in the hands of the myriad revolutionary committees based in Libya and abroad. These committees, he says, are using dummy corporations and philanthropic organizations to gather intelligence on the activities of foreign and domestic enemies.

Abdullah is correct in saying that the committees gather intelligence both at home and abroad. He is wrong in saying they control the Libyan leader—certainly it is the other way around.

In *The Green Book*, Qadhafi declared that "popular congresses are the only means to achieve popular democracy. Any system of government other than popular congresses is undemocratic." Qadhafi introduced the first revolutionary committees in November 1977. The PCLS would be one of them. He claimed at the time that he was giving up some of his own powers. In fact, the committees are no more than extensions of his own power base. These "shock troops of the revolution," as some have called them, enjoy special access to the Libyan leader. They are permitted to send delegates to the General People's Congress, where they wield much influence.

Since the early 1980s the revolutionary committees have become notorious for their "corruption" trials, at which "counter-revolutionaries" are called to account for their crimes. The committees even have the power to order executions. Often these trials are held behind closed doors, with no legal counsel present to defend the accused. The revolutionary committees are greatly feared in Libya, and their existence has largely exposed Qadhafi's "popular democracy" as a sham. There is only one power in Libya, and it is the Libyan colonel, who controls the committees. In the simplest terms, Mu'ammar Qadhafi *is* Libya.

To an outsider, Libyan foreign policy is bureaucratized anarchy: governmental branches involved in its formation include, at any given time, the Libyan Foreign Liaison Secretariat, the Secretariat for Internal Security, the Secretariat of Justice, General Intelligence, Military Intelligence, the Islamic Call Society, and the Libyan Special Security Forces. In recent years the revolutionary committees have achieved near-total dominance of Libyan foreign missions, which are now officially referred to as People's Bureaus. Since 1970 these bureaus have been staffed with few, if any, trained diplomats. Revolutionary committee members, usually students, now serve as Libya's ambassadors in the small number of Western nations that still permit an official Libyan presence.

The revolutionary committees found in these Western nations are noted for many things. Subtlety is not one of them. Their members describe themselves as diplomats, but often they are little more than terrorist operatives.

Early on, Libya's government recognized that these revolutionary committees were *too* revolutionary, and that if it hoped to maintain any sort of political and economic ties with the outside world, it would have to find another approach. The solution: front organizations. Commercial, financial, educational, cultural, and journalistic organizations—all as phony as three-dollar bills.

Abdullah of the NFSL says that the *modus operandi* of the Libyan front organizations is well-known: "They go and meet people, they establish contacts. They gather information on Libyan dissidents, and they see what Libyan students and the opposition are doing. Often, they give money to extremist groups. These people think they are dealing with Libyan freedom fighters—but they're not. They're dealing with terrorists."

In the same month that Donald Bartnik was assigned to Operation Friendly Skies, he was approached by a Libyan graduate student named Mahmoud Buazzi, who had an interesting story: militant students had taken control of the People's Committee for Libyan Students and were busily plotting to break a host of American laws. Helping them was the Palestinian travel agent with offices in Washington and Ottawa. His name was Mousa Hawamda, and his travel agencies were, of course, front companies—two of dozens in existence around the globe.

Buazzi had been an FBI informant for three years. Shortly after he met Bartnik he started passing on a wealth of material to the FBI about Hawamda and his Libyan co-conspirators. The documents clearly showed that Hawamda and the PCLS had been busily laundering money for many months. Says Bartnik, "The funds were used to defray expenses for travel, room and board of non-students in anti-U.S. groups who were sympathetic to the Qadhafi government. To mask the scheme, false bills were presented to the PCLS purportedly requesting payments for activities permitted by the [U.S. Treasury Department's] licence. Or requests were submitted for refunds on airline tickets issued to Libyan students. But the money generated by the refunds was used to [pay for] non-student, pro-Libyan activities."

Many of the photocopied records Buazzi gave to the FBI dealt with the April 1987 peace conference from which Christoph Halens never returned. Two separate billings—one for $200,000, the other for $35,000—had been sent by Hawamda to the PCLS. After comparing the invoices with Alitalia and TransWorld Airline records, Bartnik concluded that "the names of the individuals listed on the billings submitted by Hawamda to the PCLS were not Libyan students. They therefore were not entitled to have their travel expenses defrayed by the PCLS." The individuals who were given the airline tickets were known members of groups and organizations that were opposed to the foreign policy of the American government and sympathetic to the policies of Libya.

According to Buazzi, Hawamda and the PCLS gang—all of them enthusiastic followers of Mu'ammar Qadhafi—were plotting to assassinate Lieutenant-Colonel Oliver North, the former White House aide. They were also violating the trade embargo that President Reagan imposed on Libya in January 1986. In addition, they were compiling hit lists that included the names of FBI and CIA agents, army and air force personnel, and Defense Department officials. To top it all off, they were funding a number of violent ultra-leftist and ultra-rightist political groups. Their objective, Buazzi put it simply, was to destabilize Reagan's America, which Hawamda described as "the enemy of humanity."

Bartnik believed the Libyan student. The man had been a reliable paid informant since February 1985, and his information made sense in the context of the bitter relations between the United States and Libya. As well, he was on the inside of Qadhafi's most active North American spy ring. To protect Buazzi's identity, the FBI refrained from naming him in their files: on all documents, they used a code name—CI-1.

Before arriving in the United States in 1981, Buazzi had been personally acquainted with Qadhafi, although the two could not be described as friends. Buazzi was intelligent and idealistic. It was obvious to the CIA and the FBI that he was going places. When Buazzi spoke of a massive Libyan espionage effort underway in Canada and the United States, Bartnik told his FBI colleagues, he probably knew what he was talking about.

It was helpful, too, that Buazzi's motives were not complicated: like many average Libyans, he believed that Qadhafi's revolution had been an utter failure. He wanted to remain in the United States as a refugee. According to a six-page affidavit Bartnik would later file in a Virginia district court, Buazzi had agreed that in return for this refugee status, he would help the FBI to gather information "concerning any intelligence-gathering activities being conducted in the United States on behalf of the Libyan government, and also any information concerning any potential acts of violence to be committed on behalf of the Libyan government." After this deal was struck, Buazzi was instructed not to remove any type of physical or documentary evidence relating to Friendly Skies: his task was to be an observer, not a hero.

Buazzi was a consistently valuable source for the FBI, but he was not without blemish. During a polygraph test the FBI gave him in March 1985, he had apparently lied about details relating to the Libyan government's effort to assassinate anti-Qadhafi dissidents in the United States. And according to the CIA, Buazzi had also lied to them, on March 13, 1987, while being questioned about the funding of the peace conference.

But Bartnik's faith was not shaken. Buazzi was thoroughly familiar with the operations of the PCLS. Bartnik had spent considerable time with him and had been able to corroborate his information through other Libyan dissidents. He would later tell a U.S. District Court judge, "I believe him to be a most reliable source."

The American agents sensed that Buazzi was as ambitious as he was bright. In 1986 he told the CIA and the FBI that he wanted to move up the "chain of command" at the PCLS. His objective, he said, was to enhance his reputation among his Libyan peers. Soon after, with Tripoli's approval, he was elected chief executive officer by the rest of the PCLS. This made him the senior Libyan government representative on North American soil.

When he met with FBI agents on July 29, 1987, Buazzi complained that the Libyan money the PCLS was receiving under the Treasury Department licence was being misused, despite what the committee's directors had promised Shadyac and the American authorities. Buazzi told the agents that he had secured photocopies of certain documents to protect himself. These documents, he said, contained detailed evidence of illegal transactions being made by the PCLS directors. Buazzi handed the photocopies to the FBI agents. On August 5, he resigned from his position as chairman of the PCLS board.

It is likely that Mousa Hawamda had long known that an FBI posse was preparing to come knocking on his travel agency's door. The cover was blown on his spy operation at least as early as January 1988, on page three of that month's issue of *al-Inquaad*, the low-budget, small-circulation newsletter published by the Chicago branch of the NFSL. In that issue was a brief, unsigned news item headlined "Oh Canada!" In part, the story read,

> For a considerable period, the Qadhafi regime, operating through student and business recruits of the revolutionary committees and the intelligence services, has been seeking to set up an effective base in Canada. It has been a recent favourite with the revolutionaries and they are flocking into it. They have, to a large extent, succeeded in establishing a most efficient network—something the Canadian authorities should worry about a great deal.
>
> By taking advantage of the large number of Libyan students now

in Canada, estimated to be around 1,500, and the slackness and acquiescence of the Canadian authorities, the link through the students is being extended to separatist movements in Canada and the United States including Quebec nationalists, the Black Muslims and the Red Indians.

Typically, commercial enterprises, run and financed by Libyan intelligence, have sprung up as a front for more sinister operations, including arms purchases. One such venture involves the transfer of the activities of a company known as Manara Travel Agency to Ottawa, recently, with an initial funding of over $1.5 million Canadian. The agency is run by an Arab-American named Mousa Hawamda who enjoys strong ties with Qadhafi's intelligence services, having rendered them many a service in the past.

Abu Abdullah is one of the senior NFSL activists in Europe. He says he was the author of the "Oh Canada!" item and adds that many of those who make up the Libyan student underground in North America knew of Hawamda's work as early as the spring of 1987, despite Hawamda's attempts to give his travel agency an aura of respectability. Abdullah insists that the vast majority of the hundreds of Libyan students enrolled in North American universities and colleges are visceral opponents of the Qadhafi regime. They live in perpetual fear of travelling Libyan hit squads, which are known to have assassinated dozens of anti-Qadhafi dissidents around the globe—a fact about which the Libyan leader often boasts. Despite their fears, they have built networks to share information and discuss coup attempts.

When pressed, Abdullah admits that the NFSL knows little about Hawamda and his travel agency except what was included in the newsletter. Says Abdullah, "What we do know is that Libyan intelligence has set up a number of companies like Manara in Canada and Europe. They are really front companies, and they are mainly used for laundering of funds and funding certain groups. We know

Hawamda was working with Libyan intelligence on that."

In his *al-Inquaad* column, Abdullah wrote that Qadhafi and other former leaders of the Free Unionist Officers invested "several billion dollars" in Canada between 1984 and 1988. This is an exaggeration: *millions*, not billions, have been diverted into Canada by the Libyan government in recent years. But for those Arab nationalists whose commitment to Qadhafi's Green Revolution is less than certain—Hawamda may be one of these—there is still a lot of money to be made. Says Abdullah, "Among the ringleaders of the Libyan intelligence community, there are many who are opportunists. They can make money, and they use every opportunity to do that."

Abdullah and others believe that Canada has been targeted by Qadhafi's adherents because its government is so ill-informed about Libyan espionage activity—almost to the point that it is wilfully blind. And, as Abdullah wrote in *al-Inquaad*,

> Canada also has the added attraction of being close to the United States and Central and South America, where Qadhafi has many ambitions and numerous contacts and schemes.
>
> So, and as has happened elsewhere, apparently legitimate channels and cultural exchange programs are set up as cover for intelligence and terrorist networks. A few years ago events in Greece, Italy, West Germany and Great Britain followed a similar pattern, which led, eventually, to a number of brutal killings, including the murder of an innocent policewoman in London in 1984. And although Qadhafi's terrorist and liquidation campaigns might be in limbo at the present time, when they are revived Canada will certainly be the first country to witness some action. There really is no excuse for procrastination or complacency.

Early on July 20, 1988, the top-secret Operation Friendly Skies—a tongue-in-cheek reference to Mousa Hawamda's professed business interest—became very public. At Donald Bartnik's signal, FBI agents swept through the American capital and into the homes of Hawamda and the PCLS directors. More than a dozen other agents stormed the PCLS offices in McLean, Virginia. There they found Hawamda and five of his pro-Qadhafi friends. None resisted arrest. At around the same time, in Ann Arbor, Michigan, and Denver, Colorado, FBI agents arrested the two remaining Arabs on Donald Bartnik's list. In a few days the eight men would be formally charged with money laundering, conspiracy, and violating the American embargo on trade with Libya.

In the hallway of Washington's PCLS headquarters, Bartnik turned up the volume on his cellular phone. He could hear the voice of Mahmoud Buazzi crackling through it. Because most of the evidence the FBI needed to make a case against Hawamda and the PCLS directors was in the form of documents written in Arabic, translators had been brought along to assist the bureau's search teams. Buazzi, meanwhile, had agreed to remain in constant contact with Bartnik's teams by phone. As former chief executive officer of the PCLS, Buazzi could tell them where to look for the papers they wanted.

While FBI agents swarmed around him, Bartnik spoke into his phone: "Be with you in a minute, CI-1."

The PCLS offices were untidy. Posters of Qadhafi had been taped here and there on the grubby walls. A stale odour permeated the place. On every floor of the building, FBI agents were poring through file folders and taking photographs. Bartnik had known since 1986 that the PCLS officers were involved in much more than the needs of Libyan students in North America. Even so, some of the documents his team seized were startling. In one room an agent found a document indicating that the PCLS directors had met more than once to discuss ways to disrupt the 1988 American presidential election. In another room a massive computerized list sat on a table.

It contained the name, address, phone number, and political inclinations of every single Libyan student living in North America.

Bartnik again picked up his phone. He asked an agent named Winchester what the FBI team was seizing at Hawamda's apartment in Falls Church, a few minutes away. "What have you got so far?"

Winchester scanned his inventory list: his men had found copies of Qadhafi's *Green Book*, slides containing engineering data on a metal-detector system, and lists of what Mousa Hawamda had called "progressive revolutionals" (that is, those who subscribed to the Third Position). The FBI agent continued, "Another agent has found a report by that guy from the All-African People's Revolutionary Party to Mousa Koussa...."

The name sounded familiar. Bartnik signed off for a moment to contact Buazzi. "CI-1, we have found a letter to Mousa Koussa. Does that name mean anything to you?"

"Yes," Buazzi replied. "Koussa is a well-known terrorist. He was expelled from Britain in 1980 or 1981 for his activities." Koussa, Buazzi explained, was a young and ambitious radical who was a leading figure in the International Revolutionary Committee, sometimes called the Libyan World Centre for Resistance to Imperialism, Zionism, Racism, Reactionism and Fascism. He was regarded by Western intelligence agencies as an accomplished terrorist, he added.

(Much later, in October 1991, a French judge would ask Interpol to locate Koussa for questioning in connection with the bombing of a French DC-10 over Africa in September 1989. At present, Koussa is a deputy foreign minister who runs Mataba, a Libyan organization that funds opposition groups in African states. The French government believes that Koussa and others met in Tripoli in September 1988 to plot the African operation—as well as the December 1988 bombing of the Pan Am flight over Lockerbie.)

"Thank you, CI-1," Bartnik said, pleased. He buzzed Winchester once more. "What else do you have?"

"There's something about a provisional government for the Republic of New Africa, plus a letter of invitation to the 1987 peace conference."

"What else?"

"Three bank statements," Winchester said. "From a Canadian Bank."

"Which bank?" Bartnik asked.

"The Toronto-Dominion Bank."

Elsewhere in Hawamda's apartment, FBI agents had already confiscated records issued to Hawamda by two other Toronto-based financial institutions: the Royal Bank of Canada and the Canadian headquarters of the Bank of Credit and Commerce International. These records would be vital to the FBI's case against Hawamda and the pro-Libyan activists.

In the weeks ahead, as the FBI penetrated the layers of secrecy surrounding Hawamda and his business ventures, it became obvious that the travel agency owner had visited Canada often. Hawamda had used an account at the Toronto-Dominion Bank as a money storehouse since at least the summer of 1986, long before he expanded his travel business into Canada. Within a very short time Bartnik and his colleagues would be petitioning a Canadian court for access to Hawamda's files at the Royal Bank and BCCI's Ottawa branch. The FBI would later conclude that these financial institutions had been used by the Libyan government to further its illegal objectives.

Hawamda's money-laundering scheme had been as simple as it was effective. To cover up their conspiracy, Hawamda and the PCLS directors had developed code words. For example, one "magazine" meant $1,000 in American funds. Members of radical organizations such as the American Indian Movement would request five magazines, Buazzi told Bartnik. "The Indian groups would ask for these number of magazines, and they would get $5,000 from Manara Travel," Buazzi explained. "Manara then bills the PCLS for the money, claiming that it is for travel expenses for Libyan students. And the PCLS issues a cheque for $5,000 to Manara. Do you see? It is really quite simple."

All in all, the FBI seized 60 items from Hawamda's apartment. Among them were copies of two handwritten letters to Qadhafi; documents listing those who had attended the April 1987 peace conference; detailed instructions on how to build an "explosive device"; and yellow legal note pads filled with handwritten observations about the "revolutionary groups," as the Libyans called them, that made up the Third Position movement. While all of these items were compelling, to the American media there was one document that made the Libyans' arrest very big news indeed. It would end up as the prosecution's Exhibit #50: "Personal Information on Lt. Col. North."

"He goes to pray every Sunday at the following place—The Church of the Apostles Episcopal Congregation in Fairfax, Virginia," the document read in Arabic. It went on to describe North's grey Toyota station wagon. The document took note of a bumper sticker on the vehicle: "God is Prolife." The exhibit contained other information, some of it by then well-known to readers of supermarket tabloids: "His secretary is Fawn Hall." Unidentified sources in Ronald Reagan's administration told reporters from Associated Press, United Press International, NBC, and ABC that the Libyans had planned to assassinate Oliver North. The idea, apparently, had been to blow North to bits while he drove to work.

In his 1991 autobiography, *Under Fire,* North recalls how he learned about Hawamda's plan to assassinate him. Early in 1987— North does not give a precise date or much detail—an unnamed FBI agent telephoned North's lawyer, Brendan Sullivan. North was in Sullivan's office at the time.

"We have information that leads us to believe that your client, Colonel North, may be in some jeopardy," the FBI agent told Sullivan. The cause for concern, the agent added, was not the congressional investigation of North's alleged involvement in the Iran-Contra scandal. "We have some information about the possibility that someone may be trying to kill him," the agent said. He refused to name the potential assassin or assassins.

Frustrated, Sullivan demanded to know why the FBI agent had bothered to call him. "Because Colonel North ought to have some protection," the agent replied. "[But] we're not in the business of providing protection. All we can do is notify you."

Sullivan asked what the threat was. The FBI agent would not tell him. Annoyed, Sullivan asked the FBI agent what could be done. The FBI suggested calling the Department of Defense. "Your client is in the military, and they have people who can deal with this sort of problem."

"Okay," Sullivan said. "Let me get this straight. North is the target of an attempt to kill him. You can't tell us when or where, or who it is—or anything more about it. And we're supposed to get hold of somebody I don't know at the Pentagon who might be able to get more information from you?"

By day's end, the Naval Investigative Service confirmed that the would-be assassins were Hawamda and his PCLS colleagues. The NIS agreed to assign a group of officers to watch the North family's home in Virginia. The Fairfax County Police Department was also asked to get involved in the security operation, as were representatives of the local sheriff's office. For the Marine Corps, however, the security wasn't tight enough. After an incident in which one police officer mistook North's wife for a Libyan terrorist—and almost shot her—North was ordered to move with his wife and three daughters to Camp Lejeune, North Carolina. They would be given around-the-clock security for weeks afterwards. Once the Norths left their home, NIS agents took up residence there, installing cameras and high-tech surveillance equipment, hoping to nab Hawamda and his pro-Qadhafi friends as they made their move. North approved of the strategy. "Nobody said so directly," he would later write, "but I had the feeling [the NIS] hoped to catch these guys in the act. I would have tried the same thing in my old counterterrorist job."

As a National Security Council aide, North had reportedly played a major role in organizing the April 1986 bombing raids on Tripoli and Benghazi. Abu Nidal had already threatened to kill him for it. Killing Oliver North would have been poetic justice, Qadhafi-style.

One month later, Donald Bartnik sat in the witness box at a bail hearing in Alexandria, Virginia, shifting uncomfortably. It was Friday, August 5, 1988, and for once he looked unhappy. Down at the U.S. District Court on South Washington Street, things were not going well for the prosecution in the case styled as *United States of America versus Mousa Hawamda et al.* The magistrate, Leonie Brinkema, appeared unimpressed with the evidence Bartnik was giving, just as she had been unimpressed with the arguments of U.S. Attorney Henry Hudson, the man supervising the prosecution of the pro-Qadhafi activists.

Hudson and Bartnik were in court to ask that the pro-Libyan activists—Hawamda in particular—be kept behind bars until their trial, which was expected in October. On the stand, Bartnik had just dropped the prosecution's big headline-grabber: Hawamda and the five PCLS directors had attempted to locate a certain government official in April 1987 "for the purpose of killing him." The journalists in the courtroom scribbled madly in their notebooks, but Brinkema was not biting. In her ruling she declared, "The United States further alleges that the accused, Mousa Hawamda, is an intelligence officer who has directed Libyan students to gather intelligence about an unnamed American official for the purpose of arranging for his assassination. This is an extremely serious charge. However, very little evidence was presented to support it."

Brinkema gave her decision: Hawamda would be set free upon the payment of a $250,000 bond. Four of his alleged co-conspirators would be freed after providing bails ranging from $25,000 to $50,000. Only one PCLS officer, Saleh Mohamed al-Rajhi, was denied bail. Brinkema had been told that al-Rajhi posed a "flight risk"; it was he who had compiled a hit list of the American officials who directed the April 1986 bombing raid on Libya.

Brinkema agreed to Hudson's request that the five men remain in custody pending appeal. But on Tuesday of the following week, a U.S. District Court judge named Albert Bryan concluded that Brinkema was right: Hawamda and the others should be set free.

This, the FBI would bitterly note, would turn out to be a big mistake.

A few days later, on Thursday, August 28, all eight men dutifully showed up in court to be formally indicted on charges of money-laundering, conspiracy, and violation of the 1986 trade embargo. There was no mention of the scheme to assassinate Oliver North. Speaking anonymously, Justice Department officials later told American reporters that there existed "little reliable evidence" linking Hawamda to any assassination plot. When questioned about the omission, U.S. Attorney Henry Hudson hinted that more charges were forthcoming against Hawamda and his Arab friends.

For most of the American media, the big story had been the assassination plot. Now that a decision had been made to lay no charges in that regard, Hawamda's news value had dropped substantially, though he could still draw a crowd for occasions like this.

Parts of the 61-page grand jury document that formally indicted the eight men made for interesting reading. Forty counts were laid against the pro-Libyans, as they were being called by the news media. Noted Bartnik, "Forty counts in an indictment is overkill, you might say."

While Hawamda and his co-conspirators sat in the prisoner's box, the Virginia District Court clerk read the charges to a courtroom packed with reporters wanting to hear about the Oliver North assassination plot.

It was part of the conspiracy that the defendants herein, as agents of Libya, and others, agreed to subvert the legitimate purpose of the People's Committee for Libyan Students (PCLS), which is to supply funds and assistance to Libyan students studying in the United States and Canada, by using PCLS resources and assets to further the revolutionary goals of the Libyan government.

The defendants and others, acting as agents of Libya, set out upon a calculated course to undermine the laws of the United States of America by establishing relationships with and providing financial support to selected American groups to call on them to carry out actions in support of Libya's foreign policies.

It was a further part of the conspiracy that the defendants Mousa Hawamda and Adel Sennosi [the PCLS's financial director], acting as agents for Libya, used the PCLS to acquire personal information about a high-ranking United States official.

The clerk paused for effect. There was silence in the old wood-panelled courtroom, except for the sound of reporters scratching in their notebooks.

It was further part of the conspiracy that the defendant Saleh al-Rajhi, using the facilities of the PCLS, illegally acquired the names and addresses of over one thousand federal employees working at the CIA, FBI, Defense Intelligence Agency, U.S. Air Force, U.S. Army and officials of the Department of Defense and U.S. Navy.

The clerk then read the charge that Hawamda and his friends had engaged in money laundering, repeated violations of Reagan's trade embargo, and fraud.

> It was a further part of the conspiracy that sometime between January 1, 1987, and April 14, 1987, the defendants and other unindicted co-conspirators agreed that Mousa Hawamda through the Manara Travel Agency, Inc. would illegally and fraudulently use PCLS licensed funds to cover all the expenses of sending a group of U.S. citizens to a Libyan-sponsored rally in Tripoli, Libya, to be held on April 12 to 16, 1987, to commemorate the 1986 U.S. bombing of Libya, in violation of U.S. travel restrictions.

The lengthy indictment made it clear that the PCLS had not been terribly concerned about the welfare of Libyan students. A few days later, the six Libyans—Saleh al-Rajhi, Salem Omar Zubeidy, Milad Shibani, Mahdi Mohammed Abousetta, Ramadan Taher Belgasem, and Adel Sennosi—along with one Moroccan, Mike Ben-Mohamed, and one Palestinian, Mousa Hawamda, formally pleaded not guilty to all of the charges. A trial date was set for October 17, 1988.

Till then, all of the defendants except al-Rajhi were free on bail.

A few reporters dashed out of the courtroom to make their deadlines. Hawamda seemed bored as he was led away by a court bailiff to sign bail papers.

4

MOUSA

Mousa Hawamda—also known as Mousa Hawamdah, Musa Hawamdah, Moses Hawmdah, and Mohamed Ben-Mohamed—prefers the finer things in life. He likes silk suits and tailored shirts and favours expensive Italian silk ties. He travels first-class. When in Ottawa, he lived in a very upscale Laurier Avenue West highrise in the downtown core. When he dropped by the Manara Travel Agency at 99 Metcalfe Street, usually three or four times a month, he was most often behind the wheel of a white Mercedes-Benz sedan with New York licence plates. In Washington, D.C., where he lived most of the time, he occupied a pricey 12-room apartment on Seminary Road.

He is a quiet man who rarely smiles. His mouth is usually fixed in a scowl. His nose is broad, his eyes cold and deep-set. Some say he is sensitive about his appearance. He is cursed with a receding hairline and combs his thinning locks across his bald spot.

No one is quite certain how old he is. His American passport says he was born on November 21, 1945, but his District of Columbia motor vehicle registration lists December 14, 1955. Other documents vary: one says 1943, another 1945. Hawamda is married to Maisoun Ben-Mohamed, a strikingly beautiful Moroccan woman almost half his age. They were introduced by Ahmad Eed Murad, one of

Hawamda's partners at Ottawa's Manara Travel Agency. They have two young daughters.

He was born at Samu-Herron, in Jordan—or Palestine, depending upon one's point of view—shortly before the founding of the State of Israel. Some say the issue of Palestinian sovereignty consumes him more than any other. Says Ian Verner Macdonald, "From my conversations with him, I would judge him to be a fairly ardent Palestinian nationalist. I think that is his prime motivation in life, although he appeared in Ottawa as a representative of the Libyans. I would say his primary loyalty was definitely to Palestine. He was very much concerned about the occupation of his homeland and the dispossession of his family."

Others are less complimentary. Ahmad Eed Murad, who now bears a grudge against his fellow Palestinian, is blunt: "If he could be summarized in one word, it's phony. All he wanted in his life was to be rich. For him, the means through which he reached this end was immaterial, as long as he becomes rich."

To many, the Palestinian Liberation Organization is a terrorist group. To Hawamda, the PLO leadership is weak, indecisive, and not militant enough. In this respect he is like his mentor, Mu'ammar Qadhafi.

———————

Hawamda claims that he was educated to be a nuclear physicist—a peculiar background for a travel agency owner. He even claims to hold a doctorate from an American university, though he has not said which one. In Libya, nuclear physicists are not in short supply. In 1974 the government of Argentina signed an agreement with Qadhafi's regime to train Libyan chemists in uranium extraction and to provide the technology needed for the mining of radioactive ores. Throughout the 1970s Qadhafi sent hundreds of Libyan students abroad to learn about nuclear technology. So far he still lacks both the means and the materials to produce the nuclear weaponry he has long coveted.*

Whatever Hawamda was taught, some of it he learned in Libya in the years leading up to the September 1969 revolution. While there he was active in the burgeoning Arab nationalist movement. He was also, like Qadhafi, a devotee of the Egyptian leader, Gamel Abdel Nasser. It was through his Nasserite contacts that he met one of his early mentors, a Lebanese businessman and Arab nationalist named Ahmed Murad (who is not related to Ottawa's Ahmad Eed Murad). This Murad was a self-made millionaire who owned a travel agency that in the 1970s opened branches in Beirut, Caracas, Buenos Aires, and Sao Paulo. His travel agency's name was Manara.

According to the FBI, Hawamda arrived on American shores in 1970. He became a naturalized American citizen in 1972, although he continued to carry a Jordanian passport. Hawamda later told his Arab friends that at first he was so poor he had to sell cars in California to make a living. But the FBI insists that Hawamda was no penniless refugee. One of Hawamda's closest allies is Mohamed Madjoub, who works for the Libyan Foreign Intelligence Office, where he heads the Office of Communications for the Revolutionary Committee. Madjoub is a very powerful man whose main task is to co-ordinate Libyan espionage activities in the United States. Before Hawamda arrived in Washington, Madjoub gave him approximately $35,000 to start a travel agency. In 1988, Madjoub, according to the NFSL, would supervise the activities surrounding the Lockerbie bombing.

In 1980 the Manara Travel Agency was incorporated under the laws of the District of Columbia. Manara—the word means "lighthouse" in Arabic—was operated out of a well-lit office at 2141 "K"

---

*As recently as January 1992 he was still looking. A Russian scientist, Vyacheslav Rozanov, deputy chief of the thermonuclear department at Moscow's Kurchatov Institute of Atomic Energy, reported that Libya had offered well-paying jobs to at least two of his nuclear scientists.

Street North West. Hawamda knew when he opened the agency that there were thousands of Libyans studying in the United States, and that an agency owned and run by an Arab would attract Qadhafi's dollars the way a lighthouse attracts ships. He persuaded his friend Ahmed Murad to let him call the agency Manara. His allies in Qadhafi's inner circle told him that if his business succeeded they would have him designated Libya's official travel agent in North America.

Hawamda, a confirmed entrepreneur, reasoned that there was a lot of money to be made ferrying Libyan students back and forth across the Atlantic. He was right. The Libyan government keeps a wary eye trained on its students living abroad. From time to time those students are ordered to return home for political debriefings and, occasionally, punishment. That represents a lot of plane tickets—and Madjoub's support was not going to hurt, either.

Seven years later, in late February of 1987, Hawamda coasted up Ottawa's Metcalfe Street in a Mercedes sedan. Things were going well for him: he was making lots of money, his Arab patrons were happy with him, and he was about to open a branch of Manara in the capital of Canada, again with Madjoub's money. Not bad for a former used car salesman.

Hawamda had already surveyed the area and decided to establish this second Manara agency on Metcalfe just above Laurier West. Across the street were a federal government office building and Ottawa's main public library. Two short blocks north a Canadian flag fluttered above Parliament Hill's Centre Block. Hawamda had come to Ottawa that day to sign the new agency's incorporation papers. He would open for business a few weeks later. He stepped out onto the sidewalk, taking care to avoid the mounds of slush. He stood about 5 feet, 10 inches, but his self-confident, almost regal bearing made him seem taller.

Hawamda did not attract the attention of any passers-by. There are dozens of embassies in Ottawa, so well-dressed foreigners are often seen cruising the streets in expensive cars. The Ottawa Manara Travel Agency, within the shadow of the highest seat of government in Canada. His Libyan bosses would be pleased.

Terry Jabour recalls that he met Mousa Hawamda in January or February of 1987. The two were introduced by Ahmad Eed Murad, who was one of Jabour's long-time clients. They met in Jabour's sixth-floor law offices. Murad said he was interested in setting up a company with Hawamda, who told Jabour he wanted to incorporate a Canadian branch of his Washington travel agency. He added that he had been negotiating a lease with Morguard Investments for a ground-floor office at 99 Metcalfe Street. Hawamda was unsmiling, self-contained. He did not say very much, this well-dressed Palestinian. Says Jabour, "He was very serious. Thinking, always thinking. I found him always kind of deep ... serious, let's put it that way."

Jabour asked the standard lawyer questions: Where was the corporation's registered office located? What sort of share structure was it to have? Who were the directors going to be? The first two directors, Jabour was told, were going to be Hawamda and Ahmad Eed Murad. The third would be Roger Delorme of Magog, Quebec. At that point, Jabour says, he did not know much about Delorme.

Roger Delorme cannot be described as neutral on the subject of Libya. By the time he signed on as a director of Manara Travel he had already been there 14 times. Within three months he would visit again, as a delegate to the peace conference where Christoph Halens died. In 1977, as a Progressive Conservative, he ran for a federal seat in Quebec's Eastern Townships. He lost. Now he runs a glazing firm in the area. For part of the 1970s he hosted a French-language radio hotline show with Télémedia; he claims that he was kicked off the airwaves because he offended wealthy Jewish families in Quebec. He vehemently denies that he is anti-Semitic. During the ill-fated peace conference some Canadian delegates speculated that Delorme was an arms dealer on Qadhafi's payroll. When a CBC television reporter asked him about that, Delorme said, "I don't do business with the Libyans. I don't make money with the Libyans, if you want a direct answer. I'm not involved in the weapons industry although I'm very, very interested in those involved." Two years later, when asked about the arms trade, he said, "I was never into arms, neither from close or far." He refuses to comment on the apparent contradiction and calls the CBC's televised report "sensationalism."

Delorme says he met with Mousa Hawamda and Ahmad Eed Murad in Montreal in early 1987 to discuss becoming a director of Manara's Ottawa branch. Delorme liked what the two men had to say. Hawamda told Delorme that if he agreed to let his name stand as a director, he would be granted unlimited discount travel as well as a percentage of the profits at year's end. Ownership was to remain in Hawamda's hands alone. Murad had accepted the same deal.

The two Arabs approached him, Delorme recalls, because he was already well known to the Libyan government and even to Qadhafi himself. Delorme and Murad had been close friends for years—they called each other "brother." In summer months the two men often cruised the Ottawa River in Delorme's power boat.

"I'm pretty strong in Libya," says Delorme. "I'd probably say I'm one of the most important individuals in Canada, insofar as Libya is concerned and Libyan history is concerned." He now regrets letting Hawamda list him as a director: "I never saw a penny out of Manara Travel. I never saw the books or anything. I was stolen from right and left. Used and abused. I was a little bit too naïve. But at least I know what was going on."

From Delorme's vantage point, what was going on was simply

this: Hawamda was a very powerful man with a great deal of disposable income. He was so influential that Delorme now thinks he may have been a double-agent under partial control of the CIA. Says Delorme, "Mousa knew who was going to Libya [to the peace conference], how they were going. He was supplying the plane tickets, everything."

In late February of 1987, Hawamda and Murad again visited Terry Jabour's office, this time to sign Manara Travel's articles of incorporation. After that, Jabour says, he saw little of Hawamda: "I didn't deal very much with him, except when he came in to get a document signed. Once I think we went out to lunch together with Ahmad. But I wasn't really socializing with him." He thinks for a moment. "I didn't have much to do with him, afterwards, except to read the paper and keep clippings about his problems with the U.S. authorities."

The Manara Travel Agency, 99 Metcalfe Street, Ottawa, was filled with shiny new equipment and furniture and had posters of Bermuda and Jamaica on the walls. When customers strolled in off the street—which was rarely—they stepped down a few steps into a waiting area and approached a chest-high counter, behind which a half-dozen desks were neatly arranged. Perched on most of the desks were computer terminals. Manara's travel agents had access to the top-of-the-line Sabre flight reservation system. Few travel agencies can afford the system, but Manara could.

Behind the desks there were fax machines, telex machines, and photocopiers. Just off to the right, safely shielded from wandering eyes, lay Mousa Hawamda's office.

Manara Ottawa was not a low-budget operation. Hawamda had six or seven employees at any given time, and he paid them competitive wages. The agents received just over $400 a week; the agency's office manager made as much as $500. All of the cheques were made out to an account at the Ottawa branch of the Bank of Credit and Commerce International, and they never bounced. As one employee later recalled, "Any one of us who took a paycheque there didn't even have to show identification. If the cheque was from Manara, they would just give us the money in cash, no questions asked."

When Hawamda first discussed his Canadian plans with Ahmad Eed Murad, the latter insisted that the agency hire only non-Arabs. He told him, "Look, Mousa, the law agencies here know about you. In order to avoid any headache, don't hire any Arab-speaking person in the office. Don't hire anyone who is connected with the Arabs."

So Hawamda hired a Canadian woman who was married to an officer in the Canadian Armed Forces. Murad says this move helped to give the travel agency an appearance of legitimacy.

Except in the spring of 1987, when Manara was issuing tickets for delegates to the peace conference, none of the agents were very busy. Manara did not make any money. Even Murad bought his airline tickets elsewhere.

"But Mousa wanted to go first-class all the way," says Murad. "In a place like that, you need at least five hundred a day profit, but he did not make it. It's not a secret. Maybe he was hoping relations between Libya and the United States would be restored, so that he could get into trading, or whatever."

One former Manara employee says that Murad could not be more wrong. This person, who carefully recorded all comings and goings at the office, says that Manara Ottawa had only one purpose, which had nothing to do with turning a profit, and everything to do with channelling money to Third Positionists.

"Well, let's put it this way," the former employee says, when asked whether Hawamda used the travel agency to fund Third Position types. "Certain activities that were taking place there should not go on at a travel business. They were gathering information on

Canadians, they were organizing groups—special interest groups. They organized meetings with people who had nothing to do with the travel agency."

The former employee says that extremist groups made up a significant part of the agency's clientele. He says he never challenged Hawamda on the point, but adds, "I saw some funny things on the telex. Telexes about the Nation of Islam and the U.S. Indian Movement." The employee retained copies of the telexes.

Most of the time, the former employee says, Hawamda was away, travelling. He did not seem particularly concerned about the business side of the operation: "Mousa would be there one day a week, and he'd be away for weeks at a time. Sometimes he would look in to see how travel sales were going. He was very discreet."

The former employee remembers wondering at the opulence of the agency's offices: "The square footage ... itself was costing so much that, to make the business work, we would have to sell 250,000 dollars of business a month. Even American Express didn't have offices as big as us. The majority of the travel was to route people to Europe, and then on to Libya. We had a state-of-the-art reservation system. It was expensive stuff. We were losing money, but we had fax machines, telexes ... just tons of stuff for a place that was losing money."

The only Arab employee at Manara Ottawa was a Palestinian named Emad Younis. He kept working there long after Hawamda's arrest, and long after the hurried departure of the office manager and the other employees. His job was to run errands for Hawamda and stay in telephone contact with him when he was in Washington or abroad. "The boss is my friend, my good friend," said Younis, whose current whereabouts are unknown.

Manara Travel was at street level on Metcalfe. Hawamda got the space rent-free for the first few months after telling the landlord he wanted to renovate the premises and make a few improvements. In 1987 the rent, renovations, and upkeep on the premises amounted to a staggering $823,103—for a space about the size of a double-garage. Hawamda didn't mind—he wasn't paying the bills.

———————

Ahmad Eed Murad's dark eyes scan the ceiling. On a table in the living room of his suburban Ottawa home stands a photograph of him with George Habash, leader of the terrorist Popular Front for the Liberation of Palestine. Beside it, at the base of a vase filled with white plastic tulips, is another photo of Murad, this time with Mu'ammar Qadhafi. In a third photo, this one on a bookshelf, a smiling Murad is standing beside the former prime minister of Canada, Pierre Elliott Trudeau.

Murad excuses himself. He speaks into a beige cordless telephone, in Arabic, then turns his attention to his guest. It is the summer of 1988. Mousa Hawamda is in a Virginia jail, awaiting a preliminary hearing. Somewhat reluctantly, Murad has agreed to chat about his Palestinian business partner. He apologizes and asks, "What was the question?"

Why did Mousa Hawamda come to Ottawa?

"Mousa saw a market of 5,000 Libyan students in the United States. Now, it is about 250. He thought that if he went to Canada, he would get a new market. He asked me if I would be on the board of directors. He assured me that there is nothing wrong with being on the board of directors."

Murad appears withdrawn with a somewhat shy manner. When he speaks, he addresses the wall—he does not return his guest's gaze. He says he met Hawamda at a party in Washington in 1980, a year before the closing of the Libyan embassy there. It was a heady time for the Libyans: Jimmy Carter was in the White House and the president's brother, Billy, was a registered lobbyist for Libya's government. Murad says he visited Billy Carter at his Georgia home and that the two "were very good friends." To his elected brother's chagrin, Billy Carter would later admit to receiving a $200,000 interest-free "loan" from the Libyan government. Billy Carter had wanted to introduce Murad to his brother.

Murad says he and Hawamda were not close friends: "He was suspicious of me, and I didn't like the way he portrayed himself to the Libyans." He adds that over time, the two developed a grudging respect for each other.

Murad is unashamed of his fondness for Mu'ammar Qadhafi and George Habash. To Murad, Qadhafi is the only Arab leader with the courage to deal with the Israelis, and the Americans, and all who think like them. Murad has published pro-Qadhafi advertisements in the *Ottawa Citizen* and has defended the Libyan leader in letters to Canadian newspapers. He has also led a number of Libyan-funded junkets to Tripoli, one as recently as the fall of 1989. He claims to be on a first-name basis with those Members of Parliament and senators who are not noted for their love of Israel.

"What I do is not secret," he says. "I support Qadhafi one hundred per cent. I support his policies. I think he's the best Arab leader. I think most of the terrorist accusations have been...." He searches for the right phrase. "Many things, it turns out he has nothing to do with."

Murad has lived in Canada since 1960, in Ottawa since 1978. Before that, he lived in Edmonton, Vancouver, Hamilton, and Montreal. He says he loves Canada and its people; he does not regard his political activism as inconsistent with his Canadian citizenship. Accordingly, Murad claims that he does not mind that representatives of the Canadian Security Intelligence Service have seen fit to visit him every so often—once, in 1988, to discuss Hawamda's activities. He declines to give details of his conversations with the CSIS agents.

Murad was once president of the Association of Palestinian Arab-Canadians. For much of the 1970s he was the editor of a pro-Palestinian newspaper called *The Source*. It was in this capacity, almost 15 years ago, that he first met Qadhafi. Says Murad, "Show me evidence that Qadhafi was involved with actual terrorist activities—not just allegations!"

In conversation, Murad is friendly and relaxed, though rather vague. He says he was born in Palestine in 1939—and then hurriedly adds that he regards himself as a Canadian first. Murad and his German-born wife have two young children, a girl and a boy. Photos of them fill his split-level bungalow.

His eyes fixed on a photograph of his son, Murad continues: he was somewhat skeptical when Hawamda told him about his plans to expand his travel agency into Canada. There were simply not enough Libyan students up here, he told Hawamda. Besides, his overhead was going to be too big. The office space Hawamda had picked out for Manara was in a prime downtown location. He would be sharing the building with the Canada Council and the law firm Soloway Wright. But it made sense to Hawamda.

Says Murad, "He sensed that since the Americans would not—at least in the foreseeable future—have diplomatic relations with Libya, and since the Libyans wouldn't be sending their students to the United States, the Libyans would have to send their students somewhere. And Canada would be the alternative. So he would come to Canada, open an office here, and so on and so forth. By then he was well-connected in Libya—he knew [Libyan intelligence chief] Mohamed Madjoub."

Although he is not an admirer of Hawamda, Murad forcefully rejects any suggestion that Hawamda was a spy. He becomes particularly upset when his visitor broaches the subject of Oliver North. He shakes his head emphatically, sits up straight, and makes eye contact: "I feel that the Israelis are behind most of the allegations, to tarnish the image of the Arabs. I don't blame them. They have to win Canadian public opinion, and they will do whatever they can. As far as having Manara as a cover for anything, that is nonsense."

It is pointed out to him that the U.S. Attorney's office in Alexan-

dria, Virginia, has documentary evidence detailing Libyan surveillance of North in the weeks leading up to the 1987 peace conference
in Tripoli. Conceding that he is theorizing, Murad says, "Mousa
would never knowingly involve himself with anything that would
put him in trouble with the law in the United States. For him, the
United States is paradise. And if you're in paradise, you don't want to
lose it. The Oliver North thing was either concocted by the FBI, or it
was made up by one of the Libyans who defected, Buazzi." Murad is
gathering steam. "If the FBI had [not] had the slightest doubt about
Mousa and the others wanting to kill Oliver North, they would have
charged him, wouldn't they?"

There is no answer to this—Murad is right. He waves a hand, dis-
missing the FBI's case against Hawamda and the PCLS directors.
"There are always people interested in seeing Arabs in general, and
Libya in particular, pictured as terrorists."

5

SOMEWHAT RIGHT OF CENTRE

The date was May 29, 1968. Ian Verner Macdonald was still a Canadian trade commissioner, sitting at his desk in a building on Kent Street in downtown Ottawa, listening to his secretary type in the next room.

His neatly barbered head tucked to one side, he scanned one more time the memorandum on his desk. He had titled it "Commercial Interest in Canadian Foreign Policy" and addressed it to J.P.C. Gauthier, one of his superiors at the Department of Industry, Trade and Commerce. It was a tightly written piece of prose, single-spaced, dealing with the delicate question of Arabs, Jews, and Canada's trade policy. In it Macdonald was politely taking on what he would later call the Zionist Occupation Government, referred to by right-wing extremists as ZOG—and otherwise known as the International Jewish Conspiracy.

Down the hall, J.P.C. Gauthier was growing tired of receiving such memoranda from Macdonald. He would later tell the assistant director of the department's personnel branch that his subordinate's fixation on the Arab-Jewish question showed very poor judgement. In the course of his work, Macdonald was constantly airing his views on Canada's Middle East policy, though he had been told over and over to stop. Gauthier would complain that Macdonald was sometimes "wilfully disobedient" and had often shown "a lack of perspective and judgment."

Macdonald, needless to say, felt otherwise. His classified memo read,

> We have been backing the wrong horse in the Middle East.... Israel offers very little of economic value to Canada. It is, in fact, a serious obstacle to the development of normal trade relations with the Middle East and North Africa and is at best a small, uncertain and highly protected market dependent on subsidization to maintain its austere import program.... It can be regarded as an uncompensated burden on the Canadian exchequer and an indirect threat to the West.

———————

Now, more than 20 years later, Ian Verner Macdonald, retired diplomat, stretches his slender frame in a chair in his home in Ottawa's exclusive Sandy Hill district. The Ottawa native and sixth-generation Canadian looks younger than his 67 years. He folds his hands behind his head and offers a thin smile.

"My position," he begins, "is that the Israelis exercise an unhealthy influence over North America. Unquestionably, there is no other influence on government which remotely approaches the influence of the Israeli lobby. That lobby is more influential in Canada than in the United States. They are in government. They have infiltrated the government, there's no question about it. Had that not been the case, they would have had a lot of difficulty disposing of me."

It is fair to say that Ian Verner Macdonald does not flee from controversy. If anything, the former diplomat finds it invigorating—even when he is at the centre of it. Until the Libyan peace conference met its bad end, Macdonald's most memorable misadventure had been his association with James Alexander McQuirter, Grand Wizard of the Canadian Knights of the Ku Klux Klan.

Macdonald speaks affectionately of McQuirter, almost in a fatherly tone. In his view the young Klansman "stood out among his contemporaries."

McQuirter was a close associate of Republican presidential candidate David Duke, who at one time was leader of the Louisiana Ku Klux Klan. When McQuirter visited Ottawa, Macdonald would put him up at one of his many downtown properties. "I found him to be an interesting individual," Macdonald says. "He was prepared to challenge the establishment as a young man. He was a person who would take the initiative in an age of conformity. He dared to be different."

That, at least, is true. But by February 1982 it had become obvious that McQuirter was "daring to be different" too often. That month, McQuirter, Klan lieutenant Wolfgang Droege, and six others were arrested for conspiracy to overthrow the government of the Caribbean island of Dominica. McQuirter's plan had been to establish a white supremacist Garden of Eden—by force.

It may have been Macdonald himself—albeit with the very best of intentions—who steered McQuirter into the waiting arms of the

RCMP and the FBI. In 1981 he introduced McQuirter to Lee Brandy, one of his employees. Brandy helped Macdonald with his rental properties. The two made a deal: McQuirter would give Brandy information about the Dominica plot; Brandy would write a book about the publicity-conscious McQuirter. Shortly afterwards, Brandy told a reporter about Macdonald and McQuirter and the planned invasion. McQuirter's dreams of a sunny neo-Nazi sanctuary went up in smoke when the reporter wrote about it.

At his trials, McQuirter boasted frequently of his relationship with Macdonald, his "friend in Ottawa." In July 1980, McQuirter had revealed that the Canadian Knights of the Ku Klux Klan had a secret cell in Ottawa—"one that raised a great deal of money" for his cause. Ottawa Klan members, he said, were "older intellectuals in sensitive government jobs."

In his 1983 book, *White Hoods: Canada's Ku Klux Klan,* author Julian Sher wrote that Ian Verner Macdonald was, in fact, a "wealthy Klan backer" who helped to fund the organization. On the basis of that, Macdonald began defamation proceedings against Sher and his publisher. He later abandoned the lawsuit when his lawyer was disbarred. Years afterward, Macdonald continues to deny that he belongs to the Klan, but adds, "I sympathize with the Klan, as I do with any other minority group persecuted by the Zionist establishment, having been in that situation myself. But I have never been a member of the Klan, and I have never given them as much as one nickel." Macdonald admits to having written to both the National Parole Board and Ontario's Attorney General on McQuirter's behalf, and charges that the Klan leader's conviction was "a politically motivated set-up in response to pressure from Jews and blacks."

Ernst Zundel is another well-known Canadian who is very fond of Macdonald. In 1988 the Toronto graphic artist and sometime publisher was sentenced to nine months' imprisonment for spreading false news about the Holocaust—namely, that it never happened. He is appealing the conviction and sentence. Zundel says that Macdonald has supported him since the early 1970s: "In my dealings with him, I found him to be a very typical Canadian of the old school. He is in the best tradition of English Canada, I really believe that. The fact that he writes the odd letter in my support naturally might colour my judgement."

Macdonald also sympathizes with North Africa's 3.5 million Libyans. In his view, their country has been victimized too often by the alliance between Israel and the United States. Since leaving the diplomatic service, he has visited Libya three times—in 1970, 1972, and 1987. He likes the Libyan people. Part of his fascination with the country may be explained by the business links he has forged with the Libyan establishment. He says he has negotiated more than a dozen deals with Libyan government officials. Usually, the Libyans travel to Ottawa to meet with him; almost as often, he flies to meet them in New York State.

The deals are not inconsequential: they have involved millions, sometimes billions. In the early 1980s Macdonald played a central role in putting together a consortium of Canadian companies to extract desperately needed fresh water from the Marzuk Basin of southwest Libya. A decade earlier he had successfully negotiated a Canadian presence in the hugely productive Sarir oil field near Benghazi. It would have been a joint venture with the Libyan National Oil Company, with Canada providing operational know-how. The deal was subsequently scuttled, he says, by Jewish and pro-Jewish "collaborators" within the Canadian government. Adds Macdonald, ruefully, "This great opportunity, which was unprecedented in Canadian trade development ... lost."

———————

Macdonald is a soft-spoken man. When he remembers how he lost his diplomatic credentials, he chooses his words carefully, deliberately: "The only charge brought against me was that I had strong personal beliefs. We should be cultivating Arab markets. I was doing no more than fulfilling my function, and I had a virtually unblemished record, and a complete devotion to duty. When I offended ZOG, it was obviously no problem whatever to have me dismissed."

Before being dismissed from Canada's foreign service, he was no bureaucratic peon. He was, in fact, a senior and influential member of Canada's diplomatic corps. By the late 1960s he had become the second most powerful Canadian in the entire Middle East. Even after his dismissal he stayed on in Ottawa as a senior bureaucrat. During his more than 30 years of government service he kept what could charitably be called unusual company: besides advising James Alexander McQuirter on policy, he socialized with the leaders of the Nationalist Party of Canada, a white supremacist group.

Despite his dalliances with anti-Semites and white supremacists, and despite his efforts to promote racist ideology (blacks possess "mental and social immaturity," he wrote in a 1963 memorandum), Macdonald survived and prospered as a diplomat. He was admired. In December 1968 the Public Service Commission's Appeal Board noted that Macdonald's superiors described him as "exceptional" and "brilliant." He had "considerable talents" although he sometimes displayed "poor judgment."

Stories about his judgement, poor or otherwise, are not difficult to come by. Simply ask him and he will happily rhyme off a string of memorable anecdotes about his career in Canada's foreign service. In 1953 and 1954, while stationed in Bonn, he unilaterally started negotiations for the sale of several hundred Canadian F-86 Mark VI war planes to Germany. It would have been the largest-ever sale of Canadian aircraft to any nation. Macdonald was later reprimanded for his initiative by Charles Ritchie, who at the time was Canada's ambassador to Germany. According to Macdonald, Ritchie exclaimed, "My God, what would the French think if they found out that we were trying to re-arm their [former] enemy!"

In 1955, while still in Bonn, Macdonald met with Hjalmar Schacht

"to get his side of the story." Schacht had been the Nazis' finance minister and a defendant at the Nuremberg war crimes trials. Macdonald,
an RCAF and Royal Navy veteran, says, "Had we given Hitler a free
hand and co-operated with him, all of this postwar chaos would have
been forestalled. It would have opened up a glorious era."

In 1969, while posted in Ottawa as head of the special planning
division of the Department of Trade and Commerce, Macdonald
used department funds to subscribe to the *Canadian Intelligence
Service.* This newsletter, published by an Ontario man named
Ronald Gostick, denied the Holocaust and opposed communism,
the United Church, abortion, Jews, gun control, foreign aid, fluori-
dation, and what Gostick called "race mixing, which usually brings
tension, violence, race problems and ultimately mongrelization."

Macdonald engaged in all of these unique activities while a
member of Canada's foreign service. And although his fondness for
ultra-rightist doctrine earned him more than a few reprimands
during his diplomatic career, his rise through the diplomatic ranks
continued without hindrance. In 1965 he was named senior trade
counsellor at Canada's embassy in Beirut, where he oversaw Canadian trade with virtually every Arab nation in the Middle East. He
was outranked at the time only by Canada's ambassador to Lebanon,
Jack Maybee. As Canada's senior trade envoy for the troubled region,
Macdonald actively promoted trade with Saudi Arabia, Kuwait, Iraq,
Qatar, Abu Dhabi, Muscat, Yemen, Syria, Lebanon, and Jordan.

Remarks Macdonald, "What I encountered in trying to promote
better business relations with the Arab countries were Canadian
officials, trusted public officers in Canada, who were in effect serving
non-Canadian interests, to the detriment of Canadian interests." His
manner grows derisive. "I was promoting better relations with Arab
countries, and this was not part of the Israeli plan. I found there were
people in the department who chose to give precedence to Israeli
interests over Canadian interests. They were pandering to the Israeli
lobby."

It was for this reason, Macdonald says, that he was made "non-rotational" and dismissed from the Trade Commissioner's Service in 1970. In effect, he had been stripped of his credentials as a diplomat. He was then rehired to a public service post, where he remained until his retirement in 1984. He is still very bitter that the foreign service fired him. "I am a victim of this oversimplistic labelling process," he says. "I was disposed of simply by being labelled in such a way that I was discredited in the eyes of the uninitiated."

At External Affairs, Macdonald revealed himself to be many things, but bashful was not one of them. He remained close to the locus of power for over a decade and helped to shape Canada's Middle East policy. It is impossible to determine how much damage, if any, Macdonald did to Canadian interests in that region. His former employers at the Department of External Affairs are less than forthcoming on the point, though polite about it. Spokesperson Anne Collins says she does not know why Macdonald was forced out of the foreign service in 1970. "We don't have his file here. I don't know what the circumstances were surrounding his dismissal."

Some of the papers Macdonald left behind him shed a little light on the sort of diplomacy he practised: it was sometimes anti-Semitic, sometimes racist, and always intolerant. In a classified departmental memorandum Macdonald penned in October 1963, he described the American civil rights movement as

Negro excesses…. The black African has never constructed an alphabet, created a literature or science, produced any great men, or built up a civilization. The weight of evidence is in favour of the proposition that racial differences in mental ability are innate and genetic.

Incredibly, this memorandum was not followed by any disciplinary action, much less a dismissal. In fact, it was followed by six years of promotions.

How, one might reasonably ask, did he get away with it? External Affairs refuses to comment, but there is some indication that other Canadian diplomats in the 1960s and 1970s held controversial views.

On his 1988 résumé, Macdonald listed Eugene Forsey and Robert Stanfield as references. Forsey was a Canadian senator, Stanfield was once federal leader of the Progressive Conservative party. When asked about Macdonald's racist views—and the propriety of Macdonald being permitted to proclaim those views from within the ranks of Canada's diplomatic élite—Stanfield said, "The name doesn't mean anything to me at the moment. It might be a gap in my memory. I certainly have no recollection of authorizing anyone of that name to use me as a reference."

Macdonald says that his family has known Stanfield for many years. He considers the memory lapse odd but "understandable."

The gap notwithstanding, Stanfield *has* met with Macdonald on several occasions. In June 1981 the former Tory leader accepted an invitation to speak at a two-day conference in Calgary. Macdonald was one of the organizers. The conference dealt with relations between Canada and the Arab states. While there, Stanfield urged the Canadian government to recognize the Palestine Liberation Organization. (At that time it did not.) Macdonald notes that his connections with the federal Progressive Conservatives are not insignificant. In 1983, for example, during the PC leadership campaign, he rented office space in an Ottawa building he owned to Joe Clark, who was fighting to hold on to the party leadership. Macdonald says he only charged Clark "nominal rent."

Before he died in February 1991, Forsey had this to say about Macdonald: "I don't want to be seen as endorsing his beliefs. He has formed a very poor opinion of the Jews and a very high opinion of the Arabs. I've been noncommittal on that subject in the Senate because I never knew enough about it to comment on. I knew his father and mother very well and I've known him for years. I like him very much and I think he's a good man."

Good man or not, Macdonald was investigated by the RCMP Security Service in June 1984 for allegedly passing top-secret Canadian government trade information to both Iraq and Libya. Macdonald was never charged by the RCMP and vehemently denies that the documents in question were classified.

"The police have come to my home on occasion to ask me about various people," Macdonald says, sounding amused. "It's always been on a very congenial basis."

When asked about his relationship with the regime of Iraqi dictator Saddam Hussein, Macdonald says, "If the RCMP had any grounds for regarding me as a suspect, it would have been for my involvement with the government of Iraq. But only because I was their landlord here in Ottawa for some years, and because I had frequent contact with them.

"I supplied the Iraqis with trade statistics and information on Canadian companies," Macdonald continues. "The material I had given them was in the public domain. There was nothing confidential about it. I was being subjected to a form of bureaucratic persecution by the police."

Macdonald says that Iraqi officials were keen to forge better relations with Canadian companies: "They were even ready to give Canadian companies preference over other suppliers. Their ambassador told me that Iraq would gladly increase purchases from Canada by a billion dollars per year if Canada would stop supporting Zionism, and that he knew other countries would do likewise."

Two Iraqi diplomats with whom the trade commissioner had frequent contact were declared *persona non grata* by the Canadian government in the late 1970s. One was a senior Minister-Counsellor at the Iraqi embassy in downtown Ottawa. This man was stripped of his diplomatic credentials and deported for trying to coerce Iraqi nationals living in Canada into returning home. Macdonald insists that he has little contact with Iraqis these days, but admits that he wrote to Joe Clark, who was then Canada's Secretary of State for

External Affairs, to protest Canada's involvement in the Gulf War, which he called "counter-productive."

Mousa Hawamda was enthusiastic on the subject of Ian Verner Macdonald. After all, he shared the official Libyan view on the Jewish state and was decidedly pro-Arab. Macdonald would eventually become a key activist on behalf of the Libyan government.

The two men were introduced by Ahmad Eed Murad, who alongside Macdonald had not hesitated to make his anti-Israel views public. Hawamda was impressed with Macdonald and asked him in March 1987 to help out with the Tripoli peace conference. The same month, Macdonald flew to Washington at Hawamda's expense; while there, he discussed the proposed conference with the travel agency owner and with members of the Nation of Islam and the American Indian Movement. Throughout that meeting, Hawamda made repeated references to what he called Israel's occupation of Palestine.

"We discussed various things," Macdonald says. "On his initiative, we would discuss the question of justice for the Palestinians. This would resurface every so often." On Libya itself, however, Hawamda was disinclined to say much. "He didn't really go into great detail with me on his relationship with the Libyans, although he gave me the impression he was pretty well connected over there. But he seemed to be very reticent to mention any Libyan officials by name."

The meeting was a success. Macdonald made a commitment to supply a small number of Canadian delegates with anti-Israel views. Later, when he offered to find still more delegates, Hawamda did not hesitate to offer to pay for their airfare and expenses. Macdonald was told he would be "compensated" for his efforts, although he maintains he was not.

"The reason I came in touch with Mousa in the first place was primarily to organize the Canadian delegation to the peace conference," Macdonald says. "Apart from that I had no contact with him. He was looking for someone here to locate effective delegates, and Ahmad Murad had to be in Europe or some place at the time. So, being someone with Libyan connections of long standing—commercial connections, of course—it was delegated to me. I was delegated to find the delegates."

Libya's government has been quiet about its close relationship with far-right activists like Macdonald. But it has funded the racist right more than any other government except, perhaps, that of South Africa.

At first glance, white supremacists and neo-Nazis do not appear to have much in common with Mu'ammar Qadhafi. But the Libyan leader has at least three reasons for establishing links with the racist right. First, they come cheap: for only a few hundred thousand dollars—sometimes for only a few thousand—he can "rent" far-right mercenaries who will happily fight for his Third Position. Second, the far right shares Qadhafi's contempt for Israel and for all those who support its continued existence. Third, Qadhafi and the far right have much in common: Qadhafi himself is a racial separatist and has made it clear in his speeches and writings that he is strongly opposed to race mixing. For example, in a January 1988 address to members of the American Indian Movement, Qadhafi declared that he favoured the creation of separate "states" in North America for different races.

Hawamda had done well to contact Ian Verner Macdonald. The former diplomat was a resourceful man. After he was dismissed from the foreign service, and finding himself with more spare time on his hands, Macdonald had taken to dabbling in Ottawa real estate. By the mid-1980s he owned about a dozen properties in the pricey "golden triangle" near that city's Rideau Canal. Macdonald's real estate investments were sound enough that he was able to move into a palatial home on Wilbrod Street. He has filled it with dozens of rifles; hides of game animals; and thousands of books, among them anti-Semitic favourites such as Malcolm Ross's *Web of Deceit* and Arthur R. Butz's *Hoax of the Twentieth Century.*

Macdonald was able to give the peace conference plenty of attention. During late March and early April of 1987 he looked hard throughout the country for politicians and peace activists to send to the conference.

He now admits that the peace conference turned out badly. Christoph Halens' "unfortunate" death doomed the event to failure, he says. But from Macdonald's perspective, it could have been far worse. In May 1989 he wrote in a letter,

> I have reason to believe that it was I, and not Chris Halens, who was the original target. In any case, I informed the Libyans two days prior to Chris' death that an ugly incident was about to take place and requested that I be moved to a safer environment. The following morning I moved to a downtown hotel—the day before Chris Halens died. I concluded at the time that he would have been *selected* [author's emphasis] because of his relatively high profile as a reporter and his German antecedents.

Others who attended the peace conference say that Macdonald is mistaken. They say Macdonald was annoying, but not so annoying that someone would have wanted to kill him. Eyewitnesses say Macdonald made five Nazi salutes to members of the Nation of Islam during a tour of the Tripoli museum. Asked about the incident, Macdonald admits that his "Chaplinesque" gesture may have angered the black delegates: "I might have given a friendly wave to some of the American delegates there, which could have been easily misconstrued as a salute, I suppose."

To the FBI, American law was clear: by using Libyan government funds to pay for the plane tickets used by non-Libyans to get to the conference, Mousa Hawamda had committed a criminal act. To Ian Verner Macdonald, the peace conference was none of the Americans' business: "It was a question of inviting a number of Canadian and American delegates. It's hardly the Libyans' affair that the Americans put restrictions on their own citizens. That's an infringement of their right to travel anywhere they want. This whole business of the Libyan-American confrontation has been highly contrived, in my opinion.

"Who else is going to pay, if Libya invited delegates to Libya from North America? Do they expect people to go at their own expense? If the Americans put restrictions on the transfer of currency, it wasn't known to me or Mousa, as far as I know. He just carried out what was a legitimate travel agency function in providing the tickets. He was paid through this Libyan students' committee, but there was no other way in which he could be paid. The Libyans don't have any embassy there." He adds, "I can hardly see why anyone would take exception to the staging of a peace conference."

Hawamda, who to Macdonald's bewilderment did not attend the peace conference, was annoyed by the way the whole affair ended. "I think he felt that our effort had been undermined, to some extent [by Christoph Halens' death]," Macdonald says.

In the weeks following the peace conference, Macdonald wanted a new challenge. He found one. On July 22, 1987, he became a direc-tor of Mousa Hawamda's Neutron International Trading Inc., one of Libya's biggest front companies in North America.

In 1987 and 1988, Mousa Hawamda and Ian Verner Macdonald met often at Manara Travel's office on Metcalfe Street. Ahmad Eed Murad would sometimes join these discussions, which were always off-limits to the rest of the agency's staff. According to Macdonald, he and Hawamda had decided to capitalize on their respective connections with Libya's powers-that-be.

"Libya would have been a logical place to start," Macdonald says, "since we had done this big delegation thing. We thought, rightfully or wrongly, that the connections we had established through organizing the Canadian participation in the peace conference would pay off in good will, in that market at least, and in other Arab markets."

The name of their company was to be Neutron International. Macdonald insists that he was approached by Hawamda to set up the company. At no time did he and Hawamda wish to violate Canadian export controls against Libya, which forbid trade in military hardware and "unique Western petroleum technology." Is the FBI wrong to label Neutron International a front company? "That is a self-serving suggestion," Macdonald says. "The FBI is an agency of the U.S. government. The U.S. government has actually dropped bombs [on]people in Libya without provocation. Any information received from that source would certainly be tainted."

In mid-July 1987, Hawamda and Macdonald met at the office of Terry Jabour to incorporate their new company. Hawamda chose the name. Macdonald did not know what it signified and admits, a little ruefully, "It may not have been the most auspicious choice of names." Like Manara Travel, Neutron International was going to be a private company; to avoid detection of the Neutron firm's existence, no shares would be traded publicly. To save on overhead, Neutron International would be run out of Manara Travel's office in Ottawa.

Macdonald says that the trading firm was Hawamda's idea and adds that he contributed none of his own funds to the company's accounts. He insists that Neutron International was established to export commodities from North America to countries in the Mediterranean region: pulp, raw materials, dairy products. "Libya would have been a primary target," Macdonald adds. "We wanted to strengthen our connections there.... I was a relatively passive figure in this whole business. But I was prepared to co-operate to the extent of providing a Canadian personality for them. I've been interested for many years in developing markets in Libya. But Neutron has never done any transactions. It's fairly new. Both Mousa and I were engaged in many more pressing activities."

He reflects for a moment. Then: "Neutron is yet to be activated. And as soon as Mousa can be freed from his present entanglements, probably it will function again."

The third director of Ottawa's Neutron International was Dr. Yussuf Naim Kly. Little is known about Kly, except that he once lived in Hull, Quebec, and possibly in Boston, Massachusetts, where a man by that name was a director of L'institut Canadien pour le Développement et le Transfert de Technologie. After the *Ottawa Citizen* revealed the existence of Neutron International in a front-page story on October 13, 1988, a man identifying himself as Kly telephoned the newspaper's editorial department from somewhere in the United States. The man, who spoke in a thick accent, told Ian MacLeod of the *Citizen* that he had signed Neutron International's papers of incorporation at a social event in Ottawa in the summer of 1987 and had not been fully aware of Neutron International's corporate objectives. He refused to say more.

Ian Verner Macdonald is no monosyllabic revisionist sloganeer. You are not likely to spot him next week on the steps of Parliament Hill, passing out copies of Ernst Zundel's pamphlet, "Did Six Million Really Die?" Nor should you soon expect to see him hauled into an Ontario court on charges that he wilfully promoted hatred against an "identifiable group," which is what Jim Keegstra did for so long in a classroom in Eckville, Alberta.

No: Macdonald is too smart, too subtle, for that sort of thing. In conversation, it is obvious that he possesses a fierce intelligence that the passage of time and the disdain of his peers have done nothing to dim. He is articulate, and he can be witty. On the central issue of his professional life—to trade or not to trade with the Arabs—he believes his own position is unassailable: "I was twenty years ahead of my time."

This sort of fervour, which Macdonald calls "anti-Zionist," has not diminished at all in his retirement. But except for his business partnership with Mousa Hawamda in Neutron International, which he says has not been consummated, and except for occasional skirmishes about the Holocaust when David Irving comes to town*—he looks and sounds like any other senior citizen. He talks longingly about full retirement, about taking it easy for a change. He still keeps in touch with his anti-Semitic buddies, and he still praises Libya and other Arab nations to whoever will listen.

But he now keeps his distance from people like Alex McQuirter and from those Third Positionists who would bring about societal change with bombs and guns. He no longer tries to sell Canadian war planes to Germany without permission, and he is no longer seen in the company of suspected war criminals like Hjalmar Schacht. Most significantly, he no longer preaches against Zionism from within the ranks of Canada's diplomatic corps—he can't. Instead, he sits in his big old house in Ottawa, typing letters on his IBM electric. He is, after all, Ian Verner Macdonald, and he has much to say.

He writes to immigration ministers: "Canada's immigration policy has not come to grips with the more important problems, which include the difficulty or impossibility of assimilating large numbers of coloured, particularly Negro, immigrants."

---

*David Irving is a British writer, a self-described "moderate fascist" who denies that the Holocaust happened. In 1989 Macdonald and others arranged a speaking engagement for him at the Chateau Laurier in Ottawa. Three hundred people attended. A similar engagement in 1991 was cancelled as a result of protests.

And he writes to newspaper editors: "Little or no attempt has been made to disprove … the inordinate and dangerous influence exercised by Zionists in national and international affairs.... We serve an alien master. He controls us through a network of agents, collaborators and sympathizers and some outright mercenaries."

And to provincial premiers: "Jewish antipathy to Christianity transcends mere criticism and ridicule. The Holy Land has been the scene of countless abominations since 1948, perpetrated by Jews against Christians."

Ian Verner Macdonald gives another tight smile.

"Taking a conventional view," he says, "I would put myself somewhat right of centre."

6

MU'AMMAR'S FASCIST FRIENDS

In the United States, Libya has not enjoyed much success in convincing white supremacists to rally to the Third Positionist cause, which is too convoluted for the old cross-burning Ku Klux Klan types. The Canadian ultra-right has been easier to win over.

Few American racist groups have been willing to cash in their bigoted principles for Libyan dinars. One that has is the National Democratic Front, which is based in Maryland and has strong ties to the National Front in Britain. But most American neo-Nazi groups are solidly anti-Libyan. The most vocal of these is the White Aryan Resistance, which is based in Fallbrook, California, and led by Tom Metzger. Metzger, who calls himself a Third Positionist, is a full-time television repairman and a part-time host of a cable-television program called "Race and Reason." WAR has a current membership of about 2,000 and is growing at an alarming rate, mainly because so many skinhead youths are being seduced by modern-day Nazism.

Metzger is the *éminence grise* of the West Coast racists. He is a short, pear-shaped man who sports a cheap-looking toupé. His association with far-right circles goes back 30 years. At various times he has been a Republican, a high-profile activist with the John Birch Society, an organizer of the ultra-secretive Minutemen, Grand Dragon of California's Knights of the Ku Klux Klan, and a founding member of both the White Brotherhood and the White American Political Association. While with WAPA, Metzger ran for the U.S. Senate in California and garnered 80,000 votes.

He founded WAR in 1982 as a Third Positionist alliance dedicated to overthrowing "the Zionist Occupation Government." He held onto his Klan-type views, however: the following year he was charged with a misdemeanour after a cross-burning incident in a black neighbourhood. (He was convicted of that charge in 1991.) Metzger is also an unabashed fan of The Order, an Aryan Nations offshoot that carried out a campaign of murder and robbery in the American Northwest in 1983 and 1984. One of their victims was Al Berg, the controversial talk show host, whom they shot to death outside a Denver townhouse. The neo-Nazi terrorist cell has since been portrayed in the Hollywood movies *Betrayed* and *Talk Radio*.

In late October of 1990, WAR was handed a courtroom defeat from which it may never recover. An Oregon jury assessed more than $12 million in damages against that group, Metzger, and his son John for inciting three Portland skinheads to attack an Ethiopian immigrant. The skinheads beat the man to death. The award made American legal history for its size and for the precedent it set. It may signal the end of Metzger's racist empire. He has been forced to sell his home and other belongings to pay off the judgement against him.

A few months before the $12 million setback, Metzger sat in his home in Fallbrook, which is midway between Los Angeles and San Diego, and answered questions. He said that Libyan government operatives like Mousa Hawamda had taken control of much of North America's racist right. In his nasal mid-Western twang, Metzger added that the neo-Nazi movement was going to the dogs and that Mu'ammar Qadhafi was largely to blame: "Qadhafi has been passing out money around the world to different nationalist groups, but it's got so many strings attached to it that they eventually turn out material that looks like it was printed in Tripoli. There's a lot of that going on, but we don't want to see our movement taken off in that particular direction."

Libyan involvement with North American fascist organizations was now such an acute problem, Metzger said, that he no longer referred to WAR as a Third Positionist group. To distance himself from the pro-Libyan racist right, he was now calling WAR "the Third Force": "We are becoming increasingly alarmed at the inroads the Libyans are making among legitimate nationalist groups. It's one thing to give them money, but it's another to distort their entire program. Qadhafi has pretty much taken over one wing of the National Front in Great Britain, you know. As far as we are concerned, when people lose their racial consciousness, and drift off into some race-mixing political attitude, we don't want anything to do with them."

Metzger was one of the 200 Americans—and the only representative of WAR—invited by Mousa Hawamda to attend the peace conference in Tripoli. At the time, however, WAR's leader was embroiled in another court battle and could not attend. "In retrospect," he later said, "I'm glad I didn't go. This Qadhafi thing is getting out of hand."

When pressed on the subject, Metzger insisted that he did not know which Third Positionist and neo-Nazi groups were receiving funding from Hawamda and his PCLS allies. Then he contradicted himself: "You can always tell when they get the money. They almost start to sound like Libyan nationalists. I don't think they know how silly they make themselves look."

But Metzger was careful not to sound too critical of his good friend Don Andrews, leader of the Nationalist Party of Canada. He added, a little hastily, "I think the Don Andrews people are legitimately interested in Mu'ammar Qadhafi on some issues. I don't see any evidence they have been taken over by Qadhafi's people."

Don Andrews would have been pleased to hear that. He has waged many battles for Canada's neo-Nazi movement. He is many things, but "silly" is not one of them.

Until he was ten years old, his name was Vilim Zlomislic. He was born in the Serbian region of what was then Yugoslavia in 1942 and did not have a good childhood. The Nazis killed his father, he says, and his mother was shipped off to a labour camp in Germany. Young Vilim was placed in an orphanage. Soon after the war ended he became an outstanding member of the Young Pioneers, a Yugoslav Communist youth group. In 1952 the International Red Cross tracked him down and sent him to Canada, where his mother had remarried and was living in Toronto with her new husband. The couple renamed the boy Donald Clarke Andrews.

He was a sickly youth. During his early teens he was hospitalized with osteomyelitis, a bone disease. Unable to play sports, he became a voracious reader. He excelled in school, but his family could not afford to send him to university. He made do by taking public health courses at Ryerson Polytechnic Institute, where a scholarship was available for him. He worked as a public health inspector for 14 years in Toronto.

He had once been a shining example of youthful communism; now he was lurching toward the opposite extreme on the political spectrum: fascism. Until he was 21 years old, Andrews was a social democrat. But at some point in the 1960s, he discovered anticommunism. He became a founder of Toronto's Edmund Burke Society. (Burke, ironically, was the British parliamentarian who said that "the only thing necessary for the triumph of evil is for good men to do nothing".) Andrews and his fellow Burke Society members proclaimed their opposition to communism and moral degeneration. In practice, their group was little more than a repository for mean-spirited racists and anti-Semites.

The Edmund Burke Society was violent—in the early 1970s it often engaged in bloody clashes with leftist demonstrators. Apparently, though, it wasn't hard-line enough for Andrews. He looked around for a group with a less ambiguous political program and discovered the Western Guard, whose most recent leader, John Ross Taylor, held the view that Adolf Hitler had been a "softie" on the Jews. Andrews had found a home.

During his five-year tenure as the Western Guard's leader, which began in 1972, the organization was overtly racist and anti-Jewish. Its members published a hate sheet called "Straight Talk" and regularly celebrated the birthdays of Adolf Hitler and Benito Mussolini. Andrews ran for mayor of Toronto in 1972, 1974, and 1976. In 1976 he and two other men were charged with plotting arson, possession of weapons and explosives, and mischief. Their objective, Crown prosecutors maintained, had been to disrupt a pre-Olympic soccer game at Varsity Stadium involving an Israeli team. During the trial Andrews enthusiastically asserted that blacks were "human and organic garbage." He was sentenced to two years in prison and ordered to stay away from the Western Guard when he got out.

Ever the industrious white supremacist, Andrews simply decided to form a new group. In 1977, after his early release from prison, he formed the National Citizens Alliance; in June 1977 he renamed it the Nationalist Party of Canada. Hundreds of Western Guard enthusiasts signed up. One was James Alexander McQuirter, who would go on to notoriety as the leader of Canada's Ku Klux Klan.

The legal authorities would never lose their interest in Andrews. In 1985 he and another Nationalist Party member were convicted of promoting hatred against non-whites in one of the group's publications. Their conviction was later affirmed by the Ontario Court of Appeal. In March 1990 the Supreme Court of Canada heard arguments on their case. Months later the high court ruled that the law under which Andrews was charged *was* constitutional—meaning that his conviction would continue to stand.

While he was founding the NPC, Andrews began to assume a decidedly moderate stance toward the Arab world. The NPC's official newsletter, the *Nationalist Report,* noted that Islam, unlike Christianity, was incompatible with communism. Another issue carried a letter from Iran's foreign ministry thanking Andrews for a letter congratulating the Ayatollah Khomeini on his return to power. His pro-Arab stance did not go unnoticed in Libya. In early 1987, Ian Verner Macdonald asked Mousa Hawamda if he could invite a few of his NPC friends to the Tripoli peace conference. Hawamda agreed. (Though Macdonald's name can be found on an NPC membership list, he denies he is a member of Andrews' group.)

Andrews did not attend the peace conference but did join a group of NPC members that visited Tripoli in September 1989. He says that the engineers of the Green Revolution have always been kind to NPC members—paying for their plane tickets, "feasting" them, and occasionally passing along small interest-free loans. Andrews is an unabashed fan of Qadhafi's regime and dismisses those in the ultra-right fringe who are uncomfortable with that fact.

"In varying degrees," he says, "varying elements of the white nationalist movement will have to agree on some sort of participation with the Libyans. It's very important not to be an Archie Bunker-type bigot. That is a losing philosophy. We want to preserve our own Aryan racial identity, and what we are out to do is represent those who want to preserve their own racial identity, too." Like the Libyans.

The NPC delegation that attended the September 1989 celebration marking Qadhafi's 20 years in power included Andrews, his wife Nicola, the couple's three-month-old son, Ku Klux Klan member Wolfgang Droege, and a smattering of others—in all, ten men, seven women, and the Andrews' baby. While returning to Canada on

September 4, the group's Alitalia flight stopped in Chicago, where Droege was arrested by officers of the U.S. Immigration and Naturalization Service. Droege was one of the co-conspirators in James Alexander McQuirter's plot to overthrow the government of Dominica. He had spent three years in an American prison for his role in the conspiracy and had later been extradited to Canada. The American government had told him then not to return.

After questioning Droege in Chicago for a few hours, the American immigration officials permitted him to return to Canada. The videotapes he and Andrews had shot in Tripoli were confiscated by the FBI.*

According to Andrews, the funding the NPC has received from Libya is "negligible.... They give us maybe a thousand dollars for expenses. How far does a thousand dollars go? Not very. We spend ten thousand a year on literature."

How does he respond to Tom Metzger's criticism—that recipients of Libyan patronage must ultimately lose control of their racist "program"?

"I think we should start from the real racist perspective," Andrews asserts. "We should respect other races who do their own labour and respect their own racial origin. The Libyans have treated us well on two trips. They paid for everything ... but we're not required to do anything in particular when we're in Libya, other than to be friendly." Asked how well he knew Mousa Hawamda, Donald Andrews becomes uncharacteristically discreet. "I won't answer those questions. Needless to say, we have met all the main players."

---

*Droege and four other Nationalist Party members hit the headlines again in March 1992 when the *Toronto Sun* revealed they had joined the Reform Party in Toronto.

MU'AMMAR'S REVOLUTIONARY FRIENDS

"The blacks will prevail in the world," reads one section in the third volume of Mu'ammar Qadhafi's *Green Book.* In one of that book's memorable passages, Qadhafi plays amateur sociologist and comes off sounding like a bigot.

> The black race is now in a very backward social situation. But such backwardness helps to bring about numerical superiority of the blacks because their low standard of living has protected them from getting to know the means and ways of birth control and family planning. Also their backward social traditions are a reason why there is no limit to marriage, leading to their unlimited growth, while the population of other races has decreased because of birth

control, restrictions on marriage and continuous occupation in work, unlike the blacks who are sluggish in a climate which is always hot.

It is vintage Qadhafi: uninformed, unrealistic, and unpleasant.

During Qadhafi's two-decade-long reign a number of controversial black leaders and organizations have benefited from Libya's generosity. Some recipients have been less infamous than others. Idi Amin, the deposed Ugandan dictator, was loaned a few planeloads of Libyan troops in 1979; in the United States, Qadhafi has quietly funded pocket-sized groups of militants with names like the Republic of New Africa and Black Argus. Few of these groups last long.

For almost a decade the Libyan leader's strongest ally in the American black community has been Louis Farrakhan and his Nation of Islam. In the mid-1980s the Nation of Islam's leaders often visited Manara Travel in Washington, D.C. In the weeks leading up to the 1987 Tripoli peace conference, its organizers were a common sight there, making long-distance phone calls, photocopying documents, and meeting with Hawamda or the six PCLS officers—all of this under FBI surveillance. Hawamda liked the group: it was better-organized and more politically sophisticated than the neo-Nazi groups.

The Nation of Islam had been around for a long time. Its beginnings can be traced back to the summer of 1930. That year, a black man calling himself Wallace Fard Muhammad appeared in Detroit, Michigan, proclaiming that he had just returned from the holy city of Mecca, where he had found his life's mission—to teach blacks the truth about whites. He told black audiences to prepare for Armageddon, which would be the final confrontation between blacks and whites. Over the long, hard days of the Great Depression, Muhammad established his first Temple of Islam, where he preached that Allah was God, whites were the devil incarnate, and blacks were "the cream of the planet earth." By the end of 1930 he had recruited an estimated 8,000 followers in Detroit alone.

One of the 8,000 was a 32-year-old auto worker named Elijah Poole. Born in 1898 in Georgia, the son of a Baptist minister, Poole moved his wife and two children to Detroit when he was 25 years old. There he worked at a Chevrolet auto plant until 1929, when he lost his job, like so many others, to the ravages of the Depression. In 1930 he was initiated into Wallace Fard Muhammad's sect and began a rapid rise through its ranks. Fard renamed him Elijah Muhammad and picked him to be Chief Minister of his burgeoning Nation of Islam. After Fard vanished mysteriously in June 1934—some believe he was the Messiah and had returned to Heaven—Elijah Muhammad assumed control of the organization. He would continue to rule it for the next four decades.

It is fair to say that Elijah Muhammad's teachings were malevolent. His ministry counselled hatred and race war. Regarding whites, he preached, "The enemies of Allah are known at present as the white race or European race." Regarding Jesus Christ, "Never any more will you fool us to bow and pray to a dead Jesus. There is no hope in Christianity; it is a religion organized by the enemies of the Black Nation to enslave us to the white man's rule." Muhammad's hate-filled diatribes were rejected by the mainstream black community. Even some of the NOI converts—among them one of the most esteemed African-Americans of the century, Malcolm X—eventually renounced Elijah Muhammad's black supremacist views. The fact remains, though, that the organization grew at an exponential rate in the United States while he was its leader. By 1962 its membership had exploded, and there were more than 100 Nation of Islam temples in the United States.

In the early 1970s, while Elijah Muhammad was still its leader, the Nation of Islam began accepting Libyan cash. It was sent quietly and received quietly. The Anti-Defamation League of the B'nai Brith, a human rights organization that monitors anti-Semitic activity in the United States and Canada, estimates that its leaders received millions from Qadhafi during this period.

When Elijah Muhammad died of heart failure in February 1975, his seventh son, Wallace Warith Deen Muhammad, was declared the new leader of the Nation of Islam. The younger Muhammad was closer to Malcolm X's style of leadership than he was to that of his own father. To emphasize his commitment to traditional Islam, he renamed the group the World Community of al-Islam in the West; he rejected his father's deification of Wallace Fard Muhammad; and, significantly, he denounced those who regarded whites as "devils," and actually invited non-blacks to join.

Wallace Muhammad's reversal of decades of Nation of Islam-style racism did not sit well with Louis Farrakhan, minister of Harlem's mosque number seven, the organization's most powerful temple outside Chicago. Farrakhan, born Louis Eugene Walcott in New York in 1933, had a unique start for a preacher: he dropped out of teachers' college to work as a calypso singer. Calling himself Calypso Gene, he achieved a certain degree of fame. In 1955 he met Malcolm X and his life was irrevocably changed. Soon, Farrakhan was a powerful and respected member of the Nation's inner circle, the designated national spokesman for Elijah Muhammad.

Angered by Wallace Muhammad's antiracist reforms, Farrakhan left the World Community of al-Islam in the West in December 1977 to re-form the Nation of Islam. Under Farrakhan's leadership the "new" Nation of Islam promoted black nationalism and self-reliance. It also returned to the black supremacist teachings of Elijah Muhammad, with their hatred of Christianity and Judaism, deification of Wallace Fard Muhammad, and advocacy of genocide against whites. Other, newer notions have crept into the group's philosophy during Farrakhan's reign, such as his belief that he is the Messiah: "The Jesus you have been seeking and waiting for His return has been in your midst for 40 years." In various issues of the group's official publication, *Final Call*, blacks have been told that Jews are "our enemies"; whites have been referred to as "devils"; and blacks have been urged to avoid "the evil and filth of the white race."

Calypso Gene does not have a generous heart.

Although Farrakhan should not be regarded as an anticapitalist crusader—he lives in a massive fortified home in central Chicago that is surrounded by expensive automobiles—neither should he be seen as a leftist in the traditional sense. His sect rejects capitalism because it is the system that permitted the enslavement of African-Americans, but Farrakhan is no communist. Rather, he and his followers are true Third Positionists, awaiting the final revolution that will destroy the "white devils."

While awaiting this racial Armageddon, Farrakhan and his followers lobby for separate homelands for the races—a position that has earned them accolades from neo-Nazi groups such as Tom Metzger's White Aryan Resistance and Richard Butler's Aryan Nations. But it was only in 1984 that Farrakhan attracted the attention of the American national media. In March of that year, while campaigning for the Reverend Jesse Jackson during the Democratic primaries, he stated that "Hitler was a very great man." In July he added that Judaism was a "gutter religion." Jackson, who has called New York City "Hymietown," parted ways with Farrakhan when the Nation of Islam's leader became a political liability.

Farrakhan's unflinching commitment to racism and anti-Semitism has gained him the enthusiastic support of Mu'ammar Qadhafi. In April 1983, at Libya's expense, two of Farrakhan's aides attended the annual Green Book Conference in Tripoli. And in February 1985 Farrakhan invited Qadhafi to be the keynote speaker during the Nation's annual Saviour's Day celebrations. The Libyan leader accepted: on October 7, by satellite, he addressed 13,000 Nation of Islam members for half an hour. He called upon black Americans to desert the American armed forces and form their own paramilitary organization. "Defeat your enemy!" Qadhafi told the delegates. "Destroy white America!"

As Farrakhan led his supporters in a series of standing ovations, Qadhafi called the United States "the castle of imperialism" and repeated his call for a black territorial preserve in North America. "Fight together," Qadhafi told the black nationalists, "to defeat the colonialization, racism, imperialism—to get rid of exploitation and oppression!"

Farrakhan's decision to allow Qadhafi a few minutes' speaking time had the desired effect: two months later, in a speech at the Kennedy Center in Washington, D.C., he announced that the Libyan government had just promised the Nation an interest-free loan of $5 million. His 3,000 followers in the hall went wild.

Abdul Wali Muhammad, editor of *Final Call*, confirmed in December 1991 that the $5 million did arrive, by way of a Libyan "charitable organization" named the Islamic Call Society. The money was earmarked to launch the Nation of Islam's "Clean and Fresh" line of personal health care products. According to the NFSL and Western intelligence services, the Islamic Call Society, which pretends to be a pro-Arab cultural organization, is in fact one of the most active Libyan front organizations in North America.

In March 1986, the year after the Nation received the $5 million, Mousa Hawamda and his PCLS allies arranged a visit to Libya by Farrakhan himself. In going, Farrakhan defied the American ban on travel to that country. He was not prosecuted for doing so.

In Libya, Farrakhan attended the "Second International General Conference to a World Forum to Combat Imperialism, Zionism, Racism, Reaction and Fascism." In a speech to that body, he told Qadhafi, "During these 20 years of your guidance and instruction to the Libyan people, we have watched you grow, and we have grown with you. The ruin, the disgrace, the destruction that has been planned for you, Allah is bringing it swiftly upon your enemies....

"It is clear from the many attempts of the CIA, MOSSAD and intelligence institutions of other nations whose sole aim was to destroy Mu'ammar al-Qadhafi and the great al-Fateh Revolution, that all of their efforts have been, are, and shall by Allah's help continue to be a dismal failure, as Allah exalts you and the Revolution to greater and greater heights with each passing day!"

———————

Although Qadhafi calls his nation the Socialist People's Libyan Arab Jamahiriya, his efforts on behalf of international socialism are hardly noteworthy—they have been lip service at best. In recent years Qadhafi has permitted and in some cases actually encouraged the growth of private enterprise. More goods are finding their way into Tripoli's *souk*—its central marketplace—and small-scale capitalism seems to be flourishing. Most state markets have closed and restrictions on the private sector have been eased, so that some Libyans are now speaking of "green *perestroika.*" Qadhafi is hardly a socialist now, if he ever was.

Even so, Qadhafi remains an unqualified supporter of a number of ultra-left groups, including Germany's Red Army Faction, Portugal's Popular Forces of April 25, and France's Action Direct. Many of these groups are now committed to the Third Position's cause and have become as stridently opposed to the former Soviet Union's embrace of communism as they always were to American-style capitalism. Without exception these groups do philosophical battle— and sometimes physical battle—with Israel and "Zionism." They would deny strongly that they are promoting anti-Semitism; that they are doing just that is indisputable.

So when Mousa Hawamda asked Ian Verner Macdonald to recruit delegates for the 1987 peace conference, the former trade diplomat recognized immediately that he would find plenty of candidates among the revolutionary thinkers on the left, particularly those in the peace movement. It was through Ottawa's peace circles that Christoph Halens first learned of the event that would later claim his life.

Macdonald says he was prepared to offer plane tickets to Canadians anywhere on the ideological spectrum, as long as they opposed the State of Israel. On that requirement he would not compromise: "I don't ask people whom I meet what their political position might be. My only stipulation was that if they were going to Libya, they should be anti-Zionist."

Among those who may or may not have met this requirement were a senior representative of a Canadian postal union, a South African anti-apartheid activist, a Marxist bookstore employee, members of the Carleton University Women's Centre, and a member of the World Peace Council, a Moscow-funded straw group. Most were very active in the Canadian peace movement, but not all of the peace activists were anti-Zionist. In fact, some were astounded by Macdonald's stipulation. John Lamb, who at that time was director of the Canadian Centre for Arms Control, remembers receiving a late-night phone call from the former diplomat at his home. The ensuing conversation was "bizarre in the extreme," Lamb later said.

Macdonald told Lamb about the conference's objectives. "It's anti-American," he said, "and I guess you could say it is anti-Israel."

"That's a little strange," Lamb told him. "I don't think that's the kind of thing I want to be involved in."

But others were not as reluctant. Of the 95 Canadian delegates, better than four out of five were members of peace organizations.

Libya's contacts with Canada's left have been spotty at best. Some high-profile activists, such as Eibie Weizfeld of the Parliament Hill Peace Camp, have travelled to Libya, and defended the North African republic on a regular basis. But moderate left-wing groups are generally sophisticated enough to recognize that any association with Libya is "filled with more minuses than pluses," as one Ottawa-based socialist puts it. This long-time activist with the International Socialists remembers seeing Hawamda at a 1987 anti-American demonstration on Parliament Hill. The Palestinian was holding a stack of anti-Israel leaflets and chatting about a planned Tripoli peace conference. He found few takers.

"We are opposed to Israel because of the Palestinian question, and because its government violates the human rights of Palestinians," says the International Socialists member. "But we don't oppose Israel because we are anti-Semites, like Hawamda."

In Europe, this hair is split less often. There, for most of the 1970s and 1980s, Qadhafi found eager converts in the international peace movement. With Libyan support, Europe's Third Positionists started to declare their support for environmental activism, women's rights, and disenfranchised youth. In Italy in the late 1970s, far-right organizations decided to stop attacking the Red Brigades and other such groups.

"This was a period of great change for the right wing," a cell chief with the fascist Armed Revolutionary Nuclei told an Italian court. "New ideas and new needs sprang up. We changed our attitude toward the ultra-left-wing groups. The guy with the long hair was no longer our enemy. We realized that we were victims of the same system, and we started to grow our hair long and use the same terminology that was typical of the extreme left-wing. We felt a generational bond with left-wing youth, and we appreciated their anti-bourgeois attitude....

"We understood that left-wing and right-wing revolutionists had to stop killing each other."

———

The time was 11:00 a.m., FBI records show. The date was May 13, 1985. The place was a room at the headquarters of the People's Committee for Libyan Students in McLean, Virginia. Saleh al-Rajhi was the committee's cultural officer. He was also Mousa Hawamda's right-hand man and one of the more excitable members of the PCLS board of directors. At that moment he stood to address his colleagues, afire with revolutionary passion:

"We have the responsibility to continue the revolutionary battle,

Christoph Halens in Ottawa, September 1986. *(photo courtesy Rosemary Knes)*

Ahmad Eed Murad (centre) checking the tickets of Canadian peace conference delegates at Mirabel Airport, April 1987. *(photo courtesyTerry Jabour)*

The Zanzour Tourist Village, Tripoli, where Canadian delegates to the April 1987 peace conference stayed. The Gulf of Sidra is in the background. *(photo courtesy Terry Jabour)*

The arrow shows where Christoph Halens' body was found, near the entrance to the Zanzour Tourist Village. *(photo courtesy Terry Jabour)*

Michelle Tardif, under a smiling portrait of Mu'ammar Qadhafi, at the peace conference in Tripoli, April 1987. *(photo courtesy Terry Jabour)*

LEFT: Mousa Hawamda, taken the day of his arrest, July 20, 1988. *(photo courtesy FBI)*

BELOW: The Manara Travel Agency on Metcalfe Street in Ottawa, July 1988. *(photo courtesy* Ottawa Citizen*)*

Ian Verner Macdonald in his study at his home in Ottawa, 1989. The book
Macdonald is cradling is *They Dare to Speak Out* by Paul Findley, which deals with
the alleged power of the Israeli lobby in the U.S. *(photo courtesy Tony Fouhse)*

LEFT: Mohamed Shihumi,
taken in 1988.

BELOW: Horst Schmid, former
Alberta cabinet minister,
taken in 1987.
(photo courtesy Edmonton Journal*)*

National Front News

30p

INSIDE Issue 103 March (1) 1988

MEDIA POWER

How It's Used Against Us

SEE CENTRE PAGES

A Third Way Beyond Capitalism and Communism

HELP BUILD THE PAPER - PAY THE £1 SOLIDARITY PRICE   PUBLISHED FORTNIGHTLY

THE NEW ALLIANCE

THE ERA of the Super Powers - the USA and USSR - is over! For 40 years, they have dominated the world, threatening to drag us all to destruction in their own private quarrels. But this Old Order is now falling apart at the seams. In its place there is rising a new political power bloc - the New Alliance.

Revolutionary nationalist groups, racial separatists and the anti-Zionist nations of the Middle East, are beginning to recognize a common set of interests and enemies which make closer co-operation both beneficial and inevitable.

Against our common enemies - Capitalism and Communism - we are at last beginning to develop a credible alternative: the *Third Way.*

The interest groups which are gradually coming together have many differences. Some of them support policies with which Nationalists in Britain do not agree.

But we do not seek to interfere with each other's domestic affairs, we favour tradition and religion over the rootless atheism of the Super Powers, and we recognize the rights of all peoples to self-determination - free from the grip of Wall Street banks or Soviet tanks.

SPREADING

It may be years before really close, practical, relationships are established between us, but Third Way principles are spreading everywhere.

The Soviet Union is beginning to disintegrate, as its minority nations - in Asia as well as in parts of Europe such as Estonia - struggle against rule by the Marxist empire.

The U.S.A. is losing the economic dominance which made it a Super Power. Its forces have been driven out of country after country, from Vietnam to the Lebanon.

And the Zionist occupying forces in Palestine are losing their brutal war against young boys and girls armed only with sticks and stones.

The tyrannical multi-racism imposed on every people of the world by Capitalist and Zionist media masters is also beginning to die, as White and Black racial separatists unite to work together to end race-mixing and protect the identities of our own nations.

But there is still a long way to go. Common interest must be turned into practical co-operation. Those involved must work to nail the media lies which are used by our enemies to try to divide us and make us afraid to be seen standing side by side with Third Way nations such as Libya and Iran.

POSITIVE

And we must all work to spread the positive side of the Third Way in our own countries.

Co-operative economics; political de-centralization; popular participation in government and defence; respect for the environment - these NF ideas form the basis of our "Green Revolution."

They must be developed and used to build support for the ideolgy and system which is going to dominate the world in the 21st Century - The Third Position.

NATIONAL

FRONT

ULSTER VIOLENCE - WHO IS TO BLAME ?

THE VIOLENCE which has wracked Ulster over the last few weeks has pushed that strife-torn land even nearer to the brink of Beirut-style anarchy. Who is responsible?

In spite of the lies of the mass media, no-one who knows anything about the history of Ulster can blame the loyalists for refusing to allow their unique culture to be swallowed up in an artificial "united Ireland," in which they would become an oppressed minority nation.

ATTEMPTS

Nor should anyone take any notice of the attempts of the Tory media to blame the Third Way nation, Libya. As a

matter of fact, the Libyans deny that they have recently provided the IRA with arms.

They might, through ignorance of the imperialist reality behind Fenian rhetoric, have been involved, but any such aid is dwarfed by the Communist bloc arms shipments and KGB intelligence training for the IRA, and by the Republican blood money which pours in from the United States.

The Hillsborough Agreement and kid-gloves treatment of the IRA are the fault of Thatcher and her U.S. puppet masters, nobody else.

Above all, responsibilty for the deaths at the Gibralter

Continued on Page 2

Front page of the March 1, 1988 issue of Britain's *National Front News*, spelling out the "Third Position" alliances.

LEFT: Ian MacLeod, one of the *Ottawa Citizen* journalists who first broke the story that Manara Travel was a Libyan front company.
(photo courtesy Ottawa Citizen*)*

BELOW: Mousa Hawamda's letter of October 19, 1987, showing that Manara Travel, Ottawa branch, was a money-laundering operation for Libya.

MANARA TRAVEL AGENCY, INC.
99 Metcalfe Street • Ottawa, Ontario K1P6L1 CANADA • Tel. (613) 233-4949
1-800-267-6565   Telex No. 0533965

October 19 1987

To whom it may concern:

I the undersigned, president of Manara Travel Agency Inc., Canada, do herby acknowledge that the funds of Account number 01000946 under the name of Manara Travel Agency, Inc., drawn against Bank of Credit and Commerce, Canada does solely belong to the People's Committee For Students of The Socialist People Libyan Arab Jamahiriya, a Verginia non-stock corporation.

Mousa Hawamdah
President of Manara Travel

BEIRUT • CARACAS • BUENOS AIRES • WASHINGTON, D.C. • SAO PAULO • OTTAWA and to respond to the leader's call to build bridges with other peoples of the world," al-Rajhi said. To this end, he had met with members of the radical American Indian Movement and "liberation parties" based in South Africa and El Salvador. "I held conversations with all of them about the way in which we could consolidate our struggle against imperialism and Zionism.... We must be prepared to give our lives for the leader!"

Whether the struggle was achieving results was a matter of perspective. As far as the Libyans were concerned, things were going swimmingly. Twelve months earlier, in mid-1984, Mu'ammar Qadhafi had sanctioned the mining of the Red Sea and the Gulf of Suez to punish Arab states that had gone soft on the West. In European cities during 1984 and 1985, eight Libyan student dissidents—whom Qadhafi called "stray dogs"—had been murdered by Libyan death squads. For good measure, in April 1985 the Libyan leader had called on Arabs everywhere to "rise and destroy the submissive traitors who have betrayed our nation." Western governments were learning not to trifle with Qadhafi. Libya was feared by many.

Down at PCLS headquarters in McLean, Virginia, al-Rajhi and his peers had been taking a generally less dramatic approach. Living as they did in the heartland of Middle America, they could hardly do otherwise. They had been producing vast amounts of revolutionary literature but not much else.

In a series of booklets under the general title "Research and Studies," the PCLS had written articles on a wide variety of subjects: "The Activities of the CIA, National Security [and] State Department of Intelligence"; "The Basics of Spying"; "The Military Usage of Laisars [sic] Beam"; "Surveillance"; "Exhibition of New Military Concepts"; "The American Reconnaissance Planes"; "The Names of Corporations Dealing With Military Procurement"; "Intelligence Matters and National Security"; a review of the CIA; an essay on American journalists (television personality Jane Pauley received a lot of scrutiny); a look at the Israeli military; an analysis of news story selection on ABC-TV; and, finally, "The Role of the Vice President George Bush in the American Policy and His Effect on President Reagan." For an agency that was formed merely to assist Libyans studying abroad, the production of these booklets was a bizarre pursuit. Of course, the PCLS was not a run-of-the-mill non-profit group.

To the Libyans, polemics and pamphlets were not going to be enough. Al-Rajhi knew that for the Qadhafi revolution to succeed, he and his peers would have to do more than print pamphlets and spout polemics—they would also have to crack a few heads. And the heads al-Rajhi was most interested in cracking belonged to hundreds of members of the CIA, FBI, Defense Intelligence Agency, Defense Department, U.S. Information Agency, and all branches of the American armed forces.

Al-Rajhi got to work. With the help of his wife, Layla, a computer operator with the Department of Transportation, he used a classified code to access the government's computer files—including a file maintained for setting up car pools. Layla al-Rajhi was able to get her husband the names he wanted. The list they assembled contained the names of more than 100 American government employees as well as the agencies they worked for, their home and business telephone numbers, and their home addresses.

In June 1987 al-Rajhi wrote a top-secret letter to Mohamed Madjoub, head of Libyan counterintelligence. In it he stated that the Americans on the list were involved in "Mediterranean Sea Operations." This was a small exaggeration on the Libyan's part: car-pool lists normally do not contain such information. But al-Rajhi wanted his masters in Tripoli to know that the PCLS directors had not grown soft on the enemy. He went on to detail his liaisons with what he called "secret revolutionary organizations," pointing out that "their activities are armed struggle."

Al-Rajhi called Ronald Reagan "a child murderer" and told Madjoub that he wanted to arrange a meeting between Qadhafi and the "Red Indians." Funds were needed to give the American Indians armed training in Libya, he wrote—such guerrilla exercises were "very important." The PCLS cultural officer closed his letter by telling Madjoub that he planned to continue meeting with groups such as the Irish Republican Army, a Puerto Rican independence group, and various black nationalist factions.

The FBI is not sure if the letter ever found its way to Madjoub; there is, however, evidence that al-Rajhi arranged for it to be smuggled out of the United States in a Libyan diplomatic pouch at the United Nations. The letter would eventually become a very damning piece of evidence in the case against al-Rajhi, Hawamda, and the other pro-Libyan activists.

––––––––

Much of that letter should not have surprised anyone. Qadhafi has always been fascinated with the radicals among North America's Indians. In early 1986, Ian MacLeod, a reporter on the *Ottawa Citizen,* was tipped off to a Libyan-inspired plot to blow up a plane departing from one of Canada's international airports. (Exactly which airport was never determined.) The story made big front-page headlines. According to MacLeod's sources, a native-rights activist was going to plant the bomb to show solidarity with the Libyan revolution. The man, who was never identified, allegedly paid someone $80,000 to conceal the bomb on an American-bound plane. The RCMP took MacLeod's news stories seriously. For one weekend in January 1986, air travellers were subjected to long delays as police meticulously searched their carry-on luggage. In the same week, RCMP officers picked up a Gloucester, Ontario, native activist for questioning. He was released after 18 hours of interrogation.

The bombing never happened. But, as MacLeod soon learned, the police had for months been investigating the new alliance between some radical North American Indian groups and the

Libyan government. The previous August, police told him, seven members of the American Indian Movement had flown to Tripoli for a conference sponsored by the Libyans. At first, MacLeod was skeptical: what possible connection could North American natives have with an outlaw Arab regime on the other side of the globe? After placing a few phone calls, he got the confirmation he needed: AIM *was* receiving material aid from Qadhafi's government.

The leader of AIM is an Ojibwa Indian named Vernon Bellecourt. When reached at his Minneapolis home, Bellecourt, who would later become a confidante of Mousa Hawamda, confirmed that his group had developed a friendship with the Libyans, who were now providing AIM with funds. "We went over there to develop a treaty of peace and friendship with the Libyan people," he said, adding that AIM hoped to establish cultural and educational exchanges with Libya as well as send a few natives to Tripoli for enrollment in "military academies."

"There's a link between our movement and the Libyan people, but no links between our people and what might be considered terrorism," Bellecourt continued. "When we talk about terrorism, it's a two-way street. In reality, the Indian people of North America have been terrorized for 500 years. If [you] want to talk about terrorism, we ought to talk about this sort of terrorism."

It was not AIM's first dalliance with controversy. Since the day it was founded, on the tough south side of St. Paul, Minnesota, AIM has been filled with proud revolutionaries. Like the Nation of Islam, it cannot easily be pigeonholed as left- or right-wing. AIM is anti-capitalist, but it is not a communist front, as many politicians charged during the Nixon era.

AIM was founded in 1968 by Vernon Bellecourt, his brother Clyde, and a group of natives who had been imprisoned at the Stillwater State Penitentiary in the late 1960s. After being released from Stillwater, where he had been serving time for burglary, Clyde Bellecourt organized the AIM Patrol. This was a uniformed group of

Indian men and women who monitored the way police handled natives in Minneapolis' Indian ghetto. Word spread. Within four years, AIM chapters had been established in every American state and in a few Canadian provinces as well.

In February 1973, 200 AIM activists attracted international attention when they seized the South Dakota town of Wounded Knee. Like many of AIM's activities, the occupation had symbolic value: in 1890, 300 Sioux Indians were massacred at Wounded Knee. The AIM adherents armed themselves, took 11 hostages, and declared the village a sovereign nation at war with the United States of America. In a demand letter handed to the FBI, AIM's leaders wrote, "The only two options open to the United States of America are: 1. Wipe out the old people, women, children and men by shooting and attacking us; 2. Negotiate our demands." AIM demanded that the U.S. Senate investigate abuses of Indian treaty rights and the American government's neglect of Native Americans.

In response, the Nixon administration ordered troops from the U.S. Sixth Army to surround Wounded Knee. For more than two months the American military as well as state, local, and federal police traded gunfire with the AIM warriors and their sympathizers. By the time the siege was over, two Indians had been shot dead and seven others had been wounded; 562 people had been arrested for supporting or participating in the stand-off. The 71-day occupation of Wounded Knee gave AIM the sort of publicity that had eluded it during its first five years of existence. Other occupations and protests would follow, but none were as successful as that first one. One recent AIM operation took place in the summer of 1990, when 28 AIM activists reportedly joined a Mohawk blockade near Oka, Quebec.

In 1985, Vernon Bellecourt of AIM and Bill Means of the International Treaty Council were approached by Mousa Hawamda and Saleh al-Rajhi with pledges of generous funding. Accepting money from Qadhafi's outlaw regime, Bellecourt and Means knew, would almost certainly swing the news spotlight back to their cause. They were right.

In August of that year, Bellecourt led AIM's first junket to Libya. The group did little to discourage its Libyan suitors, and would be rewarded for its friendliness: less than a year later, in April 1986, al-Rajhi organized a second junket for AIM members. This time, the Libyan government suggested that the group join the Organization of Non-aligned States, as well as take part in what al-Rajhi called "armed struggle training."

In April 1987 dozens of AIM's supporters attended the Tripoli peace conference. Bellecourt told a Canadian leftist he met there that it was "easy to talk to [the Libyan people].... We find we have a common history. Our countries were overrun by colonists for 200 years. We look to the jamahiriya as a model. Our traditional government parallels Qadhafi's concept of natural law. Theirs is Muslim. Ours was the natural law of the Great Spirit where our cultural, social, moral worlds were all as one."

In January 1988 al-Rajhi and Hawamda organized a fourth trip to Libya for AIM members. There they attended what was proclaimed as "the First International Conference of Red Indians." For al-Rajhi the conference was a major coup: native leaders from North, Central, and South America attended, all at the Libyan government's expense. It was the largest meeting of native groups ever held in Libya. The keynote speaker was Qadhafi himself. His appearance was broadcast on state-run television.

"The struggle should start from now on to set up a state for the Red Indians in North America," he declared, "...in California, Chicago, Texas and Mexico. If this is not achieved peacefully, it will have to be achieved by force and a long and tenacious fight." Qadhafi urged AIM and the other native groups present to unite with black nationalists to carve up North America into separate race-states. In this new order, the continent would have three nations: one white, one black, one red. The white race would be encouraged to move elsewhere—ideally, back to Europe. It was vital, he said, that Indians and blacks work together to combat "imperialism, Zionism, racism, fascism and reaction."

"Form an alliance," he exhorted his audience, "with your natural allies!"

8

NEUTRON INTERNATIONAL, MU'AMMAR QADHAFI, PROP.

On Tuesday, January 6, 1986, Ronald Reagan imposed a trade embargo on Libya and told all American companies to stop doing business with Mu'ammar Qadhafi's government. Official Libyan reaction was not long in coming. In a broadcast aired on Libyan state radio, Reagan was accused of trying to overthrow the Qadhafi regime by means of economic sanctions. The American president was "a dog barking in the Israeli kennel," the broadcasters declared.

A government spokesman added, "If he passes a certain line, we will shoot. He is looking for a pretext. We won't give it to him. If he attacks us, he will hurt us, and we will hurt him—but this will make Qadhafi the leader of the Arab world."

The bravado and tough talk was, like Manara Travel, largely a front. The Libyans knew that American economic sanctions, if comprehensive, could deal a serious blow to Qadhafi's regime. They were concerned, for one very good reason.

Libya has hitched its future to a single commodity—oil. Other economic opportunities do exist there. The narrow Libyan coast is very fertile and, if properly developed for agriculture, could easily support the nation's 3.5 million citizens. Shipping, trading, and even tourism are possibilities. But the unavoidable fact is that Libyans have always lacked the technical know-how to wean themselves from petroleum.

High-quality Libyan crude oil was discovered in exploitable quantities in 1959. It was popular with oil companies because of its low sulphur content, which made it relatively easy to process, and because it was close to the European market, which reduced shipping costs. Libyan crude sold well. Within a short time, oil-generated income was radically changing Libyan society. In 1950 the nation's gross domestic product was about $40 per person; by 1980 it was $11,000. In the years following World War II, Libya's main export had been scrap iron. With the discovery of vast quantities of oil—more than 20 million barrels of it at Zelten in the Cyrenaica region alone—Libya had found a means to achieve the sort of economic reforms many Third World nations can only dream about.

It may seem surprising, but Mu'ammar Qadhafi did not immediately seize control of Libyan oil production in the days following the 1969 coup. There was no sudden campaign of nationalization. Qadhafi was not stupid: he knew his countrymen did not possess the technical knowledge to keep the oil fields running. Nationalization, when it came, was incremental: take over the weaker independents first, then the majors. This meant that staggering amounts of petro-dollars continued to flow unimpeded into the country until Ronald Reagan put an end to all Libyan trade in January 1986.

Henry Schuler is an expert on Libya and the petroleum industry with the Washington-based Center of Strategic and International Studies. In the early days of the revolution he helped American inde-pendents to negotiate oil deals with Qadhafi and his right-hand man, Abdul Salaam Jalloud. (The Libyans drove tough bargains, he remembers.) He says that the American trade embargo has hurt Libya's economy. To avoid economic disaster, Qadhafi has worked to maintain trade links with European nations—particularly Greece and Italy. But the Libyan leader has also established front companies in countries such as Canada.

"The Reagan sanctions are imposing a significant financial cost on Libya," Schuler continues. "The Libyans obviously will do every-thing they can to avoid the sanctions. Some things you can substitute fairly readily, but with other things that's not true." By way of example, he cites the General Electric turbines used to operate pumps in the oil fields. When the turbines break down, a replace-ment part cannot be fudged: the precise part must be used. "The Libyan oil fields were developed by and large by American compa-nies. That means they must use American equipment and spare parts and technology. But they can't get any of that out of the U.S. right now."

He notes that Canada's own embargo was not particularly onerous for Qadhafi's Libya: "The Libyans are obviously attempting to keep their oil fields running. Therefore, the logical thing to do would be to set up an operation in Canada. It's an entirely logical avenue to pursue."

Enter Mohamed Shihumi, logical Libyan.

At first glance, Mohamed Shihumi looked like what he had so often professed to be: a Libyan-born small businessman, a convert from Qadhafi-style socialism to Western capitalism. While living in Edmonton, Alberta, he worked in a small office above a strip mall on 42nd Street. It was a tough part of town—there were plenty of break-ins, and plenty of bearded truckers on the streets. His trading firm did not seem to do much business.

When he was back home in Tripoli, he cut a far higher profile: there, he was an important oil executive and a personal associate of Mu'ammar Qadhafi. Until 1986 he had been chairman of the National Oil Well Services Company, which the Libyan government owned. The last year he ran it, NOWSCO had employed some 400 workers and earned a profit of $100 million.

Like Mousa Hawamda in Ottawa, Shihumi while in Alberta was involved in many initiatives that had little or nothing to do with his modest-sized trading firm.

Shihumi was a very intriguing man. He was born in Libya on December 12, 1948. In 1968 he left for Algeria, where he obtained a degree in engineering. He then spent a year at the Halliburton Institute in Duncan, Oklahoma, where he studied oil well servicing technology. In 1982 he completed his engineering studies at the University of Alfatih in Tripoli.

Some of those who met him in the West say his manner was quiet, almost deferential. When he was back home in Libya, however, he displayed an aggressiveness that verged on cruelty and was known to settle arguments with his fists. In Libya, those who knew him respected him—or feared him. He was not taken lightly.

His clout was not restricted to the secular world. According to many, he regularly attended Edmonton's mosque, and was revered by that city's Islamic community. It is reported that Edmonton's imam, on meeting him for the first time, fell to his knees and kissed his hand.

None of this was reflected in his appearance. Behind his large, tinted glasses, his eyes betrayed nothing. He had a thatch of curly black hair. Sideburns framed his pale, moonish face. He favoured ill-fitting jackets, and ties that didn't match his shirts.

In 1982 he made his first visit to Alberta. Thereafter he was often seen at oil industry trade shows in Calgary and Edmonton. In and of itself, this was not unusual: at the time, he still ran NOWSCO. It was in this capacity that Shihumi first learned that Libyan business practices are not always understood, or appreciated, by Canadians.

In the view of four Edmonton-area oil men who worked for NOWSCO between 1985 and 1987, Shihumi was not an ideal employer. According to these four—Lester Francis, Herman Bruinsma, Sebastianus (Buzz) Sweep, and John Enns—Shihumi's underlings threatened to have them all thrown in a Libyan jail. Basically all the four men had done was complain about late paycheques and gripe about wanting to go home. For that, says Francis, a rig worker, NOWSCO representatives threatened to have him executed. Bruinsma says he was told that if he ever returned to Libya, he would be sent to the desert, never to return.

The four men say they left recession-bound Alberta in 1985 after Shihumi personally promised them big wages and subsidized travel. The promises were never kept, the men now say. Instead, their passports were confiscated and they were forced to sign contracts that were made out in Arabic, which none of them could understand. Later, they were told that Shihumi would use his "political influence" to have the Edmonton residents "jailed or executed." Shihumi later denied promising anything to the four Edmontonians and disavowed all knowledge of any threats made on his behalf.

Upon his return to Canada, Francis, the group's unofficial leader, wrote to Prime Minister Brian Mulroney to blast the federal government for permitting Shihumi to take up residence in Canada. The letter was passed on to the RCMP and CSIS. Francis, Sweep, and Bruinsma were all interviewed, once by a CSIS agent and more than once by the RCMP. Neither the Mounties nor the civilian spy agency will comment on their discussions with the oil men.

Lester Francis and Buzz Sweep will. Both men say they told the RCMP and CSIS that Shihumi was hugely influential in Libya and had close ties to Qadhafi himself. In Libya, says Sweep, "Shihumi could move heaven and hell." In 1987 Sweep and Francis met a Libyan employee of another state-run firm, the National Oil Corporation. Francis says that according to this man, who was apparently no fan of Shihumi, the NOWSCO boss was given $4 million to come to Canada to "get parts for their planes, parts for their oil fields, parts for everything." A former Canadian associate of Shihumi confirms Francis' story, adding that Shihumi "was never short for cash."

Buzz Sweep is like his nickname: colloquial, unpretentious, to-the-point. In Alberta, where he lives, such men call themselves "rigpigs." They are the ones who aren't afraid to get their hands dirty. The ones who keep the province's oil rigs running.

Sweep makes it clear, in his peppery way, that he doesn't like politicians ("those pissheads in public office," he calls them) or hypocrisy, or Canadians who live abroad. He also does not like Libyans in general. And he does not like Mohamed Shihumi in particular. "That snake never seems to come up with any blood on his hands," Sweep says, his disgust plain. "I'd like to see his ass hung out to dry."

When he was in Libya, Sweep kept his feelings about Shihumi to himself. There, Sweep says, you learn to keep your mouth shut and your ears open. Asked why, he dryly notes that it was well-known Shihumi had a cache of automatic weapons in the trunk of his jeep. Sometimes he carried a pistol strapped to his side. The powerful Libyan did not abide any sort of criticism, Sweep says.

According to Sweep, his experiences in Libya were among the worst of his life: he lost wages Shihumi had promised him and some of his own savings. He was even threatened with death for criticizing the treatment he was receiving. It was a mistake, Sweep concedes now, to consider working for a man who had nothing but contempt for the West. One day in 1985 he heard something that confirmed all his misgivings.

Sweep was stationed at a NOWSCO camp at Nafora on the road to Kufra and the Chadian border. During the month he was stationed there he got to know one of Shihumi's more senior employees, who called himself Muhammad Shibli. Shibli was a troubled man, Sweep says: "I know he had a lot of very violent nightmares and dreams, because he bunked across from the trailer I was in, and I could hear him. In the morning, his eyes would be all bloodshot from lack of sleep."

The two men got to know each other. Shibli knew some English, while Sweep had picked up some Arabic on his various trips to the Middle East. At the end of the workday, over a fire, the two would talk. Slowly, Sweep began to hear Shibli's incredible story.

In the spring of 1984, Shibli was studying in London, England. He was a radical. With Qadhafi's blessing, he and dozens of other members of a revolutionary committee had seized control of Libya's embassy in St. James Square. They rechristened the mission the Libyan People's Bureau. The British authorities did not yet know that a large number of firearms had been smuggled into the bureau in diplomatic pouches: automatic pistols, submachine guns, even eight flak jackets. It would not be long before trouble began.

On Tuesday, April 14, 1984, "trouble" took the form of a few dozen chanting Libyan expatriates. Most of them were students who were fed up with Qadhafi and had come to protest his regime's human rights abuses. Standing guard near the anti-Qadhafi students, not far from the aging five-storey building where the Libyan embassy was housed, were members of London's police force. Among them was a 25-year-old policewoman named Yvonne Fletcher.

Up on the second floor, at a window facing the square, Muhammad Shibli stood very still, his hands caressing the stock of a Sterling submachine gun.

Sweep pauses in his narrative. He remembers how Shibli's hands shook at the memory of that day. "You spend a month or two in a camp with a guy, particularly in an isolation situation where you see him day-to-day, the guy can't act forever, you know?" He stops to picture his fellow worker. "I think Shibli was remorseful in a sense for what he did, but he could not say it was a wrong thing to do."

A few minutes into the demonstration, Shibli stepped up to the window and fired out on St. James Square. The machine gun sounded like firecrackers: *pop-pop-pop*. There was pandemonium: people were screaming and scrambling for cover. Within a few seconds Shibli had wounded 11 demonstrators and killed Yvonne Fletcher.

For the next 11 days, police sharpshooters surrounded the building. Throughout that time an international debate raged over what to do with the Libyans holed up inside. On the ninth day the government of Britain severed all diplomatic relations with Libya. On the final day, Shibli and his 29 fellow revolutionaries were escorted out of the Libyan People's Bureau. Because all of the Libyans claimed to be diplomatic personnel, none could be detained or charged in connection with Fletcher's murder. Shibli was put on a plane back to Tripoli.

"He didn't leave any question in my mind that he pulled the trigger on the policewoman in England," Sweep says. "I don't think he realized the magnitude of the problem it would create. It was very politically damaging to the Libyans, but it was also in a sense patriotic to them, you know? I think they wanted to create some hell, but I don't think they wanted a woman killed. That was the last thing they wanted to happen. The sense I got from Shibli was that it wasn't *real* until after he fired, and she went down. Before that, it had all been a game."

The shameful murder of Yvonne Fletcher may have been an embarrassment to Libya's rulers, as Sweep suggests. But as far as

Mohamed Shihumi was concerned, it merely looked good on Shibli's *curriculum vitae*. The NOWSCO chairman hired him as a "den mother" for the state-run oil company's foreign workers: his task was to keep men like Buzz Sweep under surveillance and report back on their movements. "He didn't do diddly-shit," Sweep says. "All he did was cover us, follow us around, record us, or whatever."

Buzz Sweep lets loose with a derisive snort. "*Libyans,*" he says. "What a bunch of fucking terrorists."

———————

For a time, Shihumi and his wife and four young sons lived in a well-to-do neighbourhood in southwest Calgary. In November 1985, while still running NOWSCO, he and two Canadian oil men incorporated the Canadian Arabian Development Corporation. Shihumi was vice-president in charge of international relations. A few months later, in April 1986, he loaned CADCO $300,000 for start-up costs. He wrote the cheques on his personal account.

According to a business proposal Shihumi helped to prepare in July 1987, CADCO was founded

> to establish new markets and maintain existing markets for Canadian oilfield equipment technology and personnel in the Middle East and the African Countries. The establishment of these new markets will create new jobs and maintain existing jobs in the oil and gas sector of the Alberta labour force either directly through overseas placement or indirectly through increased production in Canada and export overseas.

The proposal continued,

> There are many exporters/importers who purport to have influential contacts in the Middle East. Such claims lack credibility

with most Canadian businesspeople. However, Mr. Shihumi's technical background and record speaks for itself. Mr. Shihumi's numerous Chamber of Commerce directorships have been instrumental in this regard. It is difficult if not impossible for an individual foreign company to transact business in the Middle East. In some countries, permanent resident agents are mandatory. Before business can take place, a level of trust must be established. The building of a trust relationship can take years.

The two Albertans who trusted Shihumi enough to assist him with CADCO were Allan Frame, a partner in Yorkton Securities in Calgary, and his brother, Ian Frame, a former executive with Dreco Energy Services Ltd. Dreco was a division of Kremco, a company that completed a $13 million oil rig project in Libya in 1986. The Saskatchewan-born brothers had years of experience in the petroleum industry on which the fledgling company could draw. Allan Frame agreed to serve as its president; Ian Frame took on the post of marketing vice-president. They were sure they were on to a good thing.

Statistics Canada trade figures show why. Exports from Alberta to Libya had been steadily increasing for most of the 1980s. In 1983 the province's oil and gas industry sold $76,000 in drilling equipment, turbines, and parts to Qadhafi's government. By 1985, the year CADCO was formed, the total was over $3.5 million. Alberta's total exports to Libya that year were 46 times what they had been in 1982. With Reagan's trade embargo forcing American firms to pull up stakes in Libya, Canadian ventures like CADCO were in a position to make a fortune.

But CADCO and other Alberta firms would have to be careful. Three months earlier, on January 10, 1986, following the Americans' lead, the Canadian government had imposed export controls on Libyan-bound drilling equipment containing "unique Western technology." These export controls were more than justifiable under

Canada's long-held foreign policy. Libya posed a threat to Canada or its allies (such as Israel), and was involved in hostilities with other nations (such as Chad), and its government had a "persistent record" of human rights violations. Export controls were an obvious response.

There were problems with the Canadian government's move. To start with, the Canadian restrictions were not as explicit or finite as the American ones—for example, what did "unique" mean? As more than one Alberta oil man pointed out, "unique" is the sort of word with which lawyers can make fortunes. As if to emphasize this point, CADCO's 1987 prospectus flatly stated that the firm planned to "emphasize uniquely Canadian techology."

Also, the Canadian export controls were not popular in Alberta, where many people are critical of government interference in business. Hundreds of thousands of foreign workers from Africa, Europe, North America, the Orient, and other Arab states had flowed into Libya in the previous three decades to cash in on its oil boom. Of the estimated 1,500 Canadians working in the North African republic in any given year, the overwhelming majority were Albertan oil workers. Many were enthusiastic about Reagan's trade ban—but not for a reason the American president would have liked. In the week following his announcement, one Calgary firm that specializes in recruiting oil workers received more than 1,000 job applications for positions in Libya. As an Alberta rig worker based in Tripoli said, following Ottawa's decision, "As long as they keep paying me, I'll keep coming."

Many Alberta companies expressed open contempt for the law. "If we can take business there, we will take it," said one Calgary oil consultant. "The Libyans pay on time and there are no problems." An Edmonton oil executive agreed: "We look at it as a political discussion, and we're not going to get caught in the middle of a political discussion."

Twice, Canada's federal government has resorted to trade sanctions to show its disapproval of Qadhafi's outlaw regime—the first time in 1981, the second in 1986. But it has yet to enact the sort of legislation that would hurt Libya to the degree that Reagan did with his 1986 trade embargo. The Canadian government does not hand out tough penalties to Canadian companies doing business with Libya; under Brian Mulroney it has done little more than implore Canadian firms to go along with voluntary sanctions. These appeals have not worked.

For example, in a statement on January 16, 1986, Joe Clark harshly condemned Libya's support of international terrorist movements, calling it "a scourge [that] the Canadian government … is determined to act against." But he was not going to enforce the export controls. "Let me reiterate my appeal to Canadian firms to refrain from taking advantage of commercial opportunities arising as a result of the withdrawal of American personnel and technology from Libya," he said. "In the same spirit, we have urged Canadian citizens not to seek to fill these jobs which are being vacated by Americans leaving Libya."

Appeals and urgings have never been enough when the country in question is Libya. And there is a sizable gap between what Ottawa says and what it actually does. Into this gap have stepped people like Mohamed Shihumi.

For CADCO the American trade embargo did not translate into a windfall. Sitting at his desk in a Fifth Avenue office building in downtown Calgary, CADCO president Allan Frame says, "We formed the Canadian Arabian Development Corporation with the intent of trying to arrange different trade between Canadian companies, particularly ones involved in the oil and gas business, to get them working over in North Africa and Algeria and Libya and places like that. But it turned out to be very tough work. [The Arabs] operate mainly on letters of credit. And most of the Canadian companies out here in the West are smarting a little bit too much to want to take any risk money over there. So we really didn't get too far, and

I really didn't pursue it all that much after that."

In spite of Shihumi's best efforts, and in spite of a massive infusion of cash from Tripoli, CADCO, as Frame notes, did not do well. If Libya was going to benefit from his presence in Alberta, Shihumi would have to look for other avenues. On June 17, 1987, he found one: Neutron International.

According to the incorporation papers filed in Luxembourg in November 1985, Neutron International S.A.R.L.* was owned by two Tripoli businessmen, Mohammed Masaud Emhedad and Mohammed Saleh Musa. Emhedad had a 60 percent interest in Neutron; Musa owned the remainder. Like all of the other Neutron companies, this one was privately held, which effectively ensured complete Libyan control, not to mention secrecy.

In a later interview, when asked about Emhedad and Musa, Mohamed Shihumi would only say, "They are very well known businesspeople. They are active internationally. They are in Libya, but they are very well known elsewhere in the world." That is only part of the story: all of the Neutron companies—Shihumi's in Alberta as well as those based in Brussels, Malta, and Luxembourg—were ultimately owned and controlled by Qadhafi's government in Tripoli. They were all Libyan front companies that had been set up to obtain illegally what could not be purchased legally. According to the National Front for the Salvation of Libya, there are dozens of companies like Neutron around the globe, operating under different names. They are all hotbeds of criminal activity.

Also according to the NFSL, Emhedad and Musa have good connections in the Libyan intelligence establishment. Almost nothing

---

*S.A.R.L. is the French equivalent of "limited" or "incorporated"—*Société à responsabilité limité.*

else is known about them. NFSL spokesmen scoff at Shihumi's suggestion that the two men are merely entrepreneurs. They point out that when Neutron Alberta was operating, there was no private enterprise in Libya.

By Libyan standards Mohamed Shihumi is a well-educated man. More significantly, he knows a good deal about the nation's crucial oil industry. This made his arrival in Canada in late 1984 all the more curious. Why would Libya send one of its few highly trained oil engineers to Alberta, the hub of Canada's energy industry, to ship "tomato paste and cheese" back to Libya? But this, in fact, is what Shihumi later told the *Ottawa Citizen* he proposed to do—as manager of Neutron Alberta.

Shihumi's new company was incorporated on June 17, 1987. In Brussels two days later, Emhedad and Musa appointed him its director and general manager, with the authority to buy, sell, and enter into contracts on their behalf. The particulars of Shihumi's appointment were then relayed to the Bank of Credit and Commerce International—the same bank used by Mousa Hawamda and Manara Travel, though a different branch.

A few weeks later, with CADCO turning into a disappointing failure, Shihumi received permission from Tripoli to move the company and his family from Calgary to Edmonton. It was there that he established an office on the second floor of the Beverly Building on 42nd Street. For the first few months, business was good. There were all-expense-paid trips to Libya for Alberta businessmen, and a few small contracts were signed.

In July 1988 Shihumi started negotiations with an Argentinian oil-servicing firm. In telephone conversations with Carlos Estefas, a director of Top Service S.A. in Buenos Aires, Shihumi tried, unsuccessfully, to convince the Argentinians that they should purchase state-of-the-art American petroleum equipment, which could then be shipped to Libya. The objective, Shihumi boasted to his associates in Edmonton, was to "get around the U.S. trade embargo." It was a clever manoeuvre, because according to Canadian regulations, shipping certain American goods through Canada and then on to Libya was not strictly illegal. (American authorities disagreed: they considered such activity criminal.)

When confronted later about the Argentinian deal, Shihumi denied that he was plotting to break Canadian or American laws. "We are an export company," he said. "We are involved in clothes, tomato paste ... oil and gas equipment. Our clients contact us, and we receive their inquiries. We try to make our search for what is available. And that is how we are doing it. It's up to the client. When we receive a request, asking for spare parts or something like that, we contact the companies who are producing such kinds of things. They, the company, apply for the export licence. When we receive their guarantee that the export licence has been approved, then we answer back the client."

It was suggested to Shihumi that his company's biggest client—if not its only client—was the Qadhafi regime. It was also suggested to him that a country which openly finances terrorist movements is not likely to be concerned with the trifling matter of export licences.

Shihumi thought for a long time before replying, "What happened in the past, will not happen again."

Mohamed Shihumi was finding trouble everywhere he looked. Only 35 days after he started up Neutron Alberta, a rival branch of the same company would open for business, this one in Ottawa. And its owner would be Mousa Hawamda.

Almost 13 months after Hawamda incorporated Neutron Ottawa, and after enduring the indignities of life behind bars for most of August 1988, Hawamda and his fellow co-conspirators finally made bail. Hawamda's was posted by a bond agency. Shortly afterwards, he returned to work at Manara Travel. He didn't have much choice:

under the terms of his release he was not permitted to leave the Washington area. Besides, the court had taken away his American passport.

A few days after his release, with much weariness in his voice, he agreed to take a phone call. Following up an anonymous tip, the *Ottawa Citizen* had commissioned a corporate search of Neutron International. The paper hit paydirt: a privately owned company named Neutron International Trading Inc. had been provincially registered by lawyer Terry Jabour on July 22, 1987—and Hawamda was its first director.

Introductions were made. Hawamda listened silently as the reporter explained that there was a lot of interest in the Palestinian's predicament. After a brief effort at small talk, the reporter came to the point: what exactly did Neutron Ottawa do?

Hawamda hesitated for a long time. "I don't want to talk about it," he finally said in a flat, accented tenor.

"Isn't there anything you can say about what the company did?"

"I don't want to talk about anything. If you want to talk, call my attorney." He hung up.

A few minutes later, Drew Carroll, Hawamda's lawyer in Alexandria, Virginia, confirmed that he had heard about Neutron Ottawa's existence. But he added that he could not talk about it even if he wanted to. The company had not been named in the pre-trial disclosure documents, so it was not an issue as far as he was concerned. For the moment, Carroll said, he was concentrating on learning the identity of the government's informant. (Mahmoud Buazzi's identity would not be declassified until the end of August.) He would say nothing else about Neutron International.

In Ottawa, a former Manara employee was less reluctant to talk. This man, who insisted on anonymity, explained that Neutron Ottawa was Hawamda's "secret." Manara and Neutron shared space, fax machines, photocopiers, and even office staff, but they were different: Manara was public, while Neutron's name was seldom discussed by Manara employees. He added that everyone who worked there knew that Hawamda and his Libyan benefactors designed the company to break laws.

"Mousa ran it," said the ex-employee. "We had maybe fourteen different phone lines at Manara, and some were specifically for Neutron. If a call was made on a certain line, for example, we'd say, 'Neutron Incorporated, may I help you?' It did a lot of business."

When contacted in London, Abu Abdullah of the NFSL said that Neutron Ottawa, like Neutron Alberta and the two Manara Travel offices, was yet another Libyan front organization. "The Libyan regime has decided to restrict its terrorist activities to Libyan targets, because Western governments don't care about Libyan expatriates," he said. "That is where these front companies come in. They gather information on Libyan dissidents living abroad. They see what the Libyan students and the opposition are up to."

And that was not all they were doing, he continued. All of these companies were also funding extremist groups and helping to launder money, just as PCLS had been doing between 1986 and 1988.

Donald Bartnik, the FBI special agent, also had a good idea what Neutron Ottawa was designed to do. Choosing his words carefully— he was concerned about saying something that could be used by Drew Carroll and the other defence lawyers to secure a mistrial— Bartnik said that the FBI learned about Neutron while investigating the PCLS and Manara Travel. The prosecutors had two reasons for keeping the company's name out of the indictment. First, Bartnik said, Neutron was relatively new, "and most of our stuff, as you can see in the indictment, focusses on about the middle of 1987 and back to 1986." Second, he said, "We didn't need it. We knew everything was going to get unmasked, anyway."

According to Bartnik, it was Hawamda's intention that Manara Travel and Neutron Ottawa act as two branches of the same tree: "Obviously, you can get a little bit more out of an import-export company than you can out of a travel agency, as far as materials go.

Manara was for people and money, Neutron was for materials."

But why Canada? Why would the Libyans target a nation that had remained largely indifferent to Qadhafi's misadventures?

Bartnik laughed quietly. "Canada is fertile ground," he replied, "for other people to come in and take advantage."

Within two weeks of Hawamda's arrest, Shihumi very suddenly returned to Libya with his family. He barely gave himself time to clean out his desk and home. He reportedly told his office mate he was going, and three days later he was gone. RCMP sources believe that his sudden departure was linked to Hawamda's arrest, but do not have enough evidence to boost this beyond speculation.

A few days later, Shihumi was reached by phone in Libya. Neutron Alberta's director sounded nervous: he did not understand why the Canadian news media would be interested in him. "It's hard to understand the meaning of these questions," Shihumi said. Through the phone line, some children could be heard playing nearby. When asked who controlled Neutron Alberta, Shihumi said it was *another* Neutron company based in Luxembourg. This was untrue: Neutron's parent is located in Tripoli, not Luxembourg.

Regarding the rival Neutron branch in Ottawa, Shihumi adamantly denied the two firms were ever linked—despite the name, despite the Libyan ownership, despite the identical corporate objectives. It was all just a great big coincidence, he claimed.

Shihumi was not enjoying the phone call. He did confirm that he returned to Libya on August 5, 1988, with his wife and four sons. He left Edmonton, he said, because Neutron Alberta had for the most part failed, *not* because the RCMP and the FBI happened to be paying closer attention to the activities of suspicious Libyan nationals. Asked whether Neutron Alberta was a front for Libyan espionage and illegal trade, Shihumi sputtered, "I'm quite sure we are a legal company. We apply for import and export licences according to the Canadian laws and regulations."

Shihumi listened to more questions and gave vague, evasive answers. When asked if he knew about Hawamda and Manara Travel, Shihumi hurriedly said no, then added that he knew they existed. "They … use the same name. When we found out about it, we tried to contact them and they told us they were a Canadian company. We tried to stop them, but we could not do too much about them." He declined to say how he tried to "stop" Hawamda—or who "we" were.

But *did* he know Mousa Hawamda?

"No," he replied. "I think he is Egyptian or Syrian or something like that. They have some problem in the U.S. or something." He paused, and the long-distance telephone line crackled. "I myself have never been in Ottawa. We have no idea at all who is in Ottawa. When we try to find out who is there, they told us it is really a tourist agency. I think they called it Medina or something like that. We tried to talk to them and they said, 'Yes, we have a Canadian company.' But our Neutron International S.A.R.L. is a Luxembourg company, and we are a branch. We are an extra-provincial company in Canada."

Shihumi did, in fact, know Mousa Hawamda. The two men were not fond of each other, Ahmad Eed Murad says, but they had met face-to-face at least once, in December 1987 at Toronto's Pearson International Airport. The meeting took place in Toronto, sources say, because both men regarded the city as neutral territory.

When pressed on the point, Shihumi confirmed that the meeting took place but refused to reveal what was discussed. "I have tried to contact him two or three times [since the rendezvous in Toronto]," Shihumi admitted. "But he never calls back."

Shihumi started to sound distinctly uneasy. His answers were becoming confused, rambling. There was, perhaps, a reason for this: he knew a great deal more about Mousa Hawamda and Neutron

Ottawa than he was letting on. It is believed that he knew about Hawamda and his activities as early as the spring of 1987.

In May of that year Murad travelled to Calgary to visit Shihumi: he had been sent by Hawamda. If Murad is to be believed, Hawamda sent him west when Neutron Alberta turned up in a routine corporate search.

Shihumi was frightened when Murad appeared on his doorstep, as Murad gleefully remembers: "He had heard of my name.... When he was confronted [about Neutron Alberta] he didn't like it. I told him, 'Shihumi, look, I was told to inquire about Neutron, and I have done it. I don't know you, you don't know me.' He was very mad at me, but I told him I didn't care. Simply I was asked by Mousa, and I went to meet Shihumi for Mousa. This was the only time I met Shihumi." Murad laughs. "Mousa was intruding on Shihumi. Shihumi *should* have been mad." Murad speculates that Shihumi had been told by his firm's Libyan owners to keep his name off the Canadian corporate records. Through forgetfulness or wilfulness, he did not. The result was that Hawamda—and later the *Ottawa Citizen*—had been able to track him down.

It *is* possible, as Shihumi claims, that the two Neutrons in Canada operated independently. Both were ultimately owned and operated by Libyan intelligence, say sources at the FBI, RCMP, and CSIS, but the fact remains that there are distinct factions within Qadhafi's spy network. For example, the Libyan Foreign Liaison Secretariat is often circumvented by General Intelligence and Military Intelligence, which in turn can be circumvented by the Revolutionary Committees Bureau.

Murad and the NFSL both suggest, probably with good reason, that Shihumi's Neutron Alberta was created and financed by the Libyan government's official bureaucracy, while Hawamda's Neutron Ottawa was an "outlaw" organization set up for the benefit of the small circle of Libyan revolutionaries who were counselling a more aggressive approach toward Qadhafi's enemies. In other words, the two Neutron firms could have been operating separately to achieve the same goal—namely, to dodge the anti-Libyan trade laws in Western countries. A telex that Shihumi received from Libya in the summer of 1987 supports this thesis. In it, two Neutron International bosses—who used coded names—told Shihumi, FULL INFORMATIONS [sic] REQUESTED ABOUT THE NEUTRON BRANCH IN OTAWA [sic] VERY URGENTLY.

Ali Sharif Ghet is a Libyan director of Neutron International living in Brussels. (Ghet should not be confused with the Libyan named Ali Ghet, who was deported from Egypt in the 1970s for terrorist bombings.) Ghet says the telex was sent because Hawamda's use of the Neutron International name was unauthorized. He adds that as far as he knew, his company did not operate a branch in Ottawa. "We are a very well-known company," he says. "We deal with the whole world. We have nothing to do with smuggling."

––––––––––––

On the surface, there was nothing very remarkable about the cheque. It was dated August 31, 1987. It was drawn on account 0231335 at the Toronto-Dominion Bank on 107th Avenue in Edmonton. It was made out to Mohamed Shihumi for the sum of $10,000. An attempt had been made to cash it.

If there was anything notable about the cheque at all, it was that it was signed by "Horst A. Schmid"—the same Horst Schmid who was, for 15 years, a senior member of the Alberta cabinet: Minister of Culture, Youth and Recreation; then Minister of Government Services; and still later, Minister of State for Economic Development and International Trade. On August 31, 1987, the date he presumably signed the cheque, Schmid was Alberta's Commissioner-General of International Trade and Tourism—the highest-ranking trade official in the province.

And with the first cheque was a second one, also signed by

Schmid. It was dated May 31, 1987, and made out to CADCO for the sum of $15,000.

Copies of the two cheques were dropped off at the newsroom of the *Ottawa Citizen* by an anonymous source in the fall of 1988. A quick phone call was made to Schmid's Edmonton office. His staff was no help. Mr. Schmid, a secretary said, was out of the country on a trade mission. She was not allowed to say when he would be back, where he was, or what he was doing there. Such things were kept secret. The *Citizen* knew that if the cheques were legitimate, it had just been handed a very substantial news story. Schmid was much more than a bureaucrat: though he no longer sat in the Alberta legislature, he still moved in rich and influential circles.

He was born Horst Adolf Louis Charles Schmid in Munich, Germany, in 1933. If one believes the local folklore, he was a born organizer, a get-up-and-go sort of guy. At the age of 12, he was an air-raid warden on the shattered streets of his native city. Between 1956 and 1971, after learning English at a Munich language school, he practised his salesmanship hawking sulphur and fertilizer. In the 1960s, after moving to Canada, he studied business administration for a time at the University of Toronto. In 1971 he was elected to Alberta's legislature by the voters of Edmonton's Avonmore riding. He held that seat for the next 15 years. Throughout that period he was one of the most influential Progressive Conservatives in Alberta.

In May 1986 the PCs won yet another Alberta election. Schmid, however, lost his seat, though by 93 votes. A few months later, Alberta's premier, Don Getty, named him the province's Commissioner of International Trade and Tourism—a sort of roving trade ambassador. When a Canadian Press reporter asked Schmid if this had been a patronage appointment, Schmid reminded her rather briskly that his working hours were "legendary," and added, "Because of the contacts that I have established around the world— I'm literally welcomed with open arms everywhere I go because of the contribution Alberta has made to international trade—the investment that is there would really be sad to be lost."

Soon after his appointment was announced, Schmid made it clear to his subordinates that he alone would be responsible for dealings with the Libyans. No one argued with him. People seldom argue with Horst Schmid: he is tough, and he has very clear views on a wide range of subjects, Libya being one of them. After learning that the *Ottawa Citizen* was inquiring into his relationship with Mohamed Shihumi, Schmid immediately telephoned the newspaper's editorial department from a hotel room in Germany.

In conversation, Schmid is renowned for his high-spirited candour. On this day he seemed no different. After acknowledging that, yes, he knew Mohamed Shihumi, and, yes, the two had a financial "agreement," he politely asked that the *Citizen* keep quiet about the whole thing for a while. He made vague references to tips about even better news stories; he added that printing details of the agreement would only cause Shihumi to lose "face" back home. He sounded well-briefed on these matters: "It's a loss of face. To an Arab or a Chinese, [to have personal business made public] is the most important loss of face you can suffer."

When he discussed Shihumi, he was effusive in his praise. He hardly stopped to take a breath. "He is in fact a very good friend of mine, number one. Number two, he really tried his best, you know. I would have to say that I had the feeling he suffered under the stigma of being from Libya. I know he spent a hell of a big pile of money to create some business from Alberta to Libya. He told me many times he loved Alberta, and he wanted to make a living selling especially to the oil fields of Libya. I know he tried very hard and I really felt sorry for him, how hard he tried. He loved Canada, he wanted to make a living here. But he had to go back to Libya.

"Frankly," he added, "we called each other brother."

According to Schmid, he and Shihumi met in 1983. The Libyan had not yet moved to Alberta with his family. They hit it off right away—the gregarious Alberta cabinet minister and the soft-spoken

Libyan with the big bank account. No one really knew just how close they were, Schmid told the *Citizen*—and any money that changed hands between the two men was "a personal matter." He added that when he was Alberta's trade minister, Shihumi never attempted to lobby him on Libya's behalf.

There is no evidence available to suggest this was not the case. It is interesting, however, that Alberta's exports to Libya skyrocketed during Schmid's reign as trade minister.

When asked about the two cheques, Schmid's tone changed. He spoke slowly and deliberately. He acknowledged that the payments had to seem very odd to someone who was not familiar with the unique relationship that existed between him and Shihumi. He explained that he and the Libyan had "a personal agreement" whereby Schmid covered Shihumi's debts when the Libyan was abroad, and vice versa: "If I'm away, he pays for me. And if he's away, I pay for him." The payments were for telexes, Alberta health care premiums, phone bills, and similar. The two cheques were made out simply to repay funds that Schmid had not used on Shihumi's behalf, he explained.

The two cheques totalled $25,000. Were the costs of health care premiums and sending telexes in Alberta so very high? Schmid let loose with a testy laugh. "[The bills] weren't little. One thousand dollars in telexes, and everything else included. It wasn't just fifty dollars, no."

He insisted that Shihumi had not loaned him money in order to influence Alberta trade policy on Libya's behalf: "Heavens, no. Again, he is one of the best friends I have. If he asks me to [pay bills] for him, I will do it." Their relationship "had nothing to do with business."

On this point, Shihumi agreed. When reached at his Tripoli home, he called Schmid "one of the best people I have met in my life." The Libyan denied giving any money to Schmid, or receiving any. About the two cheques, he would explain nothing. "I know

Horst Schmid very well," he said. "He was the one who convinced me to move to Canada and start my own business there. He never asked me for anything like [an election loan] at all. I never involve myself in any political action. My relationship with [Schmid] remains as a personal relationship. I am so glad to have him as a friend…. We had no business loans at all. We had a personal relationship, but we never had any business together at all."

However, telephone records passed on to the *Citizen* by an anonymous source showed clearly that Schmid had telephoned Shihumi in mid-1987 to discuss financing for Neutron Oilwell Services Ltd. This Calgary company was owned by the Libyans. It was not related to Shihumi's Neutron Alberta. Schmid, when he was speaking to the *Citizen*, was unable to remember this telephone call. But he didn't deny that it took place.

That was not all. In late 1985 and early 1986 Shihumi and Schmid were involved in another oil industry deal—a big one. At the time, Schmid was still a member of Alberta's cabinet and Shihumi was chairman of NOWSCO. The $13 million deal involved the sale of an oil rig to Qadhafi's government by Kremco, a subsidiary of Dreco Energy Services Ltd. in Calgary. According to Kremco officials, the sale did not involve "unique" Western petroleum technology—and even if it did, the deal had been signed in 1985, before Canada's export controls were legally enforceable. Dreco's president, Glynn Davies, when asked to comment, refused to discuss Shihumi's role in the sale.

On Friday, October 28, 1988, the *Ottawa Citizen* ran a front-page story headlined, "Alberta official paid bills for Libyan." The "personal agreement" between Schmid and Shihumi had become very public. On the day the story broke in Alberta, Schmid was still in Europe on a trade mission.

The repercussions were immediate. In Alberta the New Democrats' house leader, Pam Barrett, called a press conference to demand that the provincial government immediately recall Horst

Schmid to get him to explain his five-year flirtation with Shihumi. She also demanded that Alberta's premier launch an inquiry into the relationship between Shihumi and the province's most senior trade official.

Placing her index finger on the spot where Schmid's story did not appear to make sense—the value of the two cheques—Barrett told the press conference, "That's enough money to pay my health-care premiums, your health-care premiums and probably your grand-children's health-care premiums for the rest of our lives and their lives—that's a lot of money."

Schmid's boss was Larry Shaben, Alberta's trade minister. The following Monday, Shaben said that an inquiry into the matter would be "premature." He also promised to discuss the matter with Schmid when he returned from Europe at the end of the week. In fact, Schmid came home early. On the afternoon of Wednesday, November 2, the two men met for a chat. Shaben emerged from the meeting to say he was satisfied that Schmid had not broken Alberta's code of conduct for provincial employees. But he added that in the future, Schmid would be wise to refrain from paying the bills of people who were trying to do business with Alberta: "I've made some strong recommendations to Mr. Schmid with respect to how future relationships—that is, friendship and business—are melded together, and he has agreed to my suggestions and I suspect this is the end of it."

Schmid, sounding uncharacteristically muted, accepted Shaben's recommendations. But he was not contrite. "There was no rule of conduct broken because it was a personal friendship," he said. "I'm very sad to see the press condemn a man who hasn't been shown to be proven guilty in any way, shape or form."

Still, Horst Schmid was an intelligent man: he must have known that many North Americans had come to regard Qadhafi and his regime with considerable distaste. In later interviews he would admit as much. Why, he was asked at the time, would he, a seasoned politician, choose to take a Libyan like Shihumi under his wing? "Isn't fraternizing with the likes of Mr. Shihumi a bit dangerous for someone in your position, Mr. Schmid?"

Schmid let the question hang in the air. Mohamed Shihumi, he finally said, was the finest man he had ever come across. "If I would have suspected that he had done anything that would go against Canada...." He struggled to line up his thoughts. "No, I couldn't believe it anyway. Being from Libya ... it's sad ... immediately you are brushed with a brush because of it."

When it was suggested that Libya was being censured by other governments only because Qadhafi was funding terrorism—that it had nothing to do with racism or bias—Schmid had no answer.

In 1986, when the Canadian government clamped export controls on Libyan-bound oil-industry equipment, Alberta's premier, Don Getty, who was Schmid's boss at the time, called on the province's oil companies to support the federal initiative: "I want to urge Albertans, particularly those involved in the energy industry, the oil-well servicing industry, to support Prime Minister Mulroney and Canada as a nation in not making efforts to provide services or technology to Libya. It's extremely important we stand united on this and support our federal government."

When asked if he supported those export controls, Horst Schmid's voice dripped with sarcasm. "Everything is not unique, you know. It's a very vague term, you know. There are about 1,500 Albertans working in Libya, you know. They would have more experience in oil rig technology than Shihumi would ever have...." He didn't finish the sentence. When he spoke again, his anger was plain: "What the hell is secret about oil and gas equipment? After the time the embargo was announced, [Shihumi] asked me for advice only once, and that was only for truck parts...."

"It all sounds so *curious.*"

9

EDUCATION, LIBYAN STYLE

Besides owning companies called Neutron International, Mohamed Shihumi and Mousa Hawamda had one other thing in common: a commitment to higher education. One was supposedly a travel agent, the other supposedly an exporter of commodities, but it is clear that both men knew a great deal about academe. Their interest in it, however, had more to do with loot than with learning.

When FBI agents raided Hawamda's Falls Church home, they found a box full of documents dealing with World University Services of Canada. WUSC is an Ottawa-based agency that sponsors development projects around the world. Among Hawamda's papers were minutes of WUSC meetings, organizational flow charts, and detailed notes on the agency's projects and financial structure. Also seized by the FBI, at the McLean, Virginia, offices of the PCLS, were files dealing with the Canadian Bureau for International Education and with a Libyan associated with it named Giuma Beyuk. Beyuk's file contained information about radical native groups.

The CBIE assists the Libyan and other foreign governments in finding openings for their students at Canadian colleges and universities. When Hawamda arrived in Ottawa in early 1987 to set up a branch of Manara Travel, he carried in his pocket a letter signed by senior Libyan government officials and addressed to Beyuk. The letter's purpose was to force the CBIE to use only the Manara agency when arranging travel for Libyan students in Canada.

Mohamed Shihumi also showed a sizable interest in the business side of education. The Canadian man he shared his Edmonton office with was the president of the Alberta International Education Corporation. This man has refused to speak to the media. Other sources say the two men met in June 1987, in Tripoli. The same sources add that the AIEC was Shihumi's idea; that it was established largely with Shihumi's money; and that its objective was to wrest away the Libyan government's contract from the CBIE. Like the CBIE, the AIEC was founded to provide assistance for Libyan students enrolled in Canadian colleges and universities. Unlike the CBIE, it was supposed to make a profit. After only six months at the helm, Shihumi's Canadian partner left the AIEC. He will not say why.

So, while Hawamda and Shihumi were both interested in post-secondary education, their interest could not be described as purely philanthropic. Whoever cornered the market on the Libyan foreign education industry—an industry is exactly what it was—would find riches and power. Hawamda and Shihumi both knew this.

Education has not always been a priority for Libya's rulers. In December 1951, when the United Kingdom of Libya was proclaimed by King Idris, just over a dozen Libyans were university graduates and an estimated 90 per cent of the population was illiterate. Almost immediately after Qadhafi seized power, Libyan society started to undergo a marked change: schooling, health care, and other social programs were offered free of charge to every Libyan citizen. Education became compulsory for all young children. Adult literacy programs were established. A new university was built in

Beida. Schooling soon accounted for 12 percent of the national budget.

But there were still problems, such as inadequate facilities, cultural resistance to the changes, and, most significantly, the system's chronic inability to give Libyan citizens the tools they needed to seize control of their own destiny. After the revolution more Libyans could read and write, but they still did not have the knowledge or expertise to manage their own health care, or their own oil fields, or virtually any complex technological venture. This stirred up considerable resentment. In 1984 and 1985 Qadhafi expelled an estimated 70,000 "guest workers" who had been toiling in the service industries. Even so, more than 200,000 foreigners still work in that country.

To lessen his country's dependence on foreign workers, Qadhafi has encouraged his countrymen to educate themselves abroad. At the present time, as many as 10,000 Libyans are studying in other countries, most of them in Canada, the United States, and Europe. The bulk of them are encouraged to pursue technical programs such as engineering, computer science, and oil field technology. About half are on scholarships—and some are spies. They spy on fellow Libyan students, they spy on Canadian citizens, and they spy on other foreign nationals.

In recent decades the Canadian government has taken a contradictory and erratic approach with these Libyan students. In May 1986 Joe Clark, Canada's external affairs minister, told reporters that Canada should not be allowed to become a "backfill" for Libyan students who posed a security risk. Despite this, Canada has become a virtual dumping ground for them, and more Libyans are enrolling at Canadian colleges and universities every year. In April 1986 this trend began to alarm the RCMP, whose criminal intelligence section launched a probe of the activities and backgrounds of 800 Libyans then studying in Canada.

In Canada, Ottawa's CBIE administers almost every aspect of

Libyan students' lives. In the United States, Washington's PCLS performed a similar function. The CBIE has its detractors, but there is no evidence that it has ever functioned as a front for spy activity. In fact, CBIE officials have apparently been quick to report possible national security violations to CSIS and Canada's external affairs department.

The CBIE was founded in 1966. In its literature it describes itself as a "national, non-profit association of educational institutions and individuals working together to promote international development and intercultural understanding." For reasons that are understandable, the CBIE does not advertise its contractual relationship with the Qadhafi regime, but that relationship is significant. In 1986, Libya put up $35 million for more than 900 Libyans to study at dozens of community and vocational colleges across Canada. The program, which the CBIE administered, gave employees of Libya's petroleum, aviation, and atomic energy agencies a long-sought opportunity to enhance their technological skills. Surprisingly, the program received very little media attention at the time.

The Libyan contract is a lucrative one, and it is reported that other aid organizations have lobbied for it in the past. In 1987, for example, Mousa Hawamda met in Washington with three senior officials of WUSC, which at one time was one of the CBIE's main rivals, to discuss using his influence to transfer the Libyan contract to WUSC. Hawamda's arrest derailed the negotiations. The contract has remained with the CBIE.

In a sense, the CBIE acts as a broker for the limited number of foreign-student spots at Canadian post-secondary schools. After securing a place for a foreign student at a college or university, CBIE counsellors meet the student at the airport, find an apartment for him (almost all the Libyan students are men), and place him on a monthly allowance. At present there are an estimated 600 Libyans studying at Canadian universities and colleges. Most of them are in college programs. Libyans make up the second-largest—and one of the wealthiest—contingents of foreign students at Canadian post-secondary schools. Only Morocco and Tunisia send more students to Canada.

Two Libyan men provide most of the counselling for the hundreds of Libyan students in Canada. They are not CBIE employees, though they occupy office space at the agency's Ottawa headquarters. One of the men is a former ranking officer in the Libyan armed forces. The other, Giuma Beyuk, studied English in the early 1980s in Eugene, Oregon, where he was instrumental in founding a revolutionary committee. This man, who is an employee of the Libyan Civil Aviation Authority, has been a Libyan student counsellor since 1987. He is better known to Libyan students in Canada, however, as one of the members of a powerful revolutionary committee that controlled student activity in Tripoli in early 1984. In 1988 and 1989, CSIS investigated Beyuk, who has remained in Canada.

An Ontario lawyer, who represents dozens of anti-Qadhafi students, says that Beyuk was installed at the CBIE for two reasons: to oversee his government's contract, which brings the agency an estimated $1 million each year, and to keep an eye on anti-Qadhafi students in Canada.

In 1984, after surviving yet another coup attempt—led in part by the NFSL and student dissidents at foreign universities—the Qadhafi regime took decisive action: "The Libyans called all the students back home. They were all met at the airport and taken to a military camp and given lectures, from seven in the morning to seven at night. They kept the students there for two weeks. During that time, they showed them a videotape of the hanging of two students. The tape was simply designed to deliver a message, and it has delivered that message: 'We need technical people, but we don't want you coming back as political people'."

The result is that Libyan students generally keep themselves distant from any sort of political activity in Canada. There are exceptions, such as the handful of Islamic fundamentalists who regard the Green Revolution as too secular in its policies. But for the most part, the Libyans keep a low profile. "If I invite a Libyan student to my office," the lawyer says, "they don't want to come during regular business hours. They want to make sure there's nobody else in the waiting room, first. They will even sit there with magazines covering their faces. They are very suspicious. According to them, [the Libyan student counsellors] know everything that is going on. All contacts are through the CBIE and the counsellors. When they call, you come." She shakes her head. "They are scared shitless."

When asked by a reporter from the *Ottawa Citizen* why his name figured prominently in a file seized in Mousa Hawamda's Washington home—a file about radical Indian groups—Beyuk said, "I don't know" a few times and then hung up the phone.

It is known that both Mousa Hawamda and Mohamed Shihumi were in regular contact with Beyuk. Like them, he was connected to a powerful faction back in Tripoli. Beyuk was suspicious of Mousa Hawamda. According to Hawamda's former business partner, Ahmad Eed Murad, the Libyan activist did not like the travel agency owner. "With honesty, Beyuk did not help Mousa, and he didn't want to deal with Mousa," Murad says. "He tried to tell the Libyans not to deal with Mousa. But Mousa came to Ottawa knowing that he had the connections in Libya that would force [Beyuk] and the CBIE to buy tickets from him. And a letter was sent requesting him to buy future tickets for all the students from Mousa. But this never really happened." Hawamda's arrest intervened.

Shihumi also had powerful allies back in Tripoli, and he, too, wanted the students' business. Aware that Beyuk distrusted Hawamda, he contacted the man in a vain bid to work out a deal of the same kind Hawamda was trying to force. In June 1988 he also sent the PCLS some material about his Edmonton activities—only a few days before Hawamda and the PCLS directors were arrested by the FBI.

To both Hawamda and Shihumi, the PCLS was a cash cow that could be milked for millions and millions of dollars with great regularity. Any Libyan who was an ally of the PCLS was assured power and prosperity—all thanks to Mu'ammar Qadhafi's interest in post-secondary education.

10

TERROR'S PIPELINE

On Wednesday, January 4, 1989, two American fighter jets shot down two Libyan air force planes over the Mediterranean. The American Secretary of Defense, Frank Carlucci, told reporters that the American pilots had fired their missiles in self-defence. Many doubted this. It was widely assumed that the air battle was a warning to Mu'ammar Qadhafi—a warning coming on the heels of intelligence reports that the Libyans were building a chemical weapons plant in Rabta, 95 kilometres south of Tripoli.

Rumours about the Rabta factory had been circulating for weeks. On Tuesday, January 3, a day before the dogfight over the Gulf of Sidra, the U.S. State Department declared that Libya was "on the verge" of large-scale chemical weapons production. West Germany and other European nations had been given detailed information about the serious danger posed by the Libyan facility. President Ronald Reagan refused to rule out the possibility of a "surgical strike" against the Rabta site, which had been built with a great deal of help from West German companies.

According to the Americans, the Libyans were stockpiling thiodiglycol, which can be used to make deadly mustard gas. This gas, which is outlawed under the 1925 Geneva Protocol on chemical weapons, causes extremely painful blistering of the skin and agonizing death. While thiodiglycol also has commercial uses, the fact that it was present in large quantities at Rabta strongly suggested that mustard gas production was the Libyans' ultimate objective.

As the American authorities revealed, the Libyans were mounting chemical warheads on Scud missiles. Scuds are known to be inaccurate. But as Iraq's Saddam Hussein has since shown the world, they can be lethal enough—he was able to pummel Israel and Saudi Arabia with dozens of them during the Gulf War. Nor was there any question how deadly his chemical weaponry could be. Earlier, in August 1988, he had used it on thousands of Kurdish men, women, and children near the Habun River in northern Iraq. This was the first well-documented poison gas attack anywhere since World War I. A refugee named Bahagat Nife would remember these bombs as having "quiet voices."

"There was a yellow cloud," he lived to tell a reporter. "The air be like this cloud. We smelled a beautiful, nice smell." Those who did not make it to the river—some 5,000 of them—choked to death where they fell. This was their punishment for having opposed Hussein's rule. To this day, the residue of the poison gases used in that attack still claims casualties in the area.

Both Libya and Iraq covet nuclear weapons but have not yet been able to produce them. Chemical weapons are any poor nation's Doomsday Bomb. They are simple and cheap. More significantly, they are horribly effective: they killed more than a million people in World War I. For the Libyans they have an added advantage: any commercial factory—a brewery, a fertilizer plant, a pharmaceutical facility—can be quickly retooled to produce them. And such facilities are easy to hide.

Libyan claims that the Rabta plant was designed to produce pharmaceuticals and nothing else did not reassure the Americans. Neither did the fact that, by the Libyans' own admission, there was already another pharmaceutical plant in the Rabta area. The Americans were also greatly bothered that much of the factory was underground—presumably to protect it from another U.S. bombing raid. There was other incriminating evidence: American surveillance satellites had photographed "air scrubbers" over the plant's external vents, and the piping was too intricate for a simple pharmaceutical plant.

Construction of the plant had been going on for months, much of it during the period when Mohamed Shihumi had been in Alberta, when he had been requested to ship an intriguing array of products to his superiors in Tripoli.

"The Arabs are compelled to own and possess nuclear weapons," Mu'ammar Qadhafi said in a 1989 interview. "The Palestinian state must have the right to its own weapons—to have chemical weapons, to have nuclear weapons." In Qadhafi's view the Libyan people are also entitled to mustard and nerve gases. Among the world's leaders he is far from unique in taking this stance. Western intelligence agencies speculate that the chemical weapons club now includes Egypt, Syria, South Africa, Ethiopia, China, Israel, Czechoslovakia, Hungary, Romania, Yugoslavia, France, Bulgaria, Vietnam, Laos, Burma, Indonesia, North Korea, and Taiwan. Four countries that are confirmed members of this poisonous club are the United States, the former Soviet Union, Iran, and, as is now well-known, Iraq.

The development of Qadhafi's Rabta plant can be traced back to 1985, when a financially strapped West German pharmaceuticals company named Imhausen-Chemie made contact with the Libyan government, which was intent on building the Third World's single largest chemical weapons facility in the desert outside Rabta. The firm's manager, Jurgen Hippensteil-Imhausen, knew he would be violating German export laws if he supplied the Libyans with what they wanted. But his company was in serious financial difficulty and needed the Libyan cash in order to survive. Imhausen-Chemie agreed to help the Qadhafi regime.

Using Pen-Tsao, a Hamburg dummy corporation it controlled, Imhausen-Chemie shipped liquid-processing and testing equipment to Hong Kong, then on to Singapore, and from there to Libya. In Hong Kong, Imhausen-Chemie arranged for Asian engineers to work at the Libyan plant at salaries of about $3,000 per month. Other West German companies were involved in the conspiracy, as were companies based in Japan, Britain, France, Belgium, Italy, and Switzerland, but Imhausen-Chemie, German police now believe, was the main conduit to the Rabta factory.

Between 1986 and 1988, American and Israeli intelligence personnel quietly monitored the strange activity in the desert south of Tripoli. They watched with mounting concern as the plant neared completion. After measuring the factory's dimensions, and after months of tracking and analyzing the materials being shipped to it, the Israelis estimated that Rabta would have the capacity to produce each day more than 40 tons of mustard gas and a nerve gas called Sarin. The plant was doubly dangerous, the Israelis noted grimly, because it would be capable of switching to production of non-lethal chemicals in a single day: the perfect camouflage. Neither the Israelis nor the Americans doubted that full-scale chemical weapons production was Qadhafi's objective. The Libyan leader had ordered their use in his war against Chad in 1987.

In the last few weeks of 1988, with the Rabta plant a few weeks away from start-up, the Reagan administration decided to take action. The Pentagon dispatched a 13-ship battle group to the Mediterranean, dramatically boosting the U.S. Navy's presence off Libya. Then, on January 3, 1989, the U.S. State Department announced that Libya was "on the verge" of beginning chemical weapons production. Without naming West Germany, a State Department spokesman called on "all countries" to cut off any assistance "they or their firms" were giving the Libyans at Rabta.

A Republican senator from Maine was less subtle. The vice-chairman of the Senate's intelligence committee, following up on a report in the *New York Times,* told reporters that West German companies had been providing material assistance to the Libyan chemical weapons effort. For weeks, the West Germans had been skeptical about such claims. Within a few days of this one, however, they changed their attitude—officials in Bonn were soon admitting with red faces that Imhausen-Chemie and a number of other firms were being investigated by West German police. As a result of this probe, Jurgen Hippensteil-Imhausen would be sentenced to five years in prison. After listening to expert testimony, Chief Judge Jurgen Henniger would call the industrialist a "merchant of death" and declare that the Rabta plant "was clearly intended for the production of chemical warfare agents."

Off the Libyan coast, meanwhile, tensions were growing with each passing minute. At 5:00 a.m. Eastern Standard Time on Wednesday, January 4, the tension spilled over into the fourth clash between the Americans and the Libyans since 1981. U.S. F-14 jets shot two Libyan MiG-23s out of the sky just north of the coastal town of Tobruk. The Libyan foreign ministry said the MiGs had been in international airspace when the American fighters carried out "a premeditated attack."

Qadhafi took to the state-run airwaves, where in a radio speech he called the incident "American terrorism" and hinted darkly that "the Libyans will meet challenge with challenge."

"If America has prevailed because it is a superpower in the air and the sea," he declared, "it will inevitably be defeated on land. We, as well as the fish, are awaiting them."

In the fall of 1988 an anonymous source sent the *Ottawa Citizen* a sheaf of documents dealing with Mohamed Shihumi and Neutron Alberta. At first glance, one of the documents did not appear to be of much significance. It was a photocopy of a small scrap of paper, partly in Arabic, partly in English. It contained an Ottawa-area phone number and a name—Bill. The notation in Arabic read "The Embassy, Ottawa." It was clear that the telephone number belonged to a federal government department. (In Ottawa, most government phone numbers begin with 99.) But the slip of paper did not indicate which department.

Two reporters from the *Citizen* called the number. A man answered but did not identify himself. He was clearly astonished that the newspaper had called. He was even more surprised to learn that the number had been extracted from a pile of papers belonging to a person the reporter referred to as a suspected Libyan spy.

By the end of the working day the reporters knew they had stumbled onto an interesting news story: the phone number belonged to the NATO Comcentre in Ottawa's Department of External Affairs. The top-secret communications centre is located in the basement of the Lester B. Pearson Building on Sussex Drive, several blocks from the prime minister's official residence. The people who work in Comcentre handle highly sensitive coded messages to and from Canada's diplomats in other countries. They also transmit coded telexes to and from NATO headquarters in Brussels. It is without a doubt one of the most secretive units within any Canadian federal department. No private citizen is permitted near Comcentre, or to phone it. It is even off-limits to ranking foreign service officers.

But Mohamed Shihumi, Libyan businessman, had been in contact with someone who worked there. Someone named "Bill."

Officials at External Affairs were completely at a loss to explain how Libya's man in Edmonton even knew that Comcentre existed, let alone the name of a telecommunications operator assigned to work there. Like everyone employed by the unit, "Bill" had the highest possible security clearance. Christian Sarrazin, director of media relations at External Affairs, had only this to say: "It could be a freak call. We've had several freak calls. Perhaps Mr. Shihumi might have been trying to contact a particular area of the department, but he just misplaced his call."

Sarrazin confirmed that "Bill" did, in fact, exist. He would not say whether Bill had been reassigned or disciplined. He was asked how Shihumi could possibly know the name of one of the area's telecommunications operators, considering the public was not supposed to know the unit existed.

"It's a mystery to us at this stage," Sarrazin said.

After a supporter of the National Front for the Salvation of Libya was asked about it, Shihumi's connection to Comcentre appeared to be less of a mystery. According to this man, the Neutron International companies run by Hawamda and Shihumi had been set up to export military technology and know-how to Libya. If someone working inside the federal government—for example, at Comcentre—could be persuaded to help Libya in its drive to arm itself, he said, that person could end up being very wealthy.

"I know a little," said another source at the NFSL. "I know that Neutron has an account at the Bank of Credit and Commerce, and that Mousa Hawamda and his gang have been using Neutron to recruit engineers and technicians for Libya. They have even advertised for the engineers in the *Citizen* newspaper."

But what kind of engineers?

"They are after some sort of nuclear stuff," the source said. "And they are trying to figure out how to export it to Libya."

It is likely that Shihumi got the Comcentre number for "Bill" through a pro-Qadhafi source in Ottawa. There was no doubt that the Comcentre employee was acting improperly—or why else would the RCMP devote weeks to the case?

———————

That Mu'ammar Qadhafi was seeking nuclear weapons technology was nothing new. It had been public knowledge since 1981 that the Libyan leader was interested in beefing up Libya's arsenal with the Ultimate Weapon. Qadhafi sent his right-hand man, Abdul Salaam Jalloud, to Egypt in 1970 to consult with Gamal Abdel Nasser on the matter of purchasing an atomic bomb. Using a fake passport and travelling incognito, Jalloud had already been to China on a similar mission.

Later, the Libyans pestered the French, Germans, Italians, Canadians, and Americans for some nuclear technology. In each case they were rebuffed. In or around 1979, Qadhafi offered to pay India a gargantuan $15.5 billion for its nuclear weapons technology. That would have wiped out India's entire foreign debt. The Indians declined the offer.

Were Qadhafi's three Canadian front companies in Ottawa and Edmonton—the Neutron International firms and Manara Travel— set up as part of Libya's decades-long quest for an atomic bomb? No one is certain. Unlike its sister company, Manara Travel, the Neutron International account at the Ottawa branch of the Bank of Credit and Commerce International never contained the sorts of sums Mousa Hawamda had hoped for. The bank's manager, a former resident of Pakistan named Anwar Khan, told his senior staff in the summer of 1987 that Neutron International was going to be "a big account" for their branch. But it never worked out that way.

At the outset, Neutron Ottawa showed a lot of promise. There were plans to rent half a floor of office space at 50 O'Connor Street, the office tower where BCCI was located. There were also plans to hire a large staff to meet the needs of Qadhafi's regime. That the venture did not get off the ground was not surprising. One former bank employee later recalled that "Mousa and his friends didn't seem very organized. They were looking at something very splashy, but they never made it clear what they were doing. For example, they would come to the bank's officers with shopping lists of the things they wanted. They were after things to do with the oil industry, but more on the high-tech side. But then they were also looking for vegetables and sugar. Tons and tons of it. So we'd ask them how much sugar they wanted, for example, and they'd just say they'd be getting back to us. But they never did."

He could not explain why Hawamda would approach a bank for help in tracking down commodities, and admitted that it would have been far less costly to approach a broker in such goods. But, as he pointed out, saving money was not Hawamda's primary concern.

The same source mentioned that Hawamda generally preferred to deal with only a small number of people, since this minimized the risk that damaging information would be "leaked." He also confirmed the NFSL's allegation—namely, that Hawamda and Neutron Ottawa *were* clearly interested in acquiring the services of engineers and technicians. Hawamda himself would often speak of his training as a nuclear physicist. "They wanted manpower more than anything else," the ex-employee recalled. "That was their main interest—people. I remember they wanted chemical engineers in particular."

Sources at the RCMP and CSIS say that Neutron Ottawa was set up to circumvent the Canadian laws that make a crime out of providing Libya with military hardware or unique Western petroleum technology; neither the Mounties nor the security agents will give an official, on-the-record statement about it. Ian Verner Macdonald, the former trade diplomat, does have a thing or two to say about it, however.

Standing on the front porch of his large home, Macdonald surveys the embassies crowding his well-appointed street while he listens to a summary of the Mounties' suspicions about Neutron— that it may have been involved in the weapons trade. Macdonald, a director of the company, will not take the bait. He will only say, "It is not only out of proportion, it is grossly distorted to put this sort of an espionage complexion on what had been a normal international commercial interest."

Was Neutron involved in the export or trade of weapons of any type, then?

Macdonald shoots a sour look at his questioner. "Not to my knowledge."

If Ian Verner Macdonald is to be believed, Ottawa's Neutron International resisted the urge to peddle arms to Libya and other Arab nations. But surprisingly few Western firms have done the same.

Analysts calculate that since the early 1960s, the Middle East has been inundated with a staggering $1.6 trillion in armaments. According to the U.S. Arms Control and Disarmament Agency, between 1980 and 1988 Saddam Hussein's regime in Iraq paid out $50.6 billion for arms. Libya, meanwhile, bought close to $18 billion in weaponry. Only two other Arab nations spent more than that in the same period—Saudi Arabia and Syria. The Arab nations, taken together, spent more than $150 billion on arms imports during the 1980s.

Saddam Hussein showed the world the folly of pumping the Arab world full of arms. But for the arms merchants, cutting off the supply is an unattractive proposition at best. According to the U.S. Commerce Department, regulations aimed at tightening export controls on certain materials—materials that could be used to produce chemical weapons—would cost American firms as much as $75 billion a year.

Canadian firms would also stand to lose if domestic export controls were toughened. Although Canada's government banned the sale of military technology to Iraq during its seven-year war with Iran, Canadian-made technology still found its way to Baghdad. Engines built in Montreal powered some of the Iraqi air force planes that slaughtered Kurdish dissidents in northern Iraq in August 1988.

Not surprisingly, Alberta firms did most of Canada's arms

trading with Iraq. Provincial trade statistics show that Alberta companies sold more than $200,000 in aircraft parts, radar equipment, and explosives to the Iraqi military in 1989. When asked whether there had been any more such sales after Canada joined the UN embargo against Iraq, Alberta's trade minister, Peter Elzinga, said he didn't know, and added, "It's up to the federal government to enforce the embargo."

In the fall of 1990, Mu'ammar Qadhafi saw an unprecedented opportunity to associate himself with something more palatable than international terrorism. His benefactor in this regard was Saddam Hussein.

When the Iraqi dictator invaded Kuwait in August 1990, the Arab world was turned on its head. The myth of a nationalistic pan-Arab state was shattered, perhaps forever. Within weeks, Egypt, Syria, Saudi Arabia, and almost every other important country in the Arab world had lined up behind "the Great Satan," U.S. President George Bush, to form an anti-Hussein coalition. Although he is known to have supplied Iraq with at least 400 armoured vehicles during the 1980s, Qadhafi knew a political opening when he saw one. In early January, a few days before the American-led coalition began its pulverizing air assault on Iraqi military targets, Qadhafi told the Egyptian president Hosni Mubarak, "We want to unify our efforts."

By the end of January 1991 the Qadhafi charm offensive was gaining momentum. While expressing muted concern that Western troops were taking up residence on Arab soil, Qadhafi allowed that Saddam Hussein had been wrong to occupy Kuwait. He also agreed that the Iraqis should withdraw from the tiny nation.

The strategy paid dividends. In early March of 1991, Egyptian officials began trying to nudge the United States into a friendlier stance toward Libya. One of Mubarak's advisors told the American ambassador to Egypt that the Libyans were showing "a lot of self-restraint, despite their opposition to foreign forces in the region."

But why? Had Qadhafi mellowed in his old age? Or was his "charm offensive" part of a larger plan? In the opinion of Western diplomats, Mubarak himself was wooing Qadhafi—"trying to get him to listen to someone besides his nutty advisors," as one diplomat put it.

The Americans weren't about to start trusting Qadhafi. As a State Department spokesman said in Washington, "While [the Libyans] seem to have laid off a bit in sponsoring the major kinds of terrorist acts we used to associate with them, they are still meddling around in the Caribbean and Africa.

"And they are still developing chemical weapons."

A few weeks before the United States shot down Libya's MiG-23 jets north of Tobruk, the same anonymous source sent an envelope to the newsroom of the *Ottawa Citizen*. Inside it were dozens of telexes written in Arabic, all addressed to Mohamed Shihumi. Many were coded. The newspaper duly had them translated.

Many of the telexes looked run-of-the-mill—they were requests by Shihumi's bosses for bank statements, or incorporation documents for Neutron Alberta. But others showed a fixation with secrecy that was very striking, in that Shihumi had been claiming that Neutron Alberta was a broker of foodstuffs and legally exportable technology. Many of the telexes urged him to exercise extreme caution. One of them, received in January 1988, advised him to use only "the special route" because "danger has arrived."

It is fair to say that Neutron Alberta was interested in far more than flour and vegetable paste. The telexes indicated that the Alberta company, like its Ottawa counterpart, had clearly devoted much of its time to securing war-related goods and the personnel to service them.

For the Libyans, Shihumi had been asked to locate thousands of square feet of thick insulated metal sheets, high-density plastics, and "isolating materials." Among the chemicals requested were toxic cyanates, alloy agents, and a number of compounds the nature of which a team of American chemical weapons experts could not explain.

One of the most interesting telexes was sent to Shihumi on January 26, 1987. It instructed Neutron's European and Canadian branches to locate a number of chemical compounds—tons of them. Many were harmless enough: sulphur, mica, high-density polyurethane. But one of the compounds listed was T-D-I—that is, toluene 2,4 di-isocyanate. This chemical, which is used most often in the making of foam, has a sharp, pungent odour and is associated with skin and bronchial irritations. A related isocyanate killed more than 3,000 people near the Union Carbide pesticide plant in Bhopal, India, in December 1984.

There was no doubt that most of the materials listed on the telexes could be of some use at the chemical weapons facility, the experts said. It was impossible to locate the "smoking gun" in the telexes the *Citizen* obtained, but one of them, which Shihumi received in Calgary in late January of 1987, was more intriguing than most: "Please communicate with us through telex only, not through telegrams," instructed Neutron's anonymous bosses in Tripoli. They went on to request proposals and materials related to "the project"—a "factory," the location of which was not mentioned.

In late 1988, when the *Citizen* called Shihumi at his house in Tripoli, it asked him if Neutron Alberta was involved in exporting materials that could have anything to do with chemical or nuclear weapons. He sounded agitated. "We try to be active in everything we can be," he said. "Mainly we are active in the oil sector, equipment supply and manpower recruitment."

"But what about weapons, Mr. Shihumi? The Canadian police authorities suspect that's what you were involved in when you were here."

"I am quite sure we do not have anything illegal," he said. "Myself, I will not be involved in anything illegal." He then repeated his earlier claim: "We are in the commodity business—wheat flour, vegetable paste."

"Most of the countries that have chemical weapons programs, and are having difficulty getting materials, set up front companies," says Elisa Harris, who is a senior research analyst at Washington's Brookings Institution and an authority on chemical weapons. "Or they find unscrupulous traders to get them the materials they need." Other experts note that countries such as Libya and Iraq have been fairly sophisticated in their efforts to obtain the building blocks of chemical weaponry. For example, they tuck the names of the chemicals they need for producing mustard gas into lists of other, completely harmless chemicals. Or they refer to the materials they are really seeking by innocuous code words.

That Neutron Alberta was a Libyan front is beyond dispute. But was it trafficking in chemicals or materials with a military application? Was it recruiting personnel for the same purpose? Abdulmagid Sugair, an NFSL spokesman in New York City, says that the answer to both questions is an emphatic yes. Sugair, who has reviewed the telexes sent to Mohamed Shihumi by Neutron International's Tripoli headquarters, insists that Shihumi's claim that his company traded primarily in foodstuffs is "absurd."

"You have to admit it is very, very strange," Sugair says. "Eggs, butter, and margarine. Why would they go all the way to Alberta, to Canada, to get this stuff?" He notes that the telexes betray a bizarre obsession with secrecy, even to the point of using words that make no sense in Arabic, English, or French. He also points out that many of the Tripoli addresses referred to in the telexes are "totally imaginary." "The fact is [Neutron International] was trying to get some chemicals. And they were trying to build factories where they could use these chemicals in some way."

Spokesmen for Libya's government have always denied that the Rabta plant has anything to do with chemical weapons. They continue to insist that the Rabta facility does nothing more than manufacture pharmaceuticals. NFSL spokesmen, however, counter that there is no shortage of evidence that Rabta is *not* what Libya's government claims it to be.

———————

In January 1989, days after American jet fighters shot down two Libyan MiGs north of Tobruk, Qadhafi said he was ready to let American chemical weapons experts visit the Rabta facility for a one-time-only inspection. American officials rejected the offer as a meaningless publicity stunt. One official told the media that shortly after the American battle group arrived in the Mediterranean, the Libyan government had ordered large stockpiles of industrial chemicals to be moved from Rabta to another site. The fact that the facility could be converted into a bona fide pharmaceutical factory within 24 hours also supported the American government's contention that an inspection tour would be "inadequate." That same month a group of Western journalists was permitted to visit Rabta. The plant was guarded by soldiers, tanks, and surface-to-air missiles. The journalists were not allowed inside.

By January 1990 the Rabta plant was almost ready to begin production—if not already producing. A few weeks later, in February, anonymous sources in the West German government were reporting that the Libyans had already achieved full-scale production and had stockpiled enough mustard and Sarin gas to outfit more than 1,000 artillery shells. The same week, sources in the Bush administration told the Associated Press that they believed the Libyans had been producing chemical weapons for most of 1989, though the amounts were probably very small.

The Libyans soon had another cause for concern: on March 7, in a widely publicized White House press briefing, spokesman Marlin Fitzwater refused to rule out a military strike against the Rabta facility. Within a few hours of that briefing, Qadhafi's government would come up with a plan to fool the all-seeing eyes of the American spy satellites.

On March 14, 1990, a press spokesman at Libya's UN mission told reporters that the Rabta "pharmaceuticals plant" was ablaze. A spokesman for the Interior Ministry of Libya's northwest neighbour, Tunisia, confirmed the report. The Libyan government feigned outrage and called the fire the work of saboteurs—most likely the Americans, the Israelis, or the West Germans. Speaking that same day on state-run radio, Qadhafi speculated that the West Germans were at fault. He repeated his claims that the factory had been built to produce only pharmaceuticals, but added that Libya would pay millions of dollars to any company that would help it to build a chemical weapons facility. He added, "In such eventuality, I will sign the contract myself unhesitatingly."

At first, the Libyan ruse was a smashing success. At a press briefing on March 16 a Pentagon spokesman said that according to American satellite photographs, the Rabta facility had suffered massive damage. Fitzwater declared that "common sense would tell you [Rabta] is not functioning." Even George Bush was fooled. "I don't lament what happened," he said on March 17, "but I can't tell you I know the cause of it."

Some nations were more doubtful that Rabta was destroyed. At around 10:00 a.m. on March 18 a French SPOT-1 commercial satellite beamed back to Earth a number of very clear photographs of the Rabta facility. If there had been a fire at all, the French concluded from these photos, it had been far from the main weapons facility. The satellite company's president told an international symposium in Colorado that the black areas on the SPOT-1's photos were "probably mostly paint." A few days later, in April, Bush administration officials admitted that the whole affair had likely been a hoax engineered by the Libyans.

A few months later, in August 1990, Iraq's forces invaded and occupied Kuwait, and stories about Qadhafi's chemical weapons plant slipped from the front pages. The Americans' favourite bogeyman, Qadhafi, had been overtaken by another—Iraq's Saddam Hussein.

In mid-December, as the Americans and their coalition allies were preparing for war, one American official told Britain's *Independent* that "Colonel Qadhafi [is] a long way down on our agenda these days."

Qadhafi, as students of the Libyan leader might expect, welcomed this development, since it meant that while Uncle Sam's spy satellites were trained on the Persian Gulf region, he would be able to redouble his efforts at Rabta. According to the CIA, that is precisely what he did. In March 1991 the Libyans started to produce poison gas weapons in large quantities for the first time since the plant was completed.

The CIA and sources in the U.S. Congress called the Rabta plant one of the largest of its kind in the developing world, and added that Libya was digging a warren of tunnels and underground storage sites close to the facility. The tunnels were designed to protect Soviet-made Scud-B missiles from the sort of barrage that Iraq had suffered during the Gulf War. It is not known where Mu'ammar Qadhafi plans to aim his Scuds. But the world can be sure what their warheads contain.

THE BANK OF CROOKS AND CREEPS INTERNATIONAL

Mousa Hawamda sat in a conference room at the Washington offices of the People's Committee for Libyan Students, a single sheet of paper in front of him. It was March 20, 1987. He glanced down at the note. He did not look impressed. Across the room, watching him, was the PCLS chairman—and ever-watchful FBI informant—Mahmoud Buazzi. At the doorway Buazzi's designated successor, Milad Shibani, examined his fingernails, waiting.

Hawamda reread the note, which was written in awkward English.

> I, Mousa Hawamda, agree to pay the necessary funds to cover the expenses of the rally held to commemorate the first annual attack on Jamahiriya by America, the enemy of the people and humanity, on the condition the office of the PCLS will cover all expenses by preparing enough travel requisitions to cover all the expenses of the American Indian organization, and the leftists, and a few black organizations.

Hawamda signed his name to it. Buazzi would later tell the FBI that Hawamda did not like what the note had to say, for two reasons: first, it connected his name with activities the American authorities saw as illegal; and second, it demonstrated that the Libyans who ran the PCLS—Buazzi in particular—still did not trust him. Hawamda knew that many of the PCLS directors saw him as an outsider—as a too-smooth Palestinian who was taking advantage of his Libyan patrons.

Hawamda's travel agencies were front organizations while Washington's PCLS was backed by Libya's revolutionary committees. In such circumstances, feuding was almost inevitable. Hawamda, when he opened Manara, was allied with one of the most powerful factions in Tripoli. By the time he was arrested, the faction backing the PCLS was stronger. The events in Washington and Ottawa in 1988 would reflect this.

Hawamda stood up and passed the note to Mahmoud Buazzi. In six months' time it would be labelled the prosecution's Exhibit #53. To the American government it amounted to proof that money which had been intended solely for Libyan scholarship students was, in fact, passed on to radical black and Indian leaders. It went without saying, the FBI pointed out, that the Libyans used the money to promote a "foreign revolutionary policy" and to gather and transmit intelligence information.

Ever since Ronald Reagan's January 1986 trade embargo, the U.S. Treasury Department had been tightening its restrictions on the PCLS's bank account in Washington. Hawamda and the PCLS directors faced a dilemma. They needed a safe haven for Libya's money: a bank that was discreet, adept at quick transfers of large amounts of cash, and, above all, based outside the continental United States. They turned to the Bank of Credit and Commerce International.

BCCI is no longer a going concern. While it was, its Ottawa branch was located at 50 O'Connor Street at the corner of Queen, very near the West Block entrance to Canada's Parliament. The offices were bright, airy, and street level. It was an expensive location. BCC Ottawa's upstairs neighbours included three major law firms, a well-heeled group of lobbyists, and the Ecuadorian and Israeli embassies.

At its branches outside Canada, at one time or another, BCCI's clientele included Iraqi leader Saddam Hussein; deposed Panamanian dictator Manuel Noriega; Philippine strongman Ferdinand Marcos; Contra boss Adolfo Calero; arms dealer Adnan Khashoggi; Palestinian terrorist Abu Nidal; Colombia's Medellin cartel; Islamic Jihad; and several African and Middle Eastern dictators. BCC Canada's customers were less notable, but interesting nonetheless: retired Canadian diplomat Ian Verner Macdonald; the Manara Travel Agency; Neutron International's two Canadian front companies; the People's Committee for Libyan Students; Mohamed Shihumi; and, of course, Mousa Hawamda.

BCCI, which controlled all of Canada's BCC branches, had an image problem almost from the start. In May 1990 the *Wall Street Journal* called it "the world's largest rogue bank." One former executive at BCC Ottawa was more direct: "We called ourselves the Bank of Crooks and Creeps International."

According to the bank's glossy promotional brochures, BCCI was founded in 1972

> by a group of investors whose original intention was to provide commercial banking services internationally. Its operations were first started in the Gulf Region. Since then, the bank has grown extensively to become an international financial organization with operations in five major regions around the globe.

In describing its operating strategy and management philosophy, the bank drew attention to one of the things that presumably made it so popular with some of its shadier clients.

> Although it is subject to the regulations of all countries in which it operates, its small base of shareholders has enabled BCC[I] to operate with relatively low visibility. It is well known within the international community but not to the general public.

The hazy language obscured the fact that BCCI was without a doubt the largest and most successful Arab-owned bank in the world. The shareholders—euphemistically referred to as "a group of investors"—were very powerful men. Five members of the family of a powerful Saudi Arabian sheikh named Khalid Salem Bin Mahfouz controlled at least 20 percent of BCCI. (They also held majority control of their country's National Commercial Bank.) The family of Sheikh Zayed Bin Sultan al-Nahayan, president of the United Arab Emirates, controlled 40 percent. (They also controlled the U.A.R.'s Abu Dhabi Investment Authority.) A number of wealthy families and investment groups in the Arab world controlled the remaining 40 percent. (In 1990, after a global streamlining of the bank's operations, Sheikh Zayed took effective control of the bank and moved its headquarters from London to Abu Dhabi.)

The bank was founded by a Shiite Muslim named Agha Hasan

Abedi. Abedi was born in 1924 in Allahabad, India, and was president of the United Bank of Pakistan between 1959 and 1972. In the late 1960s and early 1970s he became a close associate of a number of Arab princelings who were studying in Pakistan at the time. It is reported that he took them on hunting trips in air-conditioned jeeps and offered them financial advice. In 1973, directly after the Pakistani government nationalized the United Bank of Pakistan, Abedi founded BCCI with $2.5 million from Sheikh Zayed and another $2.5 million from the Bank of America.

At the time, the Bank of America was the world's largest commercial bank. It saw the BCCI deal as a marriage of convenience: the California-based banking giant wanted Abedi's help to gain access to the Arab families in the oil-rich Middle East; Abedi wanted the prestige the Bank of America could bring to his new venture. During the eight years it was associated with BCCI (it sold its 25 percent share in 1980), the Bank of America gave Abedi's empire something it desperately needed: legitimacy.

From the start, Abedi wanted to make BCCI the biggest bank in the world. He told his employees to target what he called HNWs—people with "high net worths." The strategy worked. In 1973 the bank's operations were largely confined to the Persian Gulf region, and it held assets of about $200 million. By the end of 1988 its assets totalled $20.6 billion, and it boasted more than 400 offices in 73 countries, as well as a staff of more than 14,000. BCCI had become the fifth-largest privately owned bank in the world.

But by then there were problems. The bank's huge loans were not being properly documented, and it was violating money-exchange controls—which are the laws that govern the movement of capital in and out of a country—in almost every nation in which it operated. Law enforcement agencies were investigating the bank's internal affairs in Bermuda, Brazil, the Cayman Islands, Cyprus, France, Great Britain, Luxembourg, Nigeria, Singapore, the United States—and Canada.

The bank could not even give money away without controversy. For example, Abedi donated $2.5 million to Global 2000, a charitable foundation run by his close friend, Jimmy Carter. As well, the former American president apparently used BCCI corporate jets quite often for his charitable projects. Unfortunately, Carter and Abedi had been introduced by a BCCI consultant named Bert Lance, who at one time was Carter's budget director. In 1978 the U.S. Securities Exchange Commission had sued both Lance and BCCI for failing to meet disclosure regulations. The suit was settled out of court in 1981.*

For the most part, BCCI weathered the bad publicity it got. It persevered. But in 1988 the bank got enmeshed in a scandal from which it never escaped: the Tampa affair.

In the 1980s, in a mad scramble to find more HNWs, BCCI turned to one of the fastest-growing industries around—the drug trade. In December of 1987, officers from BCCI's Colombian branches began meeting with cartel moneymen in Paris, London, Miami, and other cities to discuss using the bank's international network for laundering drug profits. They reached an agreement, unaware that undercover police were taping some of these meetings. The U.S. Customs

---

*In the summer of 1991 Lance testified before the Senate Subcommittee on Terrorism, Narcotics and International Operations about his relationship with BCCI. Lance and a number of other prominent American Democrats were being questioned about their close ties with BCCI. Lance told the subcommittee that he was largely ignorant of the bank's true motives: "I don't know what the truth is about BCCI." He also testified that, one month after he left the Carter administration in 1977, he had urged Abedi to "get into banking" in the United States. Abedi apparently took Lance's advice—by arranging for the covert purchase of another financial institution favoured by Mousa Hawamda, the First American Bank.

Service, the FBI, and other police agencies were able to establish that the bankers knew the money they were laundering was drug-related, and prepared a "sting."

The money-laundering scheme worked as follows: officers at BCCI's American banks placed drug money in certificates of deposit at BCCI branches around the globe. They then prepared the paperwork for a loan at another branch and permitted the drug traffickers to withdraw the funds. Shortly afterwards, BCCI officers in Tampa, Florida, used the certificates of deposit to repay the original loan.

On October 11, 1988, BCCI paid dearly for this: nine of its officers in Tampa were charged with laundering more than $32 million for the Medellin cartel. This was the first time an international financial institution had been indicted in the United States.

Concerned that it would be ordered to shut down its American operations, BCCI offered to assist the Americans in prosecuting a second matter in which its officers were implicated: the Manuel Noriega case. In September 1988, BCCI's former branch manager in Panama told a subcommittee of the U.S. Senate that that country's dictator had been funnelling drug profits through a BCCI account since early 1982.

Noriega surrendered to an American invasion force on January 3, 1990, and was soon facing a prosecution in Florida. Also in January 1990, BCCI pleaded guilty to money-laundering. In return, some of the 26 charges it was facing were dropped. BCCI also agreed to forfeit $14 million that had been frozen by American authorities.

By 1988 Agha Hasan Abedi had suffered two heart attacks, as well as a debilitating stroke. After undergoing a heart transplant, he handed over control of the beleaguered bank to his long-time deputy, Swaleh Naqvi. In 1990, in an open letter to BCCI employees, Naqvi called for an end to the unethical—and criminal—practices the bank had once enthusiastically embraced. "Never again," Naqvi wrote, "shall we allow our bank's good name to be smeared or tarnished by carelessness or negligence or lack of vigilance."

This would turn out to be wishful thinking on Naqvi's part.

———————

In its heyday BCCI had eight Canadian branches: two in Vancouver, two in Toronto, one in Calgary, one in Edmonton, one in Montreal, and one in Ottawa. In July 1990, BCC Canada announced that its Alberta branches were closing, and that Toronto and Vancouver would soon lose one branch each.

Between late 1987 and its closing in 1991, BCC Ottawa was managed by Anwar Khan. Khan was born in Pakistan's northwest, not far from his country's border with Afghanistan. After attending university and doing a short stint at Lufthansa's accounting department, Khan joined the Beirut office of Pakistan's Habib Bank. By 1971 he had risen through its ranks to become that branch's manager.

Khan looks very much like a banker: slight of stature, balding, inscrutable. But according to former BCC Ottawa employees, he is no shrinking violet—at least, he wasn't while stationed in Beirut: after the Lebanese Civil War broke out, he kept the Habib Bank's important loan documentation in the trunk of his car for safekeeping, in the quite possible event that one of his branches was blown up during the night. It was in Beirut that Khan first met the leaders of the Arab paramilitary groups, among them Yasser Arafat, chairman of the Palestine Liberation Organization. Like BCCI's founder, Agha Hasan Abedi, Khan recognized the importance of cultivating Arab power-brokers.

By February 1, 1985, Khan, with his family, was on the other side of the globe, happily living in Alberta, working for BCCI as an "advisor." He became a well-known figure in that province's Progressive Conservative circles, attending party events and helping to raise funds. In the fall of 1985 he joined a trade mission to Pakistan with Horst Schmid, who was then Alberta's Minister of International Trade and Tourism. The two men became fast friends. Khan admits he "worked" for the Tory minister: "Sometimes I offered my help, maybe, at the time of elections and so on."

The two men remained close even after Khan moved to Ottawa. Schmid maintained two accounts at BCC Ottawa while Khan was manager there. Schmid would sometimes telephone that branch to speak to him or to move funds between accounts. Schmid did not visit Ottawa often, but during one of those visits, in 1988, Khan escorted him around the bank, introducing him to employees as "my very good friend Horst Schmid."

In Edmonton, Khan was popular with his employees, and he did well. His achievements caught the attention of BCCI's management. In the spring of 1987 he was promoted and transferred to Ottawa to replace the outgoing manager, Amer Mahmood. During 1987, former employees say, BCC Ottawa was a good place to work: the pay was good, morale was high, and the bank did smashing business with the city's diplomatic community. "We cleared *millions* through the bank in 1987 and early 1988," says one person who worked there.

While in Alberta, Khan was one of Mohamed Shihumi's bankers. It is not known whether Khan's dealings with Shihumi led to the formation of Neutron Ottawa. "Did Khan put the idea in Mousa's head?" asks Ian Verner Macdonald. Then he answers his own question: "As far as I know, he played no role in the formation of the company. I doubt it."

Macdonald's comments notwithstanding, Neutron Ottawa *was* incorporated five weeks after Khan arrived in Ottawa. And according to Khan's former employees, he played a pivotal role in that company's early development: he opened its BCC account and helped it to find space and recruit personnel.

Khan denies this. In November 1991 the banker was called to appear before a special parliamentary committee that was investigating BCCI's Canadian activities. On November 18, when questioned about Neutron Ottawa, Khan told the committee that all he knew about the Libyan front company came from what he had read in the media. Herb Gray, the Liberal Party's finance critic, asked him if the company had an account at BCC Ottawa.

"Yes, I am telling you, sir, we did have an account. The account was established in 1987—January 1987—at the same time when Manara Travel's account was established. [But] I never opened this account and I did not know the principals of this account."

Gray asked Khan if the Neutron International account had been set up by Mousa Hawamda. "No sir," Khan replied. "He was not the person who was operating this account."

"Well," Gray continued, "did you know that it has been alleged that Mr. Hawamda was seeking nuclear-related technology for Neutron International?"

Khan looked sucker-punched. "Sir, I am really surprised. To me, [Hawamda] was completely illiterate. I mean, I have seen his written letters, I have seen the level of his English language, his education. Of course, I wish I had the opportunity to ask him, did he have some engineering degree or if he knew about nuclear engineering or something. But as far as my knowledge goes, to me he was not that much educated."

He continued: "I am really surprised. I do not know anything about it, and I would be surprised if a man with that character had that much ability or intelligence to get to the information for a nuclear device or something. But, again, he has never even discussed [it], jokingly or casually. I have never heard anything about it."

When interviewed by the *Ottawa Citizen* in 1988, Anwar Khan attributed BCCI's success to its willingness to locate where other banks would not. "The Middle East is an area of prime focus," he pointed out. He also claimed that BCCI had the "quickest available transfer facilities. No other bank can do that. You will be surprised to know that we have been able to set up so many links around the world. We provide the cheapest transfer of funds." The bank was able to move large sums across international borders in a matter of seconds. This was what had made BCCI so attractive to the Medellin cartel and Manuel Noriega—and to Mousa Hawamda.

Khan stressed, correctly, that BCCI had no formal connection with Libya—which made good business and practical sense, given that most of the Arab world has a well-documented aversion to Mu'ammar Qadhafi's radical politics. Even so, the Libyans had not hesitated to use the bank's excellent international wire-transfer networks to their advantage. In the case of Neutron Alberta, hundreds of thousands of dollars were redirected from the company's account at BCCI's Luxembourg branch to Mohamed Shihumi's personal account at BCC Alberta.

In Hawamda's case the financial transactions were more complex. The travel agency owner maintained a number of accounts at BCC Ottawa. Some of them held millions of dollars, others just a few thousand. Number 01000946 was a U.S. funds account used mainly by Manara Travel. Number 02004293 was Hawamda's personal account; it, too, contained American dollars. Manara Travel also opened a savings account, as well as a Canadian funds account for its employee payroll. One former employee of BCC Ottawa says that the most active account was 01000946: "When money came in [from abroad], it would usually be for Manara Travel in U.S. funds. Most of the time, there was always about half a million in that one. It was always being replenished. Manara Travel was the money-making account for us, because it was the kind of account that paid no interest. Half a million dollars with no interest earned a *lot* for us."

There was no doubt about the money's source. "It was from the Libyan authorities, yes," says Khan.

It seems that Khan was so intent on keeping Manara's principals happy that he agreed to let the agency store its blank airline tickets in BCC Ottawa's vault.

According to the FBI, account number 01000946 was always a picture of rosy-cheeked fiscal health—especially during the U.S. Treasury Department's crackdown on the PCLS in the summer of 1987. Court records would show that on August 18, 1987, $325,458 was transferred into the account; a few days later, on August 21, $159,879.83; and, on September 4, $1,679,880.50. That is, more than $2.1 million within a single three-week period—all from the coffers of Qadhafi's government.

Hawamda's Neutron Ottawa account didn't do much business however. "I remember Mr. Khan saying Neutron International was going to be a big thing," says a former BCC employee. "It was going to be a big account for us." But that day never came.

When Libya wired money to BCC Ottawa—most often to Manara's U.S. funds account—it was first sent to New York City, to the First American Bank of New York or the Bank of America. At the time, BCCI secretly owned First American. On the back of the remittance slips, Khan later said, was stamped, FROM THE PUBLIC TRADING SECRETARY, TRIPOLI. For these transactions, cash was unheard of; the Libyan government preferred wire transfers. From New York City, the funds would be transferred to an account at the central Ottawa branch of the Royal Bank and then deposited at BCC Ottawa. Because BCC Ottawa was not an established chartered bank, but a Schedule 2 bank, it was required to pass all major transactions involving foreign jurisdictions through a Schedule 1 bank (for example, the Royal Bank or the Bank of Montreal). In theory, this enabled Canada's federal regulatory agencies to monitor suspicious transactions of Schedule 2 banks like BCCI and take preventative action. In the case of Manara Travel and BCCI, this monitoring control didn't work.

Hawamda had yet another hurdle to vault before he could draw from Manara funds. Because every cent in account 01000946—and in every other Manara account—ultimately belonged to the Libyan government, Hawamda had to obtain the approval of the PCLS chairman, Milad Shibani, before he could carry out any transaction. A letter given to the *Ottawa Citizen* by a member of the National Front for the Salvation of Libya showed the extent of Shibani's influence.

The letter was written in Arabic on PCLS letterhead, dated

August 10, 1987, and addressed to Libya's director general of finance. It stated that the U.S. Treasury Department had decided to suspend licences L-66 and L-66A—the ones that had permitted PCLS to receive and distribute Libyan funds in the United States. The Treasury Department's Office of Foreign Assets Control had informed the committee's directors that the suspension was not permanent. Even so, Shibani was clearly worried. The letter read in part,

> It has become evident that the continuity of the usage of these two licences will take some time. This will prevent us from [conducting] any financial transactions on the on-going accounts with the First American Bank. The continuous accumulation of debts on the account of the People's Bureau has reached up to one million dollars up to this date, [and] may cause its closure.... We ask you to speed the release of a financial transaction for an amount of [$1.5 million] to the BANK OF CREDIT AND COMMERCE CANADA, Ottawa Branch, Account No.: 1000946, Manara Travel Agency. Peace be upon you, Milad Mahmoud al-Shibani, Keeper of the People's Students' Committee.

Within days the $1.5 million was wired from Libya to New York City's First American Bank and then on to the Manara account at BCC Ottawa. At one secretive late-night gathering in September 1987, after the $1.5 million arrived, Hawamda and some Ottawa-based BCCI officials met at the bank to send certified cheques to hundreds of Libyan students living in North America. The cheques were posted using Manara Travel envelopes.

When asked about Shibani, Anwar Khan denied having any dealings with the PCLS officer. He allowed that Shibani was, in fact, "one of the signatories" for one of Hawamda's bank accounts. He did not appear concerned that Shibani—whom he had never met—could control so much money through cross-border facsimile transmissions. "Sometimes these instructions, when they came, [I wasn't] the one who received all these things," he said.

Late-night cheque-mailing sessions were not uncommon at BCC Ottawa. Former bank employees recall that, on at least six occasions in 1987 and 1988, bank drafts were issued on Manara Travel's behalf to Libyans studying in Canada; and that anywhere from 30 to 40 students came to BCC Ottawa regularly to cash cheques or drafts drawn on the Manara accounts.

According to Eric Kirsipuu, between December 1987 and January 1988, large amounts of money were wired to Hawamda from Tripoli: "That's when the really big money started to arrive, in that period. And we were writing a lot of cheques for the students."

Kirsipuu, a former assistant manager at BCC Ottawa, recalls that "Mousa couldn't really get at any of the money. Shibani was required to authorize everything. He had the signing authority. I don't think we ever met him. Paperwork was sent down to him by fax, and then it would be sent back to us with his signature, like magic. It was weird."

Was this the case for all of Hawamda's BCC accounts?

"Some money would come in for Mousa's personal account, but Shibani's approval was required even for that," he says. "As soon as any money arrived at the branch, Mousa needed Shibani's approval before he could do anything with it."

To ensure that Hawamda did not abscond with any Libyan government funds, on October 19, 1987, Khan asked him to sign a letter on Manara Travel letterhead that read,

> I the undersigned president of Manara Travel Agency Inc., Canada, do herby [sic] acknowledge that the funds of account number 01000946 under the name of Manara Travel Agency, drawn against Bank of Credit and Commerce, Canada does solely belong to the People's Committee for Students of the Socialist People Libyan Arab Jamahiriya, a Verginia [sic] non-stock corporation.

"I got him to sign it," Khan later testified. "It said these funds belonged to the Libyan People's Committee for Education [sic]. He told me that this money was being used for the purpose of students."

Hawamda's letter is significant for three reasons. First, it again shows that some of the PCLS directors did not completely trust him. Hawamda might have been Libya's chief North American spy, but the PCLS signed the cheques, as it were, that let him keep operating, and his influence over that committee was limited. Second, it shows that a money-laundering operation was being conducted at BCC Ottawa, probably with the bank's knowledge or complicity. Third, the document establishes that Manara Ottawa itself was little more than a front—a money conduit for funds that enabled Hawamda's group of Libyan agents to evade American law.

Leslie Hulse, one of three American prosecutors of the Libyan spies, says that the October 19 letter is important because it "clearly inculpates" Hawamda: "It shows the account was called Manara, but it was actually the PCLS. Certainly, Manara used its corporate infrastructure to launder and shield assets."

Kirsipuu balks when the allegation of money-laundering is raised. He maintains that while BCC Ottawa's dealings with Manara Travel and Mousa Hawamda may have been unusual, they were not illegal. "The Libyans had broken a law in the U.S., but not in Canada, as far as we all knew. Our attitude was, 'Let's have a judge tell us what to do.' We wanted to help out the FBI, but we didn't want to get sued by Mousa Hawamda for violating any trust agreement."

During 1987 and 1988 Libya sent staggering amounts of money to Hawamda and the PCLS directors. The FBI estimates that at least $16.6 million was deposited with Manara Travel or the PCLS during this period. One of the largest sums was sent on December 29, 1987: the PCLS account at the First American Bank in Washington, D.C., was credited that day with $1,805,294. When the U.S. Treasury

Department started to express concern about the way the PCLS was conducting its financial affairs, Hawamda and his colleagues simply asked that Libyan intelligence redirect all monies to the Manara accounts at BCC Ottawa.

According to special agent Donald Bartnik, the FBI knew that Canada was one stop on the Libyan money-laundering circuit, but not much more. It had no jurisdiction to investigate north of the border.

There was a solution to this. Shortly after Hawamda's arrest, at a special court hearing on August 16, 1988—long before a special parliamentary committee pried the lid off BCCI's Canadian operations—a U.S. District Court judge named Claude M. Hilton issued a legal document that is seldom used called a Request for Judicial Assistance.

> The United States District Court for the Eastern District of Virginia presents its compliments to the appropriate judicial authorities of Canada and has the honor to request international judicial assistance in obtaining certain banking records and sworn testimony needed in a matter pending before this court.

Hilton went on to request that officials from the main Ottawa branches of the Royal Bank of Canada and the Bank of Credit and Commerce

> search for and produce true and accurate copies of all records, for the period of January 1, 1986 to present [pertaining to] any account listed to the Manara Travel Agency, Inc. in the name of Mousa Hawamda, [his wife] Maisoun Ben Mohammed Hawamda or in any way accessed by Manara Travel, Mousa Hawamda or Maisoun Ben Mohammed Hawamda.

The judge also requested that Anwar Khan produce records of

any accounts maintained by the PCLS at his branch.

Canada's Justice Department acted quickly. Federal government lawyers appeared before a justice of Ontario's Supreme Court the following week and obtained an order under Canada's *Evidence Act.* The order required Khan and a representative of the Royal Bank to appear in District Court on September 9, 1988, to answer questions about Hawamda and Manara Travel.

Khan was unfazed by this ruling: "It's a simple thing," he told an *Ottawa Citizen* reporter. "We just have to give the evidence. We don't have to fight [the order]. We want to help them to give them the correct position."

He went on to provide a number of details about Hawamda's dealings with BCC Ottawa. Some might find this rather odd; after all, was not such information confidential? Khan simply replied that "one or two" remittances had found their way into Hawamda's BCC Ottawa account from accounts he maintained with the Royal Bank and the Toronto-Dominion Bank. He said he was "surprised" that the Justice Department had not also sought the assistance of the Toronto-Dominion Bank.

"[Hawamda] had an account with us," Khan continued. "A business account, much before I was here." (According to Kirsipuu, Khan had become BCC Ottawa's manager just as the Manara account was being set up, and opened the Neutron Ottawa account himself.) "There were I think two or three remittances of funds," Khan continued. "Then they were I think transferred back to the Royal Bank. I still have to put all the things together, so that we give the correct position before the court. But it appears to me that all the transactions appear to be as per the rules and in order."

After a moment's reflection, he added, "The bank doesn't like this." He was asked whether he disliked the fact that BCCI had been linked to Mousa Hawamda. He said yes and then added, "I think [Hawamda] is dumb. Whether deliberately or naïvely, he has done something. He has taken the consequences." It was an incredible statement for Khan to make, but the bank manager would not elaborate. He mentioned that he might speak to the media on September 9, outside the District Court, where the hearing was scheduled to take place.

In the meantime, Hawamda's American lawyer, Drew Carroll, obtained his client's consent to stall the examination of the Ottawa bank managers. Carroll immediately retained an Ottawa criminal lawyer named Leonard Shore to attend the September 9 hearing. Shore successfully argued before District Court judge Keith Flanigan that the charges Hawamda was facing in the United States were unknown to Canadian law; he then asked the court to consider whether the examination of the bank officials should proceed at all. Flanigan agreed to reflect on the matter.

Sitting near the courtroom door, looking uncomfortable, was a bespectacled wisp of a man in a dark suit—Anwar Khan. After Flanigan adjourned the proceedings, Khan turned to his lawyer, who told him that he would not be needed today, that Leonard Shore seemed intent on ensuring that the examination did not proceed at all. As he stepped toward the courthouse elevators, Khan said nothing.

Khan did not want his bank's name dragged through the mud, but the news media were not co-operating. He told his employees he was concerned about the impact the Libyan spy story would have on BCC Ottawa.

On October 12, 1988, his concern increased ten-fold. On that day the *Ottawa Citizen* ran two news stories on the front page of its morning edition: one was a long story that revealed the existence of Canada's two Neutron International firms; the other was headlined, "Bank executives charged with money laundering." The latter story, filed by the Reuter News Agency, told how nine officials of BCCI in

Tampa, Florida, had been indicted for their role in laundering cocaine money.

Khan was not available for comment, but Eric Kirsipuu, who was then still working for BCC Ottawa, was prepared to talk. He said that the money-laundering charges did not involve "the bank as a whole," but rather a few officers in Florida. "Here in Canada we have no knowledge of this whatsoever," he added.

The bank's officers liked to maintain the distinction between BCC Canada and BCCI, but it was an artificial distinction. BCC Canada was a wholly owned subsidiary that took orders from its parent.

The two Neutron firms in Canada were linked with BCC Canada branches. Shihumi used BCC Edmonton for his Neutron firm, just as Hawamda used BCC Ottawa for his Neutron and Manara. Khan had worked for both branches.

A third story, in the afternoon edition of the *Citizen,* spelled out the links between Libya, the Neutron firms, and BCC Canada. When Khan saw that edition, he hit the roof. He called the newsroom and, rambling almost incoherently, screamed at a reporter, "We never received any money from Libya! All this money came to the United States, not here!" In the background, Khan's aides could be heard begging him to get off the phone. Instead, he went on: "If [Hawamda] was doing any kind of illegal activity, why don't the RCMP arrest him? I reviewed the accounts, and he didn't do anything illegal. We have certainly not tried to suppress anything. They are very happy with us, the court authorities. We were there with the records in court."

His voice growing louder, he continued: "If you involve my name in anything, I have no other [choice] but to go to your door and do a hunger strike."

Why, he was asked, would he want to starve himself on anybody's doorstep?

"We are the innocent victims in this thing," he replied. "We are required by the court to hand over our records. We are giving full co-operation. So don't involve my branch! I've done nothing wrong!"

Eric Kirsipuu sits in a dark downtown Ottawa bar, sipping a beer. With him are two other past employees of BCC Ottawa, a man and a woman.

Kirsipuu explains that the three of them left the bank in 1988, shortly after the Libyan spy revelations became public, because they did not want to be associated with a bank that did business with clients like Hawamda, Manara, and Neutron. All have moved on to other jobs in the Ottawa area.

"Mousa Hawamda and his friends were like the bare-knuckle terrorist types," he says, and his former colleagues nod their agreement. "They looked like they had gone through a PLO training camp."

Even so, Kirsipuu says, Hawamda and Anwar Khan "were very close." Hawamda and his wife were often guests at the Khan family home in Ottawa's east end. Kirsipuu received one or two dinner invitations himself. At one such party, in 1987, he listened in amazement as Khan, Hawamda, and other pro-Libyan guests made vicious anti-Semitic remarks.

The woman sits forward, her hand tapping the tabletop for emphasis. "Another time," she recalls, "when I met with Ahmad Eed Murad and those guys at Khan's place, there was one subject and one subject only. And that's what they called the Jewish problem."

The second man agrees. He shakes his head in disbelief: "One time when I was there, the men and women separated. All the men talked about was Jews—Mousa Hawamda, Anwar Khan and some German guy. It was unreal."

Anti-Jewish sentiment was not unknown at BCC Ottawa. For example, Ian Verner Macdonald banked there often. In 1988, before he left BCCI, Khan said in an interview that he saw nothing wrong in doing business with such people. "He is our client, he is our client. But we don't subscribe to any of his policies. Our concern is all business. There is no discrimination here. Money takes the first priority."

According to the three former employees, Khan was always interested in assisting Mousa Hawamda and his Libyan friends. He told his staff that Hawamda was particularly interested in taking the Libyan student "account" away from the CBIE. "That was his big objective," says Kirsipuu. "He was even going to get someone on salary to do monthly cheques [for Libyan students]."

The Libyans presented the bank with unlimited commercial opportunities. Hawamda's accounts at BCC Ottawa were so lucrative that Khan was always eager to accommodate Libyans, the former employees say. In 1987 attempts were made at the branch to open an account for another Libyan front company called the Jerusalem Foundation. The firm was not incorporated because the chosen name was already in use elsewhere. Says Kirsipuu, "Substantial amounts of money came in for the Jerusalem Foundation's account. But there were no signing officers for it. The money came in by telex—$200,000 for the Jerusalem Foundation. It sat on my desk, and when nothing happened, we sent it back."

Where, Kirsipuu is asked, did you send it back to?

Kirsipuu shrugs. "The Libyans sent the $200,000, and it was for use by the Libyans. I can only assume it went back to Libya."

———

Finally, on Friday, July 5, 1991, at around 1:00 p.m. Greenwich time, the plug was pulled on BCCI. The Bank of Crooks and Creeps International was no more.

With stunning speed, financial regulators in seven countries—Luxembourg, Britain, the Cayman Islands, Spain, Switzerland, France, and the United States—swooped down on the bank, seizing records and freezing accounts. On the same day at around 11 a.m., after some of the bank's 110 Canadian employees were given time to withdraw their personal savings, Canada's Office of the Superintendent of Financial Institutions shut down the firm's four Canadian branches in Montreal, Toronto, Vancouver, and Ottawa. BANK OPERATIONS HAS [sic] BEEN TEMPORARILY SUSPENDED TILL FURTHER NOTICE, one employee had marked on a piece of paper that was taped to the door at BCC Ottawa. The funds stored in the bank's Canadian vaults—estimated at $165 million—would be frozen and counted, the OSFI told the press. The Canadian government's move would affect more than 2,500 depositors, including the Soviet embassy and a flood relief fund for Bangladesh.

In scope and speed the global crackdown was unprecedented. Within days 62 nations would move against the bank and its estimated assets of $20 billion. In Canada, it was only the second time that federal regulators had taken over a bank.

The previous Thursday, June 27, 1991, was the beginning of the end for Agha Hasan Abedi's mysterious bank. On that day Eddie George, the deputy governor of the Bank of England, was handed a lengthy Price Waterhouse report detailing money laundering, fraud, and other criminal activity at BCCI. George later admitted, "I didn't sleep particularly well that night."

The report provided page after page of evidence that BCCI had been running what British authorities later called "a bank within a bank." BCCI had been predicated on a fraud designed to give its operations the appearance of sound and profitable financial management. Under this carefully maintained gloss, it was in fact thoroughly rotten to the core. Regulators charged that BCCI's managers had deliberately disguised huge losses; and that they had made bad loans, offered bribes, made threats, stolen up to $15 billion in depositors' money, avoided taxes, laundered drug profits, and—among other things—assisted Libya in acquiring weapons systems. *Time* magazine even charged that BCCI had overseen a 1,500-member "black network" based in Karachi, Pakistan. According to the magazine, this network used extortion, kidnapping, and possibly even murder to achieve its ends.

BCCI, which the U.S. Federal Reserve Board would later call the author of "the largest bank fraud in world financial history," had been running a Ponzi-type fraud scheme in which depositors' cash was routinely siphoned off to cover up massive losses incurred by the friends of the bank's management. It was designed, said the *Wall Street Journal,* "to line the pockets of already-rich Persian Gulf financiers." The fraud worked for 19 years for a number of reasons. One was that BCCI excelled at moving funds quickly and quietly from one nation to another. Another was that the bank's corporate structure was highly complex, even to those who worked there. A third was that the bank's key records were all kept in Urdu. This was a deliberate choice by the BCCI managers. Urdu, which is the main language spoken in Pakistan, was incomprehensible to the English-speaking auditors at Price Waterhouse and at Ernst & Whinney. This is one of the reasons why they never discovered the bank-within-a-bank.

Sensation piled upon sensation. The *Sunday Times* reported that Abu Nidal, the Palestinian leader of one of the most blood-soaked terrorist organizations in the world, used accounts at BCCI branches in London to finance operations based in Libya. Yet another report stated that Syria, Libya, and the PLO maintained "terrorist accounts" at those same branches. American intelligence sources say that in 1988 the Abu Nidal Organization received about one-third of its funding from the Libyan government—which laundered the cash through BCCI. Eleven other Arab terrorist groups used the bank. The governor of the Bank of England, Roger Leigh-Pemberton, confirmed that the British government had known about the terrorist connections since "about March 1988." Said Leigh-Pemberton, "[We] were notified by a former employee that certain terrorist-related accounts had been and were being operated at BCCI." The CIA, meanwhile, reluctantly told a congressional committee that it, too, had kept a few accounts at the bank to assist covert operations.

As observers of the Manara Travel saga knew already, the Libyan government, like Manuel Noriega and the Medellin cartel, had been keen to employ BCCI's unique services. Worth noting in this regard is that the bank managers were well-tuned to Mu'ammar Qadhafi's philosophy. In Pakistan, where BCCI was revered as a Third World success story, a major newsmagazine noted that "the all-powerful Zionist lobby in America certainly played a crucial role in the bank's demise. The American banking industry and finance are largely controlled by Jews." Karachi's English-language *Daily News* said that "Jewish pressure" was to blame for the bank's failure. A public relations officer at BCCI made the bank's anti-Semitic corporate culture even plainer: he blamed "the Jews and the Zionist lobby in America" for the shutdown. "They do not want a Muslim bank to rise up," he insisted.

In the United States, Senator John F. Kerry, who led a congressional investigation into BCCI, said it was clear that the bank was profoundly pro-Arab. When asked by a *New York Times* reporter to describe the bank, Kerry said, "What you basically had was a Third World, a Pakistani-Saudi effort that was geared literally to try and help neutralize their sense of an uneven playing field with respect to Middle Eastern policy. I think that if it wasn't anti-Israel, it was certainly pro-Arab—with a view to neutralizing whatever influence Israel was perceived to have."

Britain's *Guardian* newspaper, meanwhile, stunned everyone by stating that since the 1970s, BCCI had been funding a secret joint operation by Argentina, Pakistan, and Libya to acquire nuclear weaponry; and that British financial regulators had found a number of "black holes" in BCCI accounts in London—black holes that added up to some $10 billion. These accounts existed to fund nuclear arms purchases by Libya and the other nations. Libya's objective was to provoke a nuclear showdown with Israel. Some of these attempts to buy nuclear components were successful, others not.

"BCCI also arranged airfreight, shipping and insurance for the components and provided operating funds for agents of the secret consortium," the *Guardian*'s Dan Atkinson wrote. "When agents were arrested and faced criminal charges—as happened in Holland in 1983—BCCI paid expenses for top legal counsel."

Coincidentally—or perhaps not—BCC Toronto gave a $447,500 letter of credit to a local businessman named Arshad Pervez in the mid-1980s. In December 1987 the Pakistan-born Pervez was convicted by a Philadelphia court of conspiring to export restricted materials to Karachi for nuclear use. The BCCI funds had been used to finance the deal, according to a spokesman for the U.S. Justice Department.

For the Canadian MPs on the Standing Committee on Finance, the news stories were all too much. (This committee, which advises the Canadian government about legislation, has the power to issue subpoenas and take evidence.) There were news reports filtering out about BCCI, Libya, and money laundering; about BCCI, Libya, and arms dealing; about BCCI, Libya, and terrorist organizations; about BCCI, Libya, and an "Islamic bomb"; and even about BCCI, Libya, and extremists calling themselves "the Third Position." With so much going on that involved BCCI and Libya, how could the Canadian government and its police know so little?

On July 30, 1991, members of the committee voted to hold special hearings about the activities of BCC Canada.

Brought in to testify in August and September were federal banking regulators, forensic accountants, and BCCI officers. Three times, the committee questioned members of the RCMP; many of the MPs were unsatisfied with the answers they heard. The committee invited Anwar Khan to appear before it on October 21. Khan's name had come up over and over in police testimony about two separate money-laundering investigations.

But Khan, who had been giving interviews all summer to news

reporters, was unable to attend. His lawyer, Frank Tanner, sent the MPs a letter explaining that Khan had cardiac problems: "By virtue of Mr. Khan's present medical condition, I understand it will not be necessary for Mr. Khan to attend before the committee this after-noon or at a future date."

The MPs were not impressed. John Manley, a Liberal, said that he and his colleagues were tired of being "jerked around." A majority of the parliamentarians voted to subpoena Khan, heart condition or no heart condition.

Khan by then was no longer BCC Ottawa's manager. He says he resigned; his bosses say he was fired.

On November 18, 1991—a Monday evening—a grim-looking Khan showed up at a West Block hearing room on Parliament Hill. With him were his wife, his daughter, and his lawyer. After a few minutes of jousting between Frank Tanner and the committee members about whether the meeting should be held *in camera,* Khan stepped up to give his evidence. An NDP member, Stephen Langdon, insisted that Khan give his evidence under oath.

Khan at first looked stiff and uncomfortable. But as the evening progressed, and as it dawned on him that no one was going to work him over, Perry Mason style, he loosened up. He smiled often; he waved his hands through the air; he even made light of BCCI's trou-bles. "Power corrupts," a straight-faced Khan told a dumbfounded Langdon. "Absolute power corrupts absolutely!"

For much of the evening, Khan was questioned extensively by Manley about BCC Canada's dealings with the Libyan government and its North American agent, Mousa Hawamda. Khan testified that Libyan government wire transfers began to flow into his branch soon after Hawamda set up the Manara Travel accounts in 1987. "Hawamda received two large remittances [in 1987]," he said. "The total amount that he received was $1.9 million. It did not stay here long. Out of that, $1.2 million was remitted to a bank in Washington. It was gone immediately. Another $200,000, [for] which they got us to issue a U.S. funds demand draft, was sent directly to the Libyan students. The rest of the money remained in his account. He paid a large amount to his landlord and also the developer for his travel business."

Khan continued without pausing: "Now, I did not envisage any risk or any complications because I was new here in the branch. But it was just out of curiosity, as any banker would do, that I asked a few questions: What is this? What is happening? Of course, I considered it a normal transaction. And let me tell you, sir, it was a judgement call. At the time, considering all the aspects of the transaction, I considered it all right. I didn't see any point which could be interpreted as money-laundering, or something against the rules."

Manley pressed on: "Were you not aware that, at that time, there were U.S. sanctions against Libya?"

"No," Khan said, curtly.

"Were you not aware of the fact that the U.S. government had *then* initiated trade sanctions against Libya?" Manley asked.

Khan shrugged. "No, I didn't know this. It was absolutely not in my knowledge."

"Was this a normal-sized deposit—$1.9 million—for Manara Travel?"

Khan frowned. "This was only once," he said, apparently unaware that large amounts had been deposited in the Manara Travel accounts on many different occasions. "The normal size [of the deposits] was only about $500,000," he added.

Manley asked Khan why he was not "troubled" by the size and source of the deposits. Khan replied that it was his "nature" to always investigate unusual transactions. In Hawamda's case, Khan said, he checked "the status of the account, the people behind it, their characters, their backgrounds, everything."

As Manley and other MPs listened, Khan recounted a conversation he had with Hawamda in the fall of 1987 regarding the $1.9 million deposit. "Where did this money come from?" Khan said he asked Hawamda. "And why did it come to Canada? Why didn't it go to the United States directly?"

Khan said that Hawamda told him, "The Libyan authorities made a mistake. But I am going to take this money."

To which, Khan said, he replied, "Please, I would like to be informed about the utilization of these funds."

Khan again told the MPs that he did not know at the time that he may have been unwittingly assisting a criminal conspiracy in the United States. Nobody at BCC Canada knew about Reagan's trade ban, he insisted. He did not regard the multimillion-dollar "mistake" as unusual.

Manley, clearly, was astonished by this. "He told you that over *one million dollars* came to his branch of a travel agency in Ottawa from Libya *by mistake?*"

Khan smiled shyly. "He said that instead of sending it there, they—by mistake—sent it here. That is what he told me. So he said he was going to send the money back." Khan was contradicting himself—not for the first time that evening. Hawamda's puzzling answer was "justified," he told the committee. "[BCCI] couldn't do anything."

Manley leaned back in his seat to confer with Herb Gray and a Liberal aide. "This guy is incredible," Manley told them. "If we were in court, and we had the time, we could really go after him. But we can't, unfortunately." Manley decided to take another approach. Turning once more to his microphone, he said, "Mr. Khan, our researchers have been told by other people in the bank that Mr. Hawamda was often in your home. But you have told me you didn't have any personal relationship with him."

"No, no," Khan said, shaking his head emphatically.

Manley didn't believe him. "It is not true? Mr. Hawamda was *never* in your home?"

"No," said Khan, who was under oath.

Khan's lawyer, Frank Tanner, leaned toward the Pakistani and whispered in his ear. Khan nodded, looking distinctly ill-at-ease, and cleared his throat.

"The other people must have ... there must have been, because I...." Khan looked like he was now wishing he had stayed home. Seconds ticked by. "*Yes.* On one social occasion. Where I had invited all of the businessmen, the guests." He hesitated, then added, "That was not my home. I rented the home when I came to Ottawa. Yes, Hawamda was one of [BCCI's] important clients. That was not personal or social ... but then I had with him two lunches...."

At that point Khan slumped in his chair.

"Thank you, Mr. Chairman," Manley said with a shake of his head. The hearing was over.

12

MU'AMMAR QADHAFI COPS A PLEA

After discussions with their lawyers, and after five days of intense negotiations with Henry Hudson, the federal prosecutor, on Friday, October 15, 1988, 48 hours before their trial was to begin in Alexandria, Virginia, Mousa Hawamda's six friends at the PCLS threw in the towel.

The Libyan men had concluded that the case against them was too strong—better to plead guilty now than to take their chances at trial. Late in the afternoon a deal was struck: in exchange for guilty pleas, most of the men could avoid prison sentences. Instead of jail time the Qadhafi activists would be handed stiff fines and one-way tickets out of the United States. They all understood that deportation was much more palatable than an undetermined number of years in a prison yard full of American rapists and murderers.

The prosecution team prepared an eight-page Statement of Facts for the Libyans to sign. "Were this matter to go to trial," it read, "the United States would present testimonial and documentary evidence that would prove beyond a reasonable doubt that…." The document then went on to state that all of the Libyan activists, as well as the Palestinian known as Mousa Hawamda, were guilty of every crime they had been charged with in July 1988. No mention was made of the alleged conspiracy to assassinate Oliver North. Even so, the Libyans must have hated to sign it.

> The PCLS was allegedly formed to service the academic, medical and legal needs of Libyan-sponsored students and their dependents studying in the United States and Canada. In fact, the evidence would show that the PCLS has also been used as a front by the defendants and others to subvert United States policy and laws by using PCLS facilities, resources and licenced funds for gathering intelligence-related information and purposes not related to the legitimate needs of Libyan students studying in the United States. The evidence would further show that the Manara Travel Agency, Inc., incorporated and located in Washington, D.C. with a branch office in Ottawa, Canada, provided travel services for Libyan students but was also used as a front organization by the defendants to subvert … United States restrictions on Libyan funds licenced for specific PCLS expenditures.

In a section titled "The Conspiracy," the final statement of facts noted that the PCLS and Manara Travel's two branches had circumvented the American trade ban "to support dissident American groups and Libyan intelligence-gathering activities." The Libyan spies' major obstacle, it continued, was the $2,000-per-cheque limit on expenditures. Revolution was difficult, if not impossible, in $2,000 increments. The solution was not complicated. Mousa

Hawamda supplied the PCLS with invoices for fictional travel by fictional students. Defendants Saleh Omar Zubeidy and Saleh al-Rajhi then issued cheques to Manara Travel for the billed amounts. The funds were then passed on to Third Position groups—or spent on such things as Christoph Halens' Alitalia flight to Tripoli.

That was not all. The statement noted that the six Libyan-born defendants agreed they had established an elaborate network of bank-to-bank wire transfers in Ottawa and Washington to get around the restrictions imposed by the Office of Foreign Assets Control.

> It was part of this conspiracy that the defendants, at the behest of Libya, set upon a calculated course to undermine the laws of the United States by providing financial support to dissident American groups, transporting some of these group members to Libya, and promising "the direct arrangement with Libya in armed struggle, such as training Indians in Libya" and financial support in their continued and shared struggle against American 'imperialism and Zionism.'

In that paragraph the prosecutors were quoting directly from a letter al-Rajhi had written to spymaster Mohamed Madjoub. The statement ended with a brief recitation of the case against al-Rajhi, who had pleaded guilty earlier that same week, on Tuesday, October 11. The prosecution team wrote that by organizing the January/February 1988 First International Conference of the Red Indians of the Americas, al-Rajhi had flagrantly violated American law. Even more damning was his top secret memorandum of June 1987, in which he revealed to Madjoub the home addresses of hundreds of members of the FBI, CIA, and a half-dozen other U.S. government agencies and departments. For his revolutionary zeal, al-Rajhi was sentenced on November 25 to five years' imprisonment. He is now serving time at a federal prison in El Reno, Oklahoma.

Meanwhile, the five other PCLS directors, whose crimes were

seen as less serious than those of al-Rajhi or Hawamda, were fined $100,000 each by Judge Albert Bryan and ordered deported by November 11. They left the American capital without incident. Their fines were paid by the Libyan government through unidentified intermediaries.

The second non-Libyan defendant was Hawamda's Moroccan-born brother-in-law, Manal "Mike" Ben-Mohamed, who was manager of Manara Washington. Ben-Mohamed, who studied briefly at Ontario's University of Waterloo in the early 1980s, did not want to be deported. While living in the United States he had met a Canadian woman he wished to marry.

While he fought the deportation order, he continued managing Manara Washington. When reached there, he sounded boastful, and contemptuous of those who had brought charges against him. "They failed," he said. "Anything they tried to do to me, they failed." He curtly refused to discuss the prosecution of Hawamda and his friends: "That thing is history now. It's something that happened, and it's gone."

Understandably, Ben-Mohamed's views on his sister and his celebrated brother-in-law had soured: "I don't really care a lot about them. It was her and her husband who got me in this problem in the first place. I'm mad, and I don't want anything to do with them. I just don't care about them."

These brave words did not explain why Ben-Mohamed was still working at Manara Travel. When pressed on the issue, he said that the business was under new ownership. He would not say who the new proprietors were. The District of Columbia's registrar of companies was more helpful: according to the department's up-to-date records, the travel agency's president was now one Maisoun Ben-Mohamed. The firm's vice-president and secretary was Mousa Hawamda.

Eventually, Mike Ben-Mohamed left Manara and went to Georgia. Assistant U.S. Attorney Lawrence Leiser, one of three prosecutors in the Libyan spy case, who worked with Donald Bartnik throughout Operation Friendly Skies, says that Ben-Mohamed may still face deportation for his role in the espionage conspiracy.

———————

Why, considering the trouble they got into with American authorities, were Mousa Hawamda and his Libyan friends able to lead such charmed lives in Canada, while indulging in the same sorts of criminal activity? Why did the RCMP show so little concern?

In October 1991, in a cavernous committee room in Parliament's Centre Block, four senior RCMP officers appeared before the House of Commons Standing Committee on Finance to answer those questions. They were summoned to help MPs to unravel the mystery surrounding the Canadian operations of the recently collapsed BCCI empire. In the course of their three hours of testimony, the Mounties publicly confirmed for the first time that yes, they *had* investigated Libya's use of Manara Travel to funnel cash to extremist groups and Third Positionists.

The Mounties were primarily represented at the committee by Deputy Commissioner Gilles Favreau. In answer to questions about the travel agency and BCCI put to him by Liberal MP John Manley, he stated that "[the Manara] investigation was under the Security Offence group. It started in 1987, when we were asked by the FBI to verify some information about the travel agency in question. We did that."

Favreau told the committee that the Mounties were "in direct relations" with the FBI throughout 1987 and 1988: "There was an exchange of information all the time." He added that the RCMP probe revealed that Libyan government money—sometimes in very large denominations—was at the time being passed through BCC Ottawa and on to Mousa Hawamda's travel agency. He rejected suggestions that the bank itself had done anything wrong.

"We had [the bank's] co-operation during the investigation," Favreau said. "We transmitted this information back and forth with the FBI and the end result was that several people in the States were charged, were arrested for diverting funds in violation of U.S. law."

If the FBI was carrying out its own investigation of BCCI, Mousa Hawamda, and Manara Travel, Manley demanded, why didn't the RCMP do the same? When Favreau, stone-faced, suggested that there was no particular reason to conduct one, an incredulous Manley asked him why not. Favreau replied, "To my knowledge, there was no illegality in Canada to start with. It was a question of Libya rerouting money to the States because of United States laws at that time."

"In other words," Manley said, "you would not regard it as offensive for a Canadian financial institution to be a co-conspirator in contravention of U.S. laws?"

Favreau bristled. "No, that is not what I said at all."

"Then clarify," Manley said, "because really that is the essence of this question, that if the bank's officers knew what was going on and knowingly helped to do it, then they were conspiring with Mr. Hawamda to breach the [law]."

"No," Favreau said, looking annoyed. "That is not correct. My recollection of the case is that there was a bank account. Some people would deposit some money in that bank account and somebody else would make withdrawals. So as to what the bank knew about it, it is a little bit going too far in assuming that they knew about it."

Manley pressed on. "The context of the question was whether you made any further investigation that would have led you to either believe—or not believe—that there was a conspiracy occurring here."

Favreau sat back in his seat and folded his arms. "There was nothing that made us believe that there was a conspiracy."

But Henry Jensen disagreed. Jensen, a former RCMP deputy

commissioner, appeared before the same committee on October 21, a few days after Favreau, and testified that a Libyan conspiracy to launder money and assist extremists seemed very plausible to him while he was still a Mountie. A 37-year veteran of the force, Jensen retired in December 1989—and then, a few weeks later, went to work for BCC Canada as a paid consultant.

Under a barrage of questions by Liberal and NDP committee members, Jensen angrily rejected any suggestion that he was in a conflict of interest for doing so. In Jensen's view, the fact that he had supervised money-laundering investigations involving the bank while still a deputy commissioner, and then gone on to advise the same bank about the same subject, did not constitute a breaking of any rules. "Clearly," a red-faced Jensen told Manley, "if there were any hint or evidence of criminal conduct on the part of any of the officers of the Bank of Credit and Commerce Canada … I would not have gone anywhere near the institution. The fact that other people use that banking institution is a different matter."

Among the "other people" using the bank, Jensen told the committee, were Mousa Hawamda and his Libyan friends.

Jensen testified that he was told about the Hawamda investigation in 1987 by an FBI agent then working out of the American embassy in Ottawa. According to Jensen, the two men had conversations "from time to time" about Libyan spy activity in North America. What the FBI agent had to say interested him very much. At the time, he regarded the Hawamda case as one of "significance." He told the committee that he discussed it with the RCMP's commissioner more than once. Exactly what did they discuss?

"The Manara Travel Agency and an individual by the name of Hawamda, as I recall it," Jensen said, without referring to any notes. "[Manara] was in fact the subject of interest by the FBI. As a consequence of their interest, the RCMP was involved in [the] investigation. And the RCMP of course acquired information that would be of assistance to the American authorities in that particular case."

While the MPs and a dozen reporters scribbled notes, Jensen continued. It soon became clear that no matter what Favreau and others had testified, the Mounties were heavily involved in the Libyan case in 1987 and 1988—from Jensen's perspective, at least.

"While [the Libyan] investigation was going on," he told the MPs, "I was very aggressive in terms of the staff of the RCMP—the intelligence directorate that was handling that particular investigation, and personnel within the economic crime directorate. It seemed to me that there ought to be a way that [Hawamda's activities] would constitute an offence in Canada.

"They exhausted every possible avenue and established to my satisfaction that, in relation to Canadian law, there was absolutely no violation whatsoever. The offence in the United States was related to a trade embargo issue, and that is not a crime in Canada. I even went so far as to ask the staff to examine an American immigration case and the law of conspiracy to determine whether or not it was possible for persons in Canada to conspire to commit what would be an offence against the regulations in the United States. And again the answer I was provided with was no, it is not possible. And I was satisfied with that."

According to at least one intelligence expert, however, the RCMP was looking at the Libyan case from the wrong end of the telescope. It made *sense* that the RCMP could not charge the Libyans with money laundering, says the expert—because at the time, Canada had no law against money laundering.

To this agent, who worked for CSIS, there was no doubt: a conspiracy existed at Manara Ottawa and BCC Ottawa to launder funds, evade trade laws, and finance Third Position extremists. (Khan admits that money was laundered at his bank, though he insists it happened without his knowledge. And Hawamda was, of course, using laundered money to help extremists.) In this agent's view, these activities should have been occupying more of the RCMP's time. So in August 1988, a CSIS counter-terrorism expert arranged a meeting between a Libyan dissident and two *Ottawa Citizen* reporters in a bar on Elgin Street a few blocks south of Parliament Hill. The *Citizen* reporters were Ian MacLeod and John Kessel, two newspaper veterans with years of experience on the police beat. The Libyan was a senior representative of the National Front for the Salvation of Libya, who identified himself only as Saleh. During the meeting Saleh confirmed beyond any doubt that CSIS was investigating Libya's support for neo-Nazis and ultra-leftists at the same time that the RCMP was stating publicly that it had no interest in the matter.

While the CSIS agent quietly sipped a beer, and while MacLeod and Kessel scribbled away in their notebooks, Saleh confirmed that there was, in fact, a very active group of anti-Qadhafi students in Canada. "But they should all be very careful," he said, "because they will be on Qadhafi's hit list if they are discovered."*

The reporters asked Saleh about Libya's use of people like Mousa Hawamda to fund political extremists and Third Positionists. Saleh told them that Qadhafi's regime was particularly interested in strengthening its connections with militant North American native groups. In the past, Saleh continued, Libya had made generous monetary gifts to the American Indian Movement in the United States and to the Mohawk Warrior Society in Canada. "Qadhafi

---

*Qadhafi has ordered the execution of Libyan student dissidents in the past, but never in Canada. As recently as June 1991, however, an Ottawa immigration lawyer's offices were broken into on the eve of a hearing in which a Libyan student was expected to claim refugee status. The lawyer, who asked that he not be identified, said that no cash or valuables were stolen. The unwanted visitor or visitors seemed to be interested only in locating Libyan client files. The lawyer attributed the break-in to pro-Qadhafi "thugs."

likes these radicals," he added.

That Qadhafi was helping AIM was nothing new—that group's leaders have been close to Qadhafi since at least August 1985. But Saleh's claim that the Mohawk Warrior Society had benefited from Libyan patronage was, in 1988, startling. At the time, the *Citizen* was unable to verify it. But two years later, in the summer of 1990, after the Mohawk Warriors' standoff at Oka, Quebec, the Libyan government itself verified it without any prompting: the Warriors received a $250,000 "human rights" award in Tripoli. The award was presented to two men and a woman representing the pro-Warrior Longhouse, in recognition of the Mohawks' "unyielding, centuries-old fight for sovereignty."

"The Libyan government is using Canada as a base in North America," Saleh went on, noting that Libya's European bases were Greece and Italy. "They are using it as a base to help these extremists." The Libyans, he added, were also channelling laundered money to Black Muslims and Marxist radicals in the United States.

The bridge between Qadhafi's regime and the Third Position types was Mousa Hawamda. "He has been active for Qadhafi for about three years, since 1985," Saleh said. "He is running Qadhafi's show in the United States. Helping Libya, this is very dangerous, because of the FBI and so on. A Libyan can't be active in the United States. But a person with U.S. citizenship, like Hawamda, can be very active."

After a brief discussion of the NFSL's plans to use Chad as a base to overthrow Qadhafi, Saleh and his CSIS escort prepared to leave the bar. "Saleh," MacLeod asked, "when did you people first learn about Mousa Hawamda and Manara Travel?" Saleh and the CSIS agent exchanged glances. The CSIS agent nodded. Saleh pulled a legal-sized sheet of paper out of his jacket pocket.

Abu Abdullah, the NFSL's London spokesman, was tipped off about Hawamda and his Ottawa travel agency in the fall of 1987, Saleh told MacLeod. It happened when one of the NFSL's contacts intercepted a letter from the PCLS headquarters in McLean, Virginia. Saleh now handed the letter to MacLeod.

The letter was crucial. It was dated August 10, 1987, signed by Milad Shibani, chairman of Washington's PCLS, and addressed to Libya's finance minister. In Arabic, it described how that group wanted to circumvent Reagan's trade embargo. It asked Libya's director general of finance to send $1.5 million to Manara Travel's bank account at BCC Ottawa.

As FBI agent Donald Bartnik now confirms, and as the PCLS letter makes clear, Hawamda's reasons for opening a branch of Manara Travel in Ottawa, and for using an account at BCC Ottawa, had very little to do with tourism or travel or plane tickets. In fact, Manara Ottawa and BCC Ottawa could be fairly regarded as offshore financial havens. They were close enough to be useful to Libya's representatives in the United States, but not so close that the American federal agents could do anything about it.

"After we reviewed the bank records of the PCLS," Bartnik says, "we found that between April 10, 1987, to May 13, 1987, alone, the PCLS wrote cheques totalling $575,000 to Manara Travel. The cheques were supposedly made out to pay for travel expenses by Libyan students—but they were all false billings."

Was Manara Ottawa a front, as the NFSL claims? Were Third Positionists getting money from it? Bartnik lets loose with a whoop of laughter. "Mousa Hawamda was a Libyan intelligence operative," he says. "And the office of Manara Travel in Ottawa ... served Libyan foreign intelligence-gathering activities. Period."

Shortly after noon on a sunny fall Thursday—September 29, 1988— Mousa Hawamda stopped by a United States Probation Office. A condition of his bail was that he would make a daily appearance there. Silently, he signed the register—for the last time. The following day he stopped by the U.S. District Courthouse in Alexandria to listen to his lawyer make pre-trial motions. He exchanged a few sombre words with his co-defendants. Moments later he stood up and walked out of the courthouse and onto the worn cobblestones of Alexandria's South Washington Street, and no one—not his lawyer, not Donald Bartnik, not the RCMP, not the CIA—has been able to find him since. Mousa Hawamda has vanished.

At first, Bartnik and his FBI colleagues thought that Hawamda might return to Canada; after all, he had a nice apartment in Ottawa, a business, and a few well-nourished bank accounts. "A guy like him, with money, can defer things for a long time," says Bartnik. "Tie up extradition with appeals and things like that."

However, sources say that since his escape, he has lived under an assumed name in Athens, Greece. "We've pulled out the stops all over the place," Bartnik continues, "but as long as he stays in countries that are not friendly to us, one way or another, he doesn't have a whole lot to fear from us."

The question Bartnik declines to answer is the obvious one: how did Hawamda do it? How did a travel agency owner outwit the well-trained FBI agents who had been assigned to shadow him?

"He escaped the very meticulous minds of the U.S. authorities," says Ahmad Eed Murad, with grudging admiration. "He made fools of them. And it was so easy, anyone could have done it."

In retrospect, Hawamda's escape does seem simple, but it was also clever. By mid-September 1988, perhaps earlier, he had concluded that the FBI and American prosecutors were intent on placing him behind bars for as many years as they could. Worse still, he knew that the evidence against him was compelling: a conviction was almost inevitable. It was time to lam out.

On September 20 he typed a brief memorandum on Manara letterhead and addressed it to Anwar Khan, the manager of BCC Ottawa. YOU ARE HERBY [sic] INSTRUCTED TO TRANSFER $1 MILLION U.S. DOLLARS FROM USD 01000946 MANARA

TRAVEL AGENCY ACCOUNT TO DR. HASEIN MOHAMED ABID VIA LUNDER BANK, VIENNA, AUSTRIA. He and his wife both signed it. The next day his wife boarded a flight for Ottawa to hand-deliver the letter. With the PCLS directors behind bars, a co-signer was apparently no longer necessary.

The Hawamdas were setting up an early retirement fund, courtesy of the Libyan government. In Murad's view, Hawamda's action was pure thievery—and a shocking betrayal of the Palestinian cause. According to him, Qadhafi's government had agreed in 1988 to show its solidarity with the Intifada uprising in Israel's occupied territories: the Libyans would provide a monthly subsidy for Palestinian students living in Canada and the United States. "Mousa was working for Libya," Murad says. "The Libyans trusted him, and he had good connections with them."

He shakes his head in disgust. "This amount of money was supposed to come every month for the Palestinian students from the West Bank and Gaza. After the Intifada, they could not receive the money from their families. The Libyan [education minister] decided that those students should be compensated for the loss of revenues. Since they couldn't send the money to the States, and because they knew Mousa, and Mousa was trusted, they said, 'Okay, we will send you a million dollars.'" With considerable bitterness, Murad admits that the Libyans made a mistake: they should not have trusted Hawamda.

The FBI agents who had been instructed to shadow Hawamda were not nearly so trusting. For him, this was not an insurmountable problem. He knew that the FBI had been observing him 24 hours a day since his release on bail. He was certain that the telephones were being tapped at his home and at Manara Washington. So he knew that his escape needed to be planned with great care.

Two days before he made his dash for freedom, Murad flew to Washington to visit him. Murad says he did not know at the time that Hawamda was planning to flee the United States. Murad will not say why, while in Washington, he rented a car on his partner's behalf.

On Friday, September 30, after making his brief appearance in court, Hawamda returned to his home in Falls Church, Virginia. He and his wife and two young daughters lived in an exclusive apartment building consisting of two multistorey highrises joined by a central administration complex. Below it was an underground garage where he parked his two cars, a 1985 Nissan two-door and a 1987 Nissan four-door. Sometime after dark, he took an elevator to that garage, where the rental car sat in a stall. He placed his suitcases in the trunk, pulled a hat over his head, pasted on a fake moustache, and drove out onto Seminary Road.

As he expected, the two FBI agents assigned to observe his comings and goings did not notice the switch. They had been told to watch for a clean-shaven man in a Nissan, not a man sporting a moustache behind the wheel of another make.

Hawamda immediately made his way northwest, toward Greater Pittsburgh International Airport. Upon his arrival, a few hours later, he parked Murad's rented car, threw the keys under the seat, and caught a flight to O'Hare in Chicago.

An FBI agent continues the story: "Once he got to Chicago, he bought a ticket out of O'Hare to Switzerland, but he did not get on that plane. He took another flight. His luggage showed up [in Switzerland], however. It was unclaimed for a couple of days. Nothing of significance was in it, just some clothes and personal effects. The name tags even had his real name on them. It was all later released to somebody else, on his behalf."

Using a false name and a bogus passport, Hawamda flew from Chicago to Rome and then on to Tripoli, where he checked into his favourite hotel, the Bab al-Bahar. It was a triumphant homecoming, says Ahmad Eed Murad: "The Libyans said to him, 'Thanks be to God, you are here. You have evaded the American authorities, and have managed to come here.'"

Murad says that after congratulating Hawamda on his cunning

escape, the Libyans grew businesslike. They wanted to know where the $1 million was—the money they had told Hawamda to pass on to Palestinian students living in North America. Hawamda told them that his wife had forged his signature on the September 20 memorandum addressed to Anwar Khan at BCC Ottawa. His wife had the money, he told them, adding that she was in Greece, though he did not know exactly where. "This went back and forth for a few days," says Murad, "until Mousa arranged to get a travel document and left the country."

Hawamda rented a car and drove west to Tunisia. The Libya/Tunisia border is virtually wide open on most days: Hawamda was not stopped by any border patrols during his journey. The travel agency owner quickly made his way to Tunis. "Once he got to Tunis," Murad says, "that was it. He went to Europe."

Back in the United States, meanwhile, the FBI was coming to grips with a single salient fact: Mousa Hawamda had escaped. The bureau will not say when it became aware of this, but Murad insists that Hawamda had been overseas for at least three full days— perhaps longer—before the FBI realized it had been tricked. There is evidence to support Murad's story: on Sunday, October 2, at around 9:00 p.m., he was stopped at Ogdensburg, New York, while attempting to cross into Canada in Hawamda's 1987 Nissan. Murad, who is a Canadian citizen, was interrogated by an FBI agent and American customs officials for four hours. The Nissan was seized and would remain in the United States, he was told: "They told me the owner of the car would come and pick it up. They thought it would be Mousa. I did not know up until then—and they certainly did not know— that Mousa was already gone. I found out on Monday morning, when I received a phone call from his wife in Greece. She told me Mousa had escaped."

Apparently the FBI was so confident that Mousa Hawamda was still in the United States that its agents declined to tell the U.S. Attorney's Office in Alexandria that he had disappeared. In an affidavit filed on October 6, 1988, at the U.S. District Court for the Eastern District of Virginia, Assistant U.S. Attorney Lawrence Leiser stated that he learned of Hawamda's escape an entire week after the fact. The affidavit gives details of telephone conversations between Leiser and Drew Carroll, Hawamda's lawyer, on the morning of October 6. It opens with Leiser and Carroll negotiating a time and place to discuss a plea bargain.

> Having consulted with the United States Attorney, I called Mr. Carroll and informed him that we could not meet with him until after 11 a.m. Mr. Carroll indicated that would not be good for him because by the time he went over to the FBI office, he would have to turn around and come back. He then paused and said: 'I might as well tell you now, I have not been able to contact my client since last Saturday.' Mr. Carroll then went on to say that he had heard that his client had fled, that he has made several efforts to contact his client since last Saturday and has been unable to do so. He also informed me that Mr. Hawamda's brother-in-law has contacted Mr. Carroll in an attempt to locate Mr. Hawamda. Mr. Carroll told me that he tried to contact Mr. Hawamda's wife in Canada and was unable to make any contact with her as well."

Hawamda was gone. He had fooled both the FBI and the Libyan government.

Donald Bartnik says it will be a very long time before the mysterious travel agency owner is seen again in the United States. The prospect of jail time terrifies him: "He's used to something better, you know."

But will he return to Libya now that Qadhafi's people know he stole a fortune from them? Ahmad Eed Murad laughs at the question: "If he went back to Libya, he would be making a very drastic mistake."

───────

For most of the summer of 1988, Mohamed Shihumi had been trying to convince the faceless Libyans who controlled Neutron International that he should be permitted to remain in Canada. To the very last, he was optimistic. But Neutron's bosses were not swayed by his pleas. By August 6, 1988, he and his young family were back in Tripoli.

"We have four or five deals to be closed yet," Shihumi had told his friends while he was leaving Edmonton. "Maybe I will be back … by the end of September." But he was kidding himself.

In Tripoli he quickly found out that his political masters were angry with him. Millions had been spent on Neutron Alberta, and Shihumi had very little to show for it. One of the largest deals in which he took part—the $13 million sale of an oil rig to Libya by a subsidiary of Calgary's Dreco Energy Services Ltd.—was finalized months before he took up residence in Calgary in 1985.

Shihumi's tumble was sudden and hard. During the mid-1980s he could do no wrong. In Edmonton he had $4 million in Libyan funds for a bankroll. In Tripoli during the same period, his clout was the stuff of local legend. One Canadian businessman who met him there in early 1987, shortly after Neutron opened its Alberta office, describes how he and Shihumi spent the day: "We went anywhere we wanted, without an appointment. He would just walk right into some minister's office, and sit down. And if there was a meeting going on, the other people would clear out.

"Mohamed had a lot of pull at the airport, too. He had gotten me there with only minutes to spare, and the people in the line-up parted so that he could get up to the desk. In one minute I had my boarding pass, and I never went through customs."

Soon after Shihumi returned to Libya in the summer of 1988, he came to the unpleasant conclusion that such days were gone, probably for good. Before he stopped answering his Tripoli telephone he made it clear that his Neutron International gamble had not paid dividends. "I am facing financial problems," he said. "I am struggling hard. That is my dream, to be active in these types of companies, which I think we need in both North America and Canada.

"I have not given up yet, but due to the high costs and the slow movement of trade, I...." His voice trailed off. "I am facing some personal problems." He would say no more.

———————

Horst Schmid is still Alberta's senior unelected trade representative. Before his relationship with Shihumi became public knowledge, he appeared eager to help the *Ottawa Citizen* to learn more about the manager of Neutron Alberta. After the Shihumi-Schmid story broke, he refused to ever speak to the newspaper again, loudly advising one reporter, an Irish Catholic, to "go back to Israel."

As far as Alberta's trade commissioner was concerned, Shihumi had been the target of a smear campaign by the media, and that was why he was now facing hardship at home. Loyal to the end, he added, "All I know is from the time I met him to the time he said he had to go back to Libya, because he just couldn't make it, I never had the feeling he didn't do his best to become a Canadian. I can't see where Mohamed would have done anything like [Libyan espionage], because he's just not the type, you know.

"In his case, I really wanted so much for him to have some business, because he was so serious about being a Canadian. I couldn't see him betraying his country, you know."

———————

While Mohamed Shihumi was working out his business problems in Tripoli, the *Ottawa Citizen*'s newsroom staff were having to confront their own kind of problems. The paper published three stories about Shihumi in October 1988. One of them in particular—printed on October 16, and detailing Shihumi's connections with Ottawa's top-secret NATO Comcentre—attracted the interest of the RCMP. Shortly after that front-page story was published, Ian MacLeod was told by a source high in the RCMP that he and another reporter were under RCMP surveillance. Both should "expect" that their phones were being tapped, the source said.

They discussed the tip with the *Citizen*'s city editor, Randy Denley. There was skepticism, but it was agreed that the tip should not be dismissed out of hand.

By sheer coincidence the two reporters covering the story lived in the same building in downtown Ottawa. For most of October and November they had both heard odd clicks and echoes on their unlisted home phone lines. As well, they had both noticed that a nameless utility company had parked a large trailer outside their old brick lowrise. Wiring could be seen running from nearby telephone lines to the interior of the trailer. No one had ever spotted any workers entering or leaving the trailer during daylight.

The most convincing evidence, however, came from the RCMP itself. On four separate occasions in October and November, the *Citizen* received telephone calls from an RCMP corporal named Jim Payne. Payne, the newspaper learned, was heading an investigation into the links between Shihumi and NATO's Comcentre. The RCMP believed that the Libyan may have breached the *Official Secrets Act*. For three weeks Payne and another officer had been interviewing External Affairs employees about the *Citizen*'s story of October 16. During his fourth and last call to the *Citizen*, Payne asked Ian MacLeod for copies of the documents relating to Shihumi that had been given to the newspaper. The *Citizen*'s editors conferred with their managing editor, Scott Honeyman, and decided to refuse the RCMP's request. Payne replied that he was planning to visit the newspaper's offices with a search warrant.

The *Citizen*'s publisher, Russell Mills, instructed editorial staff to place the notes and tapes relating to the investigation in a box. Within two hours of Payne's telephone call, the box was sitting in a locked vault at the downtown offices of the newspaper's law firm. The search warrant was never executed, but, as Denley said later, "Better safe than sorry."

For the *Ottawa Citizen* the RCMP's threat to obtain a search warrant was annoying but not surprising. By the time the story ended, seven months after it began, the newspaper had grown hardened to the fact that Canada's various governments did not appear to give a damn that Libyan spies were operating in Canada. That the RCMP was devoting more of its energies to tailing a pair of newsmen than to apprehending Libya's Canadian-based spies and terrorists was simply more evidence of Canadian governmental negligence.

The bad guys had gotten away. Mousa Hawamda was living the good life somewhere in Europe. Mohamed Shihumi was safe, if financially battered, in his Tripoli home. The Mounties did not, in this case, get their men.

The unresolved cases of Mousa Hawamda and Mohamed Shihumi provide a number of lessons, not the least of which is this: Canada's federal and provincial governments have grossly underestimated the attractiveness of their nation to Mu'ammar Qadhafi's outlaw regime. Because it is the United States' neighbour and has weak laws governing many of the activities in which Libya specializes, Canada is an ideal sanctuary for Libyan-sponsored wrongdoers. By establishing front companies such as Manara Ottawa and Neutron Alberta, Libya has turned Canada into a base for obtaining high-tech drilling equipment, for funding anti-Semitic Third Positionists from the ultra-right and ultra-left, and for every shady activity in between.

Some authorities, most of them in the United States, regard the Qadhafi regime as a sizable menace. Many more observers, in Europe and elsewhere, continue to dismiss Libya as no more than a bit player on the international stage: a tiny nation of radicals led by a self-aggrandizing crackpot with too much spare time on his hands. Those who embrace this latter view note, correctly, that Libya possesses neither the population nor the technological know-how to threaten Western interests in any consistent or large-scale way. They point to the great unlikelihood that a nation with fewer people than Chicago or Toronto could engage in global terrorism and espionage; they argue that Libya's military has suffered crushing defeat every time it has engaged the United States in battle. What is there to fear, they ask?

Since the beginning of the 1980s, Canada's federal government has maintained a contradictory policy toward Libya. It has been hawkish on the subject of Libya's paramilitary excursions beyond its own borders. For example, immediately after the April 1986 bombing raids on Tripoli and Benghazi by American fighter planes, most American allies condemned Ronald Reagan for ordering them. Only three foreign countries supported his decision: Britain, Israel, and Canada.

But, even while they paint Qadhafi as a threat to Western interests overseas, Canada's governments refuse to be convinced that the pro-Libyan activists living *in* Canada merit any degree of scrutiny. For proof of this one need look no further than the cases of Mousa Hawamda and Mohamed Shihumi.

The federal and provincial governments are not entirely at fault for the presence of Libyan agents on Canadian soil, although they should be assigned the greatest share of the blame. There are other reasons why Hawamda and Shihumi were able to violate Canada's *Criminal Code* and export controls with apparent impunity. Clearly, one has to do with the mindset of Canadian police agencies. Throughout the summer and fall of 1988 the *Ottawa Citizen* interviewed more than 20 police officers and CSIS agents. All of them rejected the notion that Qadhafi's regime could even find Canada on a map, let alone bestow it with strategic significance. As one officer put it, "Why would the Libyans be interested in *us*? What have we done to them?"

Libya rarely waits for another nation to "do" something to it before it takes action. In Qadhafi's mind, the entire world is politically and economically rotten, so a bomb blast or a political assassination can be justified under virtually any circumstance.

The way in which the *Ottawa Citizen*'s Libyan investigation was greeted by the nation's wire services and news outlets did little to diminish the skepticism it encountered when dealing with the RCMP or CSIS. Except at the *Edmonton Journal*, the *Calgary Herald*, and Ottawa's Southam News, where the slain writer Christoph Halens had worked, its stories attracted little attention. The suggestion that Libyan agents had been skulking about in the shadow of Parliament Hill and in Edmonton's oil patch was too far-fetched, rival news outlets claimed. Maybe such things happen to the Europeans or the Americans, but not to Canadians.

Christoph Halens' family would perhaps have a different view.

In early January of 1989, some two months after the Libyan spy story was put to bed by the *Ottawa Citizen*, a reporter received a phone call from an NFSL supporter who called himself Abdul. This was the same Abdul who months earlier had called the *Citizen* to denounce Mousa Hawamda as a Libyan spy. "Mrs. Hawamda is back in town," he said. He then hung up. He would never be heard from again.

Two reporters immediately drove to the Hawamda family's apartment building on Laurier Avenue West. Through the foyer intercom one reporter told her he was a friend of Ahmad Eed Murad's. The deception did not work. Maisoun Ben-Mohamed would not let the reporters into the building. "Go away," she said in an accented voice. "Leave me alone."

An hour later the *Citizen* tried again at Manara Travel on Metcalfe

Street. As the reporters walked into the travel agency, Mousa Hawamda's wife dashed into an office behind the reception area. The agency's manager, Dawn Huck, approached the counter.

"We're from the *Citizen* and we'd like to speak with Mrs. Hawamda," said one reporter.

"She isn't here," Huck said, her arms folded.

Huck was told that Mrs. Hawamda had just been observed walking through the door at the back of the travel agency. Huck was unimpressed.

"She isn't here," she repeated, "and if you don't leave right now, I'm going to call the police."

The *Citizen* reporters left. Now the newspaper knew where Mrs. Hawamda was—but where was her husband?

Mousa Hawamda was, in fact, in Athens, far from special agent Donald Bartnik and his FBI colleagues. Apparently he was living off the $1 million he had sent to the mysterious Dr. Hasein Mohamed Abid via the Lunder Bank in Vienna—which made him a very rich fugitive.

The FBI admits that it does not know who Dr. Abid is. The name could be a pseudonym, they say, or it could belong to one of Hawamda's powerful allies—more likely, by now, one of his *ex-allies*—in Libya's diplomatic corps. The latter is most plausible, says one former employee of BCC Ottawa.

This person, who handled all of Hawamda's bank accounts, well remembers the late-September day that Hawamda's wife appeared at BCC Ottawa with the co-signed transfer tucked in her purse: "Mousa's wife gave us the letter ordering us to send the [$1 million] to Austria's Lunder Bank. I remember that because it was such a pain in the ass to do."

She was clearly in a rush, the former employee recalls. But, strangely, after the transfer was completed through the First American Bank in New York City, the $1 million remained untouched at the Lunder Bank for weeks. This person adds that "Mousa's wife went to Vienna, but [Abid] didn't pick up the money for about a month. So Mrs. Hawamda called us from Vienna, saying she wanted us to change the order so she could get at the money. We changed the beneficiary, but about two hours before the paperwork got to the Lunder Bank, this Dr. Abid fellow picked up the money. Mrs. Hawamda was really pissed off that she didn't get the money. And she never got it, as far as I know."

During the fall of 1988, Hawamda and his young family lived quietly in Athens. Whenever they needed money, Maisoun Ben-Mohamed would call Anwar Khan. "Mousa never phoned," says the ex-employee. "It was always her, and she was a very demanding lady. Sometimes she'd even call a few times a day. She insisted on speaking with Mr. Khan—she'd say she wasn't hanging up until she could speak with him. She wouldn't take no for an answer."

Khan busied himself with keeping Hawamda's finances in good order in Canada—paying the Palestinian's legal bills in Ottawa and Washington, taking care of the rent at Manara Ottawa and at the exclusive Laurier Avenue West apartment. He would not, however, notify the RCMP that BCC Ottawa was aware of Hawamda's where-abouts. Only after being pressured on the point by two employees did Khan reluctantly telephone the Mounties. It is not surprising that Canadian authorities never petitioned the courts to have Hawamda's bank accounts frozen after he jumped bail.

A few weeks later, Hawamda's wife apparently decided that a fugitive's life was less than ideal for their two infant daughters. That is what she told Ian Verner Macdonald. Besides, she reasoned, the whole mess could be disposed of without jail terms, deportations, or stiff fines. All her husband needed was a good lawyer, she said.

Macdonald was one of the few who met with Maisoun Ben-Mohamed during her seven-week return to Canada in early 1989. He, too, remains puzzled over the woman's decision to return to the United States. "I saw her when she came through here," he says. "Naturally enough, I asked her why she was going back, and she said she was going to try to somehow or other absolve Mousa from all these charges." Macdonald gives a wry smile. "That sounded to me a little bit too optimistic."

During her stay in Ottawa she sold the couple's furniture at bargain-basement prices, paid off the lease on their apartment, and made arrangements to shut down Manara Ottawa. Then, on the evening of February 21, with her two young children in tow, she boarded a flight to National Airport in downtown Washington, D.C. The next day she was arrested by FBI agents.

Maisoun Ben-Mohamed's arrest was not related to any role she might have played in her husband's bail-jump. Rather, she was detained along with four other American residents on charges of conspiracy, wire fraud, and credit-card fraud, as well as aiding and abetting. Others arrested included a Libyan student living in Chicago; a former PCLS office employee living in Manassas, Virginia; and two Palestinian men who lived in Baltimore and Alexandria respectively. Both these men were friends of Mousa Hawamda. In a federal grand jury indictment handed down in mid-February 1989, Mousa Hawamda and Bob Brown of the All-African People's Revolutionary Party were charged as co-conspirators in an elaborate wire-fraud scheme.

According to the 23-count indictment, these pro-Libyan activists were appropriating AT&T, Sprint, and MCI confidential phone access codes as early as May 1986—perhaps even earlier. These codes were shared by Hawamda, his wife, and the others to make hundreds of free long-distance phone calls. Some calls were made to Ottawa, to Ahmad Eed Murad's home.

Bartnik and his FBI colleagues learned about the wire-fraud conspiracy while investigating Mousa Hawamda and the PCLS. Were the phone calls made by the group part of a Libyan espionage effort, or were they simply get-acquainted sessions?

Donald Bartnik says the former. "What they were doing was using other people's phone numbers, if you will. Literally thousands and thousands of dollars of charges were incurred." He adds that phone calls were made to other Libyans and Third Positionists around the world, "to facilitate their international contacts. These people have an international perspective, if you get my meaning."

More intriguing than the wire-fraud charges is Maisoun Ben-Mohamed's decision to return to the United States with her children, knowing that her arrest was inevitable. Bartnik is asked how Mousa Hawamda could remain unaffected by his wife's predicament. Does Maisoun Ben-Mohamed's return mean that Mousa Hawamda is not far behind?

Bartnik finds that suggestion funny. "I don't expect to see him any time in the near future," he says. "The children are U.S. citizens, but I don't know whether she just wanted to come back here or not. Who knows?"

A few months after her homecoming, a U.S. District Court judge found Maisoun Ben-Mohamed guilty of conspiracy and wire fraud. After losing a last-ditch appeal of her sentence in late July 1990, she was shipped off to a federal prison to serve a three-month term.

Mu'ammar Qadhafi is not kidding around.

Despite the failure of his Green Revolution, despite the collapse of his dream of a unified Arab super-state, and despite the fact that he and his tiny republic have been ostracized and vilified by most civilized nations, the Leader soldiers on. He struggles. He survives. The American government and its allies may regard him as a buffoon, a loser. But it cannot be ignored that Qadhafi has watched four American presidents come and go and that one of those—Ronald Reagan—failed to oust him though he tried for eight years.

In March 1991 it was unearthed by the American media that in the final years of his administration, Ronald Reagan sanctioned the training of anti-Qadhafi rebels in neighbouring Chad. By 1987,

American military advisors were training the Libyan dissidents in sabotage, land navigation, and other paramilitary skills. The program was downgraded after Reagan left office, partly as a budget-cutting measure and partly because the newly elected president, George Bush, does not hate Qadhafi with the visceral intensity his predecessor showed.

Qadhafi is a survivor. And those who have taken the time to study him find it reasonable to assume that he *is* serious: he *believes* in what he calls liberation movements, and in the Third Position, and that the West is a paragon of evil, and that he will one day win. He believes he is on the right side of history. In one of his more revealing interviews he said that the first 20 years of the Green Revolution were merely a suggestion of things to come: "We have just started to apply the Third Universal Theory. As I said, the last twenty years were merely an introduction."

When asked what his most important lesson had been in those 20 years, Qadhafi thought for a long time before answering: "It is very difficult to be upright in a world that is absolutely crooked."

In his heart, this is how the master of the Green Revolution and the Third Way truly sees himself—as a morally upright island surrounded by a storm-tossed sea of corruption, as a missionary with his eyes fixed on a distant horizon that very few can see. While patiently awaiting Armageddon's dawn in his tiny Islamic-socialist land, he has surrounded himself with two groups of "soldiers."

The first group includes *agents-provocateurs* like Mousa Hawamda. They are not ideologues or Third Positionists; rather, they regard the Qadhafi regime as a means to an end—the end, more often than not, being personal wealth and power. As Ahmad Eed Murad puts it, "Mousa wanted to become rich, and he didn't care what means he used to achieve his goals. He discovered that if he opened a travel agency, through his niceties and through being friends with the Libyans, he would get all the Libyan students' business." Murad curls his lip in distaste. "It is hard to describe what that son-of-a-bitch did."

The second group includes the starry-eyed ideologues who endorse the Third Position—men such as Mohamed Shihumi. They believe passionately in the Green Revolution and in the Third Universal Theory. One of Shihumi's Edmonton colleagues recalls that the Libyan rarely spoke of his nation's leader. But one afternoon he did, and the transformation was startling: "He stood there, holding a copy of the *Green Book* like it was the Bible. He told me I should read it. He talked about this Third Position crap. He said it contained all of the answers I would ever need." The Edmonton man laughs. "Mohamed really *believed* in all that stuff! Can you imagine!"

———————

The end, when it came, was not particularly dramatic for either Ottawa's Manara Travel Agency or Edmonton's Neutron International. Both ventures, which had once served as Libyan safe-houses for espionage, money laundering, assassination plots, and criminal conspiracies, quietly slipped from view.

In late March 1989, after months of non-payment of rent, the owner of 99 Metcalfe Street, Morguard Investments, changed the locks on the doors at Manara Ottawa. Few people noticed. As one Morguard employee put it, "They haven't had much business there in a long time." The employee said it was possible that the agency could reopen, but not until overdue rents were paid. That day never came. In the fall of 1989 a fast-food franchise took over the space where Libya's most powerful North American intelligence agent had plotted with Third Position extremists.

In Edmonton, Neutron Alberta's panelled offices remained empty for most of September 1988, their contents unclaimed. Mohamed Shihumi's departure had been so abrupt that he had not found the time to clean sensitive telexes out of his desk. This was fortunate for the *Ottawa Citizen,* which received batches of Neutron files that fall—all anonymously.

After the *Citizen* published the results of its investigation, Shihumi's landlord came forward to say how unhappy he was with the Libyan's business practices. Shihumi and his associates skipped in the middle of the night, he complained to the Canadian Press.

That wasn't all. Apparently, Shihumi's associates—or others—had returned to the Beverly Building in the middle of the night to survey some of the material he left behind. A few days after his departure, a number of offices on the building's second floor were broken into. As far as anyone could tell, no valuables were removed. According to the Edmonton police, the person or persons who broke in examined documents stored in boxes at Neutron Alberta's offices. They do not know if anything was removed from Shihumi's offices, because no one was around to provide them with an inventory after the break-in.

Many questions remain unanswered about Manara Ottawa, and Canada's Neutron branches, and Mousa Hawamda, and Mohamed Shihumi. Unfortunately, it seems unlikely that anyone will ever step forward to provide all of the answers: the principal characters in the Libyan spy drama are long gone. Hawamda is still in Athens, sources say, living under an assumed name. Shihumi, meanwhile, is in Tripoli, his influence and lifestyle both greatly diminished. According to some of those who know them well—and many of those who do not—Hawamda and Shihumi would be foolhardy in the extreme to return to North America. Meanwhile, Mahmoud Buazzi, who informed on the PCLS for the FBI, is in a witness protection program and attending university in the American Midwest.

In Qadhafi's Libya, there will always be many others eager to take up the banner of the Green Revolution. For those Libyan men who agree to go abroad to battle the United States and its allies—"the enemy of humanity," as Hawamda once called them—there is the promise of riches, power, and respect back home. The FBI's Donald Bartnik knows that Hawamda and Shihumi were not the first Libyan agents to operate on North American soil—and that they won't be the last.

Bartnik, who was promoted in 1989 and has passed on the Libyan file to another man at the FBI, gives a last good-natured laugh.

"If you keep digging away into these Libyan businesses," he says, "if you keep digging away at the backgrounds of these Libyan businessmen, you'd be amazed at what you will find. It would make for a good spy story, wouldn't it?"

CHAPTER NOTES

Chapter One

The sections of this chapter relating to Tripoli are based mainly on interviews with Michelle Tardif, Peter Bleyer, Terry Jabour, Ian Verner Macdonald, and Ahmad Eed Murad—as well as Abdul Sugair and Abu Abdullah of the National Front for the Salvation of Libya. The interviews were conducted between July 1988 and October 1991.

Documentary material for the introductory section was drawn from "Pondering Libya's Paradox" by Ellie Kirzner in the April 30, 1987, edition of *Now* Magazine; reports on the peace conference written by Charles Scheiner of the National Mobilization for Survival on April 22, 1987; and an undated report written by Michael Marsh of the War Resister's League. Other documentary material relied upon here is referred to in the Chapter Two notes, below.

Reliable documentary material about the Third Position is as elusive as the movement itself. When it is written about at all, it is often dismissed by reporters as an amusing oddity. For instance, in a November 1991 column in the *Globe and Mail*, Canadian writer Erna Paris detailed the historical links between the far right and the far left. But with their tongues planted firmly in cheek, the paper's editors headlined the story "Fun couples: Wedding in red." When interviewed at her Toronto home, Paris made it clear that she takes the unholy alliance between the anti-Semitic left and the anti-Semitic right far more seriously. She recalled that she had first encountered the links between neo-Nazis and ultra left-wing extremists in the early 1980s, while researching *Unhealed Wounds: France and the Klaus Barbie Affair* (New York: Grove Press, 1985). "This aspect of my book was disowned by some people in the media who were very disturbed by it," she says. They didn't want to accept it. "There was a lot of sympathy for the Palestinians—justifiable sympathy in my view—and no one wanted to hear about links between fanatics on both sides."

Paris admits that she too "was a little perplexed" at first by suggestions that there existed some kind of an extreme left/extreme right alliance. "But gradually, things started to fall into place. I learned that François Genoud, this very proud Swiss Nazi, had been to Cairo in the 1950s," she says. "That's where it began. The merger of the ultra left and the ultra right can be traced back to Nasser's Egypt."

In her excellent book about Barbie, Paris probes "the new Left-Right anti-Zionist ideology," which would later be called the Third Position. Mu'ammar Qadhafi was not the first to support it, Paris says: this bizarre ideology has a much longer pedigree. As early as the 1920s, Arab leaders could be seen forging alliances with National Socialists. In 1939, for example, the former Grand Mufti of Jerusalem fled to Nazi Germany, where he built an enduring friendship with the SS chief, Heinrich Himmler. "The struggle against Judaism is at the very heart of the natural alliance between National Socialism and those Arab Moslems who burn with a desire for freedom," Himmler told the Mufti in a note. "This alliance will endure until the final victory."

Paris writes in her book that in the 1950s, Egypt's leader, Gamal Abdel Nasser—Mu'ammar Qadhafi's lifelong idol—permitted his nation to become a base for anti-Semites of every ideology. Nasser was not afraid to assist those Europeans who shared his desire to destroy Israel, even if the Europeans were white supremacist Nazis. In that decade, François Genoud was working for Nasser's government; three of Joseph Goebbels' associates resided in Egypt; and Nasser himself was insisting that the "Third World" was a bulwark against Zionists intent on seizing Arab lands. So it should have surprised no one when an Egyptian government-run newspaper declared in 1955 that "our duty is to war against the Jews for the love of God and religion."

After the Six Day War in 1967—during which Israel's armed forces crushed the Arab invaders—some radical Arab leaders joined ranks with European neo-Nazis, as Nasser had done a decade before with the real article. "I think this whole left-right alliance thing got focussed—quite naturally—around the Palestinian question," Paris says. In April 1969 a neo-Nazi terrorist group called Neue Europaische Ordnung met in Barcelona; there, it received a request from the Palestinian Liberation Organization for funds, arms, non-Arab mercenaries, and anti-Semitic propaganda. Paris notes in her book that after the murder of Israeli athletes at the Munich Olympics in 1972, Mu'ammar Qadhafi donated $50 million to the PLO; and François Genoud advised the PLO on how to make use of those funds.

It was around this time, Paris writes, that anti-Zionist Arabs started to reach out to the far left, just as they had reached out to the far right. Swiss terrorist Bruno Bréquet, a former member of the Baader-Meinhoff band—in 1970 he was caught planting a bomb in the Israeli port city of Haifa—developed a close association with Genoud. And in the early 1980s, neo-Nazi skinheads were training at paramilitary camps in Lebanon, shoulder-to-shoulder with young terrorists from the far left. In 1985 an Armenian leftist terrorist was arrested in Paris carrying a German passport that had been stolen by members of a neo-Nazi group calling itself Aktionsgruppe Nationaler Sozialisten. This group specialized in attacking American army bases in Germany.

"These were strange alliances that surprised and disturbed many people," wrote Paris in her *Globe and Mail* column. "They shouldn't have: extremists, whether on the left or right, have more in common with each other than they do with centrists." She sombrely observes in her *Globe* piece that in France, some members of the Communist Party are now signing up with Jean-Marie Le Pen's racist National Front party.

"The [Third Positionists'] anti-Semitism is always hidden," says Paris. "The word they use is anti-Zionism. They fooled a lot of people for a long time with that. But essentially, when you look at the evidence, it becomes clear that this was a new word for a much older point of view."

Three other useful sources for the Third Position material were Britain's excellent anti-fascist magazine, *Searchlight;* the exposé written by Kevin Coogan and Martin A. Lee in the May 1987 edition of *Mother Jones;* and Ray Hill's 1988 book, *The Other Face of Terror: Inside Europe's Neo-Nazi Network* (London: Grafton, 1987). Hill, a former British white supremacist, states in his book that in Britain "there [was] a regular pattern of Arab financial backing for the extreme right," and that until the murder of Yvonne Fletcher, "the Libyan's People Bureau was becoming increasingly helpful." Hill, who served as an informant throughout the 1980s, was one of the most powerful neo-Nazis in Britain for two decades. He says that those who promote "Third Position policies ... are so worrying, [because] they are pledged to build organizations of street-hardened young political soldiers."

Much of this chapter focusses on Mu'ammar Qadhafi himself. There are a number of excellent sources of information about his background and policies. Particularly recommended are Lillian Craig Harris' indispensable *Libya: Qadhafi's Revolution and the Modern State* (Boulder, Co: Westview Press, 1986) and John K. Cooley's *Libyan Sandstorm* (New York: Holt, Rinehart and Winston, 1982). Revealing portraits of the Libyan leader are contained in T.D. Allman's "Blind Vision" in the July 1989 issue of *Vanity Fair;* an interview with Qadhafi in the November 10, 1986, edition of *U.S. News and World Report* titled "I am a mixture of Washington and Lincoln"; Marie Colvin's "Qadhafi: The man the world loves to hate" in the *Ottawa Citizen* of August 9, 1986; Southam News' portrait titled "Qadhafi cultivates many images besides financier of terrorism," in the April 19, 1985, edition of the same paper; "Libya's Qadhafi: Still in command?" by Lisa Anderson in the February 1987 edition of *Current Affairs;* and Edward Schumacher's "The United States and Libya" in the Winter 1986 edition of *Foreign Affairs.*

Chapter Two

Some of this chapter is based on interviews with Horst Halens, Rosemary Knes, Desmond Gray, Peter Bleyer, Michelle Tardif, Terry Jabour, Ian Verner Macdonald, Ingrid Beisner, Albert Nerenberg, Ahmad Eed Murad, Nick Hills, Anne Ladas, and others who asked not to be identified. The interviews were conducted between July 1988 and September 1991.

I also relied on the following documentary material: Ellie Kirzner's 1987 *Now* piece, noted above; a transcript of a March 1988 segment of "Fifth Estate" called "Death in Tripoli"; and news stories filed about Halen's death by Southam News writers Paul Koring and Jonathan Manthorpe. Particularly helpful were Manthorpe's investigative stories, which were published in

February 1988. I also recommend the news stories on the peace conference that the *Globe and Mail* ran on April 9, 1987, and other *Globe* coverage on April 15, 16, and 23 of that same year. The *Ottawa Citizen* printed stories dealing with Halens' death on April 15, 16, 23, 24, and 29, 1987, as well as Manthorpe's outstanding work on February 27, 1988.

Material relating to other delegates comes from Martin Gottlieb's story on the group in the *New York Times* of December 31, 1991; and from "Third-party candidate calls Democrats the enemy" by Doug Swanson in the *Ottawa Citizen* of October 18, 1988. Material about Eibie Weizfeld was taken in part from stories in the *Citizen* about the run-ins the "peace activist" had with the law; see September 13 and 15, 1985; October 22, 1988; December 17, 1988; January 18, 1988; February 9, 1989; and May 9, 1989.

Material concerning the bombing raid on Libya was drawn from many sources. See the extensive coverage by Bob Levin and Rae Corelli, respectively, in the April 28, 1986, and May 5, 1986, editions of *Maclean's*; also, "A New War and New Risks" by Henry Trewhitt in the *U.S. News and World Report* of April 28, 1986; also a story by James Wallace in the May 5, 1986 edition of that same magazine; also, "Targeting a Mad Dog," by Mark Whitaker and John Walcott in *Newsweek*, April 21, 1986; and other publications.

Chapter Three

This chapter is based on interviews with FBI special agent Donald Bartnik; U.S. Attorneys Henry Hudson and Lawrence Leiser; members of the FBI, CSIS, and the RCMP who spoke on the condition that they not be identified; and the NFSL's Abdullah and Sugair. The interviews were conducted between August 1988 and November 1991.

Documentary evidence for this chapter includes the following: sworn affidavits filed by the FBI and the CIA at the U.S. District Court for the Eastern District of Virginia; *Veil* by Bob Woodward (New York: Simon and Shuster, 1988); *Under Fire* by Oliver North (New York: HarperCollins, 1991); and many news stories. Regarding the latter, the following are recommended (all were published in the *Ottawa Citizen* or carried on wire services): "Libyans held in possible assassination plot," July 21, 1988; "Suspect in plot to kill North owns local firm," July 22, 1988; "Suspect in alleged death plot held," July 23, 1988; "Man linked to Ottawa firm charged with aiding Libya," July 29, 1989; "Eight suspects in alleged Libyan plot plead not guilty" by Tonda MacCharles and the author, August 6, 1988; and other news stories written by Ian MacLeod and the author in 1988 on August 9, September 1, and October 12, 13, 15, 16, 18, and 26.

In the past few years there have been literally hundreds of reports and media accounts detailing Qadhafi's recent involvement with international terrorist movements. Reliable are the following: the U.S. Department of State's *Bulletins* of June, August, and October 1986; the British/Israeli Public Affairs Committee's *Briefing* of May 1986; and the Embassy of Israel's *Policy Background* published in Ottawa in April 1986. Useful media stories concerning the spate of Libyan-sponsored terrorist incidents in the middle to late 1980s include "Libya preparing attacks around the world," from a *New York Times* wire service story published in the *Globe and Mail* on April 15, 1986; Judith Miller's "Qadhafi to give terrorists arms and training in Libya"; Bernard Weintraub's "Terrorists train at 15 Libyan sites, U.S. official says"; and David K. Shipler's "Trail of Mideast Terror: Exploring link to Libya" in the January 5, 7, and 16 editions, respectively, of the *New York Times*; a *World Press Review* cover story on Qadhafi and terrorism, published in June 1986; and a report in the April 11, 1987, edition of *The Economist.*

Although Qadhafi appears to have withdrawn, to a point, from terrorist involvement since the 1986-87 period, his dalliances with armed extremists have once again come back to haunt him. In late 1991 rumours began to circulate that Libya was again the focus of Western counterterrorism campaigns. These rumours proved to be true.

In October 1991 a French magistrate announced that he was seeking Libya's deputy foreign minister, Mousa Koussa, in connection with the September 1989 bombing of a UTA airliner over Africa. The following month two Libyan agents were indicted by the United States and Britain for their role in the bombing of Pan Am flight 103 over Lockerbie, Scotland, on December 21, 1988. The two men—Abdel Basset Ali al-Megrahi and Lamen Khalifa Fhimah—answered to Mohamed Madjoub and Mousa Koussa. At the time of the Lockerbie bombing, Madjoub was head of Libyan counter-intelligence and Koussa was a member of the International Revolutionary Committee. The two indicted men were members of the Jamahiriya Security Organization, which,

in the byzantine Libyan power establishment, ultimately reports to those revolutionary committees charged with intelligence matters. Al-Megrahi was a
high-ranking JSO official; Fhimah was a covert operative who, like many
Libyan intelligence agents, worked for Libyan Arab Airlines.

During an interview in January 1992, Abdul Sugair of the NFSL noted that
Mousa Hawamda, like al-Megrahi and Fhimah, was a close associate of
Madjoub and Koussa. He pointed out that, since Libya is a relatively small
country, most of those employed by Libyan intelligence are well-known to each
other. Koussa and Madjoub, he added, control most terrorist and intelligence-
gathering operations.

"Madjoub is the inside man," Sugair said. "He doesn't really speak any
foreign languages. He's a military man. He doesn't try to be intellectual, or ideological. Koussa is more ideological, more well-travelled. He has been in the
United States, England and all over. Together they control people like
Hawamda and the two guys who have been charged in Lockerbie."

It is likely the Lockerbie attack was planned in response to the Americans'
April 1986 bombing of Tripoli and Benghazi. In this case, at least, Reagan's
foreign policy toward Libya may have provoked rather than prevented more
terrorist attacks.

After the Lockerbie story broke in November 1991, the Bush administration
started hinting broadly that another military strike against Libya was likely if
Qadhafi did not hand over the two agents. (See "U.S. will try diplomatic action
before a military strike on Libya" by Michael Wines in the *New York Times* of
November 14, 1991; and "U.S. may retaliate against Libya" by Charles Green in
the *Ottawa Citizen* of November 15, 1991.) Some questioned whether Libya was,
in fact, the culprit, in that when the indictment was announced, the United
States was seeking improved relations with those nations that had been previ-
ously linked to the Lockerbie tragedy, namely Syria and Iran: this case was
made by Robert and Tamara Kupperman in an op-ed piece titled "The politics
of Pan Am 103" in the *New York Times* of November 16, 1991. But most com-
mentators seemed to agree that the evidence against Libya, while largely cir-
cumstantial, was overwhelming.

After repeated British and American demands that the two Libyan agents
be turned over, Qadhafi grew nervous. On November 28, 1991, after weeks of
official denials, he met with Egypt's leader, Hosni Mubarak, to discuss the

issue; on the same day, JANA announced that a Libyan magistrate investigating the Western charges was seeking American and British help. Evidently fearing a military strike or harsher economic sanctions, Qadhafi replaced the head of his External Security Agency; told a representative of Britain's Foreign Office that he was prepared to renounce terrorism; and ordered Fhimah and al-Megrahi held in captivity so that they could be tried. Foreign Minister Ibrahim Bishari said the two men would be executed if found guilty.

These were all fairly desperate attempts by Qadhafi to forestall punitive action by the United States and Britain. They were recognized as such by the West. On January 21, 1992, the United Nations Security Council ordered Qadhafi to hand over the two agents. The next day, Libya said it would co-operate with the UN's secretary-general, but refused to extradite the two intelligence agents. On March 2, 1992, the United States and Britain rejected a Libyan offer that would have seen the two men tried in a "neutral" nation. A State Department spokesperson hinted that military action might be taken.

It will be interesting to watch, in the coming year, the final act in the Lockerbie tragedy.

Chapter Four

This chapter is largely based on interviews with Ahmad Eed Murad, Terry Jabour, Roger Delorme, Anwar Khan, Ian Verner Macdonald, Eric Kirsipuu, Mike Ben-Mohamed, Donald Bartnik, and a former RCMP deputy commissioner, Henry Jensen. Other RCMP, CSIS, and FBI sources were also used. All of the interviews were conducted between July 1988 and December 1992.

Much of the documentary material for this chapter consists of sworn affidavits, search warrants, the FBI's inventory lists of seized goods, and indictments and other pleadings filed by the FBI at the U.S. District Court in Alexandria, Virginia. Background information was obtained from American officials, who also assisted me in obtaining documents I needed. These officials include U.S. Attorneys Henry Hudson and Lawrence Leiser, as well as clerks Sam Dibbley and Kathy Bartell. In Canada, the testimony given to the House of

Commons Standing Committee on Finance was helpful. Most of the media stories about Mousa Hawamda were written by Ian MacLeod and the author and published in the *Ottawa Citizen* in 1988 on July 21, 22, 23, 27, and 29; August 6 and 9; September 1; October 8, 9, 12, 13, 14, 15, 16, 18, and 26; and December 31. Also in 1989, on March 1 and 10 and April 2.

Chapter Five

This chapter is based on many interviews conducted with many people: Ian Verner Macdonald, Anne Ladas, Anne Collins, Corporal Pierre Belanger of the RCMP, Senator Eugene Forsey (now deceased), Robert Stanfield, Ernst Zundel, Ingrid Beisner, Philip Belgrave, Donald Bartnik, Ahmad Eed Murad, Yussuf Naim Kly, Julian Sher, Stanley Barrett, Terry Jabour, Michelle Tardif, and a host of anonymous sources.

Much of the documentary material about Ian Verner Macdonald comes from Macdonald himself—he does not avoid publicity, to say the least—or from sources at the RCMP. Two excellent and widely read texts on Canada's racist right contain biographical information on Macdonald. These are Julian Sher's *White Hoods: Canada's Ku Klux Klan* (Vancouver: New Star Books, 1983) and Stanley Barrett's *Is God a Racist? The Right Wing in Canada* (Toronto: UTP, 1987).

Chapter Six

This chapter is based on interviews with Tom Metzger, Donald Andrews, Ian Verner Macdonald, Anne Ladas, Ernst Zundel, Paul Fromm, Terry Long, Richard Butler, skinhead members of the Nationalist Party of Canada, and a number of others from North America's racist right. Also consulted were spokesmen for the John Brown Anti-Klan Committee and the B'nai Brith, and Bernie Farber of the Canadian Jewish Congress. The interviews were conducted between the fall of 1988 and the fall of 1991.

Documentary sources include Barrett and Sher's books (noted above); *Hate Groups in America* by the Anti-Defamation League of the B'nai Brith

(New York: B'nai Brith, 1988); James Ridgeway's excellent exposé of white supremacists in the United States, *Blood in the Face* (New York: Thunder's Mouth Press, 1991); and a host of news stories dealing with specific incidents. Among these are "Hatemongers find rights ally" by Stephen Bindman, in the *Ottawa Citizen* of December 4, 1989; "Cross-burning decision splits jury" by Murray Campbell, in the *Globe and Mail* of October 30, 1991; "19 Canadians held at Chicago airport by U.S. Customs" in the *Citizen* of September 5, 1989; Jeff Coplon's outstanding magazine article, "Skinhead Nation," in *Rolling Stone*, December 1, 1988; "Sending a $12.5 million message to a hate group," in the *New York Times* of October 26, 1990; and a number of other stories written by the author for the *Calgary Herald* and, later, the *Citizen*.

Chapter 7

This chapter is based on interviews with Donald Bartnik and other FBI spokesmen; various Nations of Islam spokesmen; and Ian Verner Macdonald, Michelle Tardif, Terry Jabour, Peter Bleyer, and other delegates to the April 1987 Tripoli peace conference. Also interviewed were Rosemary Knes, Desmond Gray, Kevin Coogan, Ian MacLeod, Vernon Bellecourt, and spokesmen for the B'nai Brith's Anti-Defamation League. Tremendously helpful was James Adams of New York's *Forward,* who has published excellent work in this area.

The chapter also draws from a wide variety of background material: Bruce Parry's *Malcolm* (New York: Stanton Hill Press, 1991); Rex Wexler's very sympathetic treatment of the American Indian Movement, *Blood of the Land* (New York: Everest House, 1982); "Killers on the Right" by Coogan and Lee, in the May 1987 issue of *Mother Jones* (this is a top-notch exposé of the inroads the Third Position is making into the racist right); *Forward* magazine's Fall 1986 article, "Hate Begotten of Hate— Louis Farrakhan and the Nation of Islam"; the Anti-Defamation League's 1990 report, "Louis Farrakhan: The campaign to manipulate public opinion"; and Errol Nazareth's "Black Nation Rising" in the August 3, 1989 issue of *Now* magazine.

The Nation of Islam's connections to Libya are not hidden—Farrakhan actually boasts about them. AIM tends to be more tight-lipped about the issue. Some interesting news stories on AIM's links to Qadhafi's regime include Ian MacLeod's "Police probe link between native group and terrorist" in the *Ottawa Citizen* of January 18, 1986; a key Canadian Press story on Qadhafi's support of AIM, dated January 31, 1988; "Rebel Yank natives gather in Oka" in the *Ottawa Sun* of August 2, 1990; Ray Smith's "Qadhafi honours standoff warriors," also in the *Sun,* June 16, 1991; and an Associated Press story, "Indians say Libya gave them $250,000," published in the *New York Times* of June 23, 1991.

Chapter Eight

Part of this chapter is based on brief interviews conducted in July and August 1988 with Mousa Hawamda and his American lawyers. Also interviewed for the material in this chapter were Ali Ghet, Mohamed Shihumi, Lester Francis, "Buzz" Sweep, Herman Bruinsma, Horst Schmid, Donald Bartnik and his colleagues, Henry Schuler, Allan and Ian Frame, Glynn Davies, and various unhelpful spokesmen for Alberta's premier, Don Getty. RCMP and CSIS spokesmen, Abdul Sugair and Abu Abdullah of the NFSL, Anwar Khan, Eric Kirsipuu, and two anonymous BCC Ottawa sources also provided information.

Documentary material about the relationship between Horst Schmid and Mohamed Shihumi was sent to the *Ottawa Citizen* by anonymous but very reliable sources in 1988 and 1989. Also useful were documents provided to Ian Macleod and the author by Buzz Sweep and Lester Francis—for example, the Statements of Claim they filed against Shihumi in Alberta's Court of Queen's Bench on July 20, 1987. News stories filed on the subject of the Canadian trade ban, Neutron International, and Schmid's relationship with Shihumi included these: "Canadian trade moves unpopular" by Leslie Pommer in the *Globe and Mail* of April 1, 1986; "Canadians unlikely to take oil jobs, oil executives say" by Matthew Fisher in the *Globe* of January 15, 1986; "Alberta companies won't stop dealing with Libya" by Mike Sadaya in the *Edmonton Journal* of January 10, 1986; "Canada moves to stop firms from making new contacts" by Hugh Winsor in the *Globe* of January 11, 1986; Maggie Fox's "More Canadians expected in Libya" in the *Globe* of January 15, 1986; Wayne Kondro's "Getty tells oilmen to honour ban" in the *Calgary Herald* of January 14, 1986; "Clark urges Canadians to leave while Libya calm," a Canadian Press story found in the

Citizen of April 22, 1986; Philip Winslow's "Clark's warning to leave baffles diplomats in Libya" in the *Citizen* of April 24, 1986; Brian D. Johnson's "Pushing the limits" in the April 21, 1986, issue of *Maclean's*; "Canada jittery about Libya policy" by James Bagnall, in the *Financial Post* of April 26, 1986; Susan Riley's "Many obstacles seen to Canada imposing sanctions against Libya" in the *Citizen* of April 26, 1986; the first Canadian news story about Shihumi, which was published in the *Edmonton Sun* on August 20, 1987; a Canadian Press story about Schmid written by Sylvia Strojek on January 28, 1987; and wire stories written about Neutron International on October 14 and November 1 and 3, 1988.

Chapter Nine

This chapter is based on interviews with Mohamed Shihumi; Ahmad Eed Murad; spokesmen for the NFSL, FBI, CSIS, and the RCMP; and with a host of other sources, including Ottawa-area lawyers and Libyan students. These were conducted in the summer and fall of 1989.

Documentary evidence includes material provided to me by the NFSL and quoted extensively in the text. Also, Patrick Best's columns on the CBIE and Libya published in the *Ottawa Citizen* on December 1, 1982, and April 2, 1986; "Libyan banned" by Barbara McLintock in the *Vancouver Province* of April 27, 1986; "Mounties check Libyans here" by Salim Jiwa in the *Province* of April 27, 1986; and "Clark cool to admitting Libyan students" in the *Globe and Mail* of May 1, 1986.

Chapter Ten

Interviewed for this chapter, in 1989, were a number of scientists and chemical weapons experts, among them Gordon Burck, Brad Roberts, Seth Carus, and Elisa Harris. In Mohamed Shihumi's business records were listed a number of strange-sounding commodities and chemical compounds—strange-sounding in the context of Mohamed Shihumi's claim that he had come to Canada to broker tomato paste and flour. The experts who were interviewed said that countries like Libya and Iraq often set up dummy corporations to seek precursor "dual use" chemicals—that is, chemicals which can be used either for legitimate purposes or for production of chemical weapons.

Spokesmen for the RCMP, CSIS, and the FBI all confirmed that this "dual use" hunch was not at all implausible. The NFSL's Abdullah and Sugair said the same thing, as did various anonymous sources.

A number of excellent articles have been written about the general chemical/nuclear weapons threat posed by nations like Libya and Iraq. Strongly recommended reading is the *Christian Science Monitor's* January 1989 special report, "Poison on the Wind." Recommended news stories and features include the *Globe and Mail's* entire coverage on January 5, 1989, relating to the downing of two Libyan jets over the Mediterranean; *Business Week's* article of January 23, 1989, "How Qadhafi built his deadly chemical plant"; Peter Goodspeed's "Superpowers move closer to ban on toxic weapons" in the *Toronto Star* of September 23, 1989; Ann McFeatter's "Banning chemical weapons not an easy task" in the *Ottawa Citizen* of September 27, 1989; Victor Simpson's "Qadhafi plans action if Germans guilty in Libyan plant fire" in the *Globe* of March 16, 1990; "Small fire, much smoke" in *The Economist* of March 31, 1990; Michael Gordon's "Weapons fears remain threat to world stability" in the *Globe* of April 9, 1990; Robert Cook's "Chemical warfare" in the *Citizen* of August 9, 1990; Malcolm W. Browne's "To Baghdad, poison gas is poor man's A-bomb" and "Iraqi chemical arms: Difficult target," both in the *New York Times* in 1990, on August 9 and September 5 respectively.

After a surge in such stories around the time of the Gulf War, such items started to appear again: "Secret project may employ Soviet nuclear scientists" in the *Ottawa Citizen* of January 20, 1992; "U.S. agents say Libya is adding and hiding chemical weapons" by Elaine Sciolino and Eric Schmitt, in the *New York Times* of January 22, 1992; Stephen Kinzer's "Germany acts to curb arms exports" in the *Times* of January 24, 1992; and "Libya denies link to arms" and "Qadhafi launches anxious bid to improve relations with West" in the January 26, 1992, *Ottawa Sun* and *Citizen* respectively.

Chapter Eleven

This chapter is based on interviews with Anwar Khan, Eric Kirsipuu, Ahmad Eed Murad, Ian Verner Macdonald, Herb Gray, John Manley, Henry Jensen, former BCC Ottawa employees, spokesmen for the FBI, CSIS, and the RCMP, and representatives of the staffs of Massachusetts Senator John Kerry and Manhattan DA Robert Morgenthau. The interviews were conducted between July 1988 and January 1992.

Before it collapsed in July 1990, a number of excellent features were written about BCCI, including John J. Fialka and Peter Truell's "Rogue bank" in the *Wall Street Journal* of May 3, 1990; "How the BCCI grew and grew" in *The Economist* of January 27, 1990; Richard Donkin's two stories on the bank's early troubles, in the *Financial Times* of January 23 and May 2, 1990; and stories about the closing of BCCI branches, in the June 1 and July 30, 1990, editions of the *Wall Street Journal* and *Globe and Mail* respectively.

When the bank was shut down by international regulators in July 1991, there followed an avalanche of news stories about BCCI's sprawling empire. I have relied mostly on the stories on BCCI published in the major North American and British newspapers and magazines. There are too many to mention. Some of the most useful: "The dirtiest bank of all" in the July 29, 1991, issue of *Time* (cover story); "Not just a bank" in the September 2, 1991, edition of that same magazine; "Seven nations charge fraud and seize a banking empire" by Stephen Prokesch in the *New York Times* of July 6, 1991; "BCCI: Big money and mysterious" by Dean Baquet in the *Times* of July 6, 1991; "The bank that liked to say yes" in London's *Financial Times* of July 8, 1991; "BCCI's demise ends a dream" and "Aggressive BCCI crossed moral boundary" by Brian Milner in the July 11 and 29, 1991, editions of the *Globe and Mail*; "The many facades of BCCI" in *The Economist* of July 13, 1991; "BCCI scandal grows: Bank of England knew facts last year" by John Cassidy and Fiona Walsh in the *Sunday Times* of July 14, 1991; Diane Francis' "Ottawa got warning on BCCI in 1984" in the *Financial Post* of July 26, 1991; "All things to all men" in *The Economist* of July 27, 1991; "MI5 knew about terrorist accounts of bank years ago, officials indicate" in the *Ottawa Citizen* of August 2, 1991; "A bank of a scandal" and "A scandal in waiting" by Marci McDonald and Brenda Dalglish respectively in the August 5, 1991, issue of *Maclean's*; "Feeling the heat" by John Greenwald in

Time, August 5, 1991; "B'nai Brith calls for probe into bank's murky ties" by Paul Lungen in the August 8, 1991, issue of *Canadian Jewish News*; "Indecent exposures" by Marci McDonald in the *Maclean's* of August 12, 1991; "At the end of a twisted trail, piggy bank for a favoured few" by Steve Lohr in the *New York Times* of August 12, 1991; "A cloud of suspicion" by Marci McDonald in the *Maclean's* of August 19, 1991; "The brave ones began to sing" by John Greenwald in *Time,* August 19, 1991; and hundreds of other news stories published in the summer and fall of 1991.

A number of major books on the collapse of BCCI are in the works at the moment. For a quick overview, London's *Financial Times* mini-book, *Behind Closed Doors* (London: Financial Times, 1991) can be recommended.

Chapter Twelve

This chapter is largely based on interviews with Donald Bartnik, Henry Jensen, Ian MacLeod, John Kessel, Mike Ben-Mohamed, Ian Verner Macdonald, Henry Hudson, Lawrence Leiser, Horst Schmid, Mohamed Shihumi, Anwar Khan, Eric Kirsipuu, Ahmad Eed Murad, various spokesmen for the FBI, CSIS, RCMP, and NFSL, and a large number of anonymous sources. These interviews were conducted between July 1988 and January 1992.

Most of the documentary material for this chapter consists of affidavits, pleadings, and similar material, all filed in the U.S. District Court in Alexandria, Virginia, or at the Ontario District Court in Ottawa. The accounts of the investigation by the House of Commons Standing Committee were taken from official transcripts. Some documents were provided by the NFSL and Ian MacLeod.

To all who helped me to research this book—especially my friend Dan Hayward—I offer a heartfelt thanks.

INDEX

The index is to names of persons and organizations. Inclusive page numbers suggest references "here and there" on the pages given, together with other subjects.